Essentials of Standardized Achievement Testing

Validity and Accountability

Thomas M. Haladyna

Arizona State University West

Allyn and Bacon

Boston • London • Toronto • Sydney • Tokyo • Singapore

Series Editor: *Arnis E. Burvikovs*
Series Editorial Assistant: *Matthew Forster*
Executive Marketing Manager: *Stephen Smith*
Manufacturing Buyer: *Julie McNeill*
Cover Designer: *hannusdesign.com*
Production Coordinator: *Pat Torelli Publishing Services*
Editorial-Production Service: *TKM Productions*
Electronic Composition: *TKM Productions*

Library of Congress Cataloging-in-Publication Data

Haladyna, Thomas M.
    Essentials of standardized achievement testing : validity and accountability / Thomas
M. Haladyna.
        p. cm.
    Includes bibliographical references (p.) and index.
    ISBN 0-205-32691-9
        1. Educational tests and measurements--Validity--United States. 2.
Examinations--Scoring. 3. Educational accountability--United States. I. Title.

    LB3060.7 .H35 2002
    371.26'01'3--dc21   2001053282

Printed in the United States of America

10 9 8 7 6 5 4 3 2 1   06 05 04 03 02

Contents

Preface

Standardized achievement testing plays a major role in U.S. society. These tests are given to millions of school children in every state in the nation. Test scores from these standardized achievement tests are used for many purposes, including admission to colleges and universities, graduate programs, and professional schools; certification or licensing decisions in professions; graduation or certification requirements for high school students; and evaluation of the educational programs in schools, school districts, and states.

Phelps (2000) reported that standardized achievement testing is a worldwide enterprise of enormous magnitude. Cizek (1998) indicated that testing is increasing in scope both nationally and worldwide, with tests administered to an estimated 140 million to over 400 million students. Standardized testing is big business that is getting bigger.

Behind this increase in achievement testing is an urgent need expressed by the public and elected officials to study the eroding standards in schools. Increases in migration make necessary the standardization of curriculum throughout the nation. There is also a growth in demand for tests to select students for programs or for college admission. The decrease in federal government testing has been followed by more locally supported testing. Additionally, test scores are increasingly being used for many purposes. Specialists in achievement testing question how tests can be validly used for so many different purposes without adequate validity evidence.

Supporters of standardized achievement testing want to know how the nation's children are doing in school, and they have a right to know. Critics of standardized achievement testing rue the undue emphasis placed on achievement test scores and do not condone the questionable tactics used to boost test scores. Regarding standardized achievement testing, Haertel and Calfee (1983) wrote:

> Standardized achievement tests are widely accepted today as trustworthy measures of educational outcomes. The yearly test is an institution in many districts; if the average scores are higher this year than last, then the schools are improving. The scores on these tests are trusted because they are quantitative, they have support of statistical theory, and they comprise a few standards for comparison over time and over programs. (p. 119)

Haertel and Calfee also stated that since these tests are general indicators of student achievement, historically there was no reason to be overly concerned. Test results were used in benign ways. However, at the time of the appearance of their essay, the authors were justifiably concerned about the validity of various test uses. Today, test interpretations and uses have proliferated, causing considerable unrest among educators, students and their parents, school boards, legislators, the media, the business community, and the public. Standardized achievement testing continues to increase in America, and its influence and consequences are enormous.

Purpose of This Book

Essentials of Standardized Achievement Testing: Validity and Accountability is dedicated to providing you with sound, clear information about standardized achievement testing to enable you to become a wise consumer of test information. This book will motivate you to think about the deeper issues underlying the validity of interpretations and uses of these test scores and the consequences of test score use on students and on society overall. As you become better informed, you will learn why tests are given, what test scores mean, what tests should be used, and how to use test results validly. You also might consider the consequences of testing students. In other words, what effect does this testing have on students? And how does testing affect parents, teachers, and the public? Are these consequences mostly positive or negative?

Audience for This Book

The audience for this book includes those wanting to be teachers, teachers, principals and other school personnel, school board members and state board of education members, legislators who are interested in the state testing that they support, and the public. All of these audiences have important roles to play in shaping the future of education.

Content of This Book

As the references scattered throughout these chapters and appearing in the References section at the end of this book attest, a good deal of theory, research, and essays have shaped the content of this book. Although the organization and content of each chapter suggest a major topic, the underlying theme of this book is simple:

Students should be tested in ways that benefit their learning.

However, the book is not solely focused on standardized achievement testing given in elementary and secondary schools. A broader view is intended. Standardized achievement tests are administered to postsecondary students and nonstudents for an incredible variety of reasons. The book argues that not all test score uses are equally valid; in fact, some uses are downright illogical and unsupported by evidence. Also, some test score uses may have negative effects on students and others. These issues are discussed and advice is given on how to evaluate and use test score information in ways that help students learn.

Organization of This Book

Part I: Foundations for Standardized Testing provides a context for the other parts of the book. This foundation includes the first three chapters.

Chapter 1, *A Model for Student Learning,* presents a tentative model that identifies the ideal outcomes of education and the factors that may cause these outcomes. The chapter gives you the opportunity to examine and evaluate a model for school learning. You can then adapt or adopt your own model that expresses your personal beliefs about how students learn and what factors influence learning. A good understanding of your personal model for school learning gives you realistic expectations of your students and better purpose and direction in your teaching and testing of student achievement.

Chapter 2, *Basic Concepts and Principles of Standardized Achievement Testing,* presents basic terms, definitions, examples, principles, and background that will help you better understand the issues in the next chapters. The chapter also explains the role of the infamous bell curve (normal distribution) in conjunction with standardized test score scales. Some basic statistical concepts are also involved.

The topic of the third chapter, *Validity,* is the most important consideration when interpreting or using a test score. The chapter examines the reasoning that goes into interpreting and using standardized testing results for various purposes. When validity is considered in a testing situation, it is more likely that test scores will be interpreted wisely and put to good use. An important aspect of validity is the idea that any interpretation or use of a test score can have positive or negative consequences on students and others. As the reasoning and evidence supporting a test score use and the positive and negative consequences of this use are evaluated, one might conclude that the use is not very valid.

Part II: Standardized Testing contains three chapters that take a comprehensive look at a major field of standardized testing.

Chapter 4, *Intelligence and Intelligence Testing,* gives you a historic view of the study of human intelligence. Many social scientists have hotly debated the one-factor versus multifactor approaches to defining intelligence. In actuality, both positions may be correct! The role of intelligence is significant in student learning, but in a very complex way. Intelligence tests have many valid purposes, as you will see, but there are invalid uses as well.

The fifth chapter, *Standardized Achievement Testing,* identifies and describes major categories of achievement tests intended to measure student learning that occurs in elementary and secondary schools. Emphasis is placed on the meaning and appropriate uses of these achievement test scores. A deeper understanding of these achievement tests will allow you to participate more actively in the enduring debate over the usefulness of these tests.

Chapter 6, *High-Stakes Testing for High School Graduation and Professional Certification and Licensing,* reviews a type of educational achievement testing that seems to be growing. The public has increasingly demanded that high school graduates be qualified before graduating and going on to college or work. A number of states have adopted graduation or certification tests as a means for increasing achievement and holding students accountable for their learning before they graduate. Those being trained for a profession or highly specialized work need to pass either certification or licensing tests. These tests lead to pass/fail decisions that affect the futures of these test takers. Indeed, the testing programs described in this chapter have serious consequences for secondary students and those preparing for professions.

Part III: Issues in Standardized Achievement Testing deals with significant issues affecting the validity of interpreting and using test scores for many purposes.

The Pollution of Test Score Interpretations and Uses, Chapter 7, discusses a problem concerning the truthfulness of test scores. The public tends to use achievement test scores as the sole indicator of student learning. Consequently, some educators, eager to please the public, engage in arguably unethical practices to increase test scores. This chapter discusses these polluting practices, how widespread they may be, and how they affect education.

Chapter 8, *Consequences of Standardized Achievement Testing,* provides a framework for thinking about the positive and negative aspects of extensive standardized testing and speculates about the benefits and deficits of testing programs. The assessment of benefits and deficits due to the creation of a testing program will help you understand the need for the testing program.

Chapter 9, *Standardized Achievement Testing of Students at Risk,* discusses three comingled populations of students who typically score low on standardized intelligence and achievement tests. That these students are performing below expectations is well documented. Federal and state laws and other regulations govern the education and testing of students at risk. The nation needs to be concerned about the education of these students and ensure that they learn sufficiently so that they can more fully participate in society. Also, one must guard against misinterpretation and misuse of of these students' test scores.

Chapter 10, *How Can Standardized Achievement Test Results Help Students Learn?* espouses many ideals about standardized achievement testing that are widely supported by educators. These ideals range from the reason for standardized achievement testing, to how to prepare for these tests, to what can be done in the classroom to make achievement testing better.

This book is intended to elicit opinions about certain practices and conditions involving achievement testing. As you read each chapter, you might build a working model in your mind about what students need to learn, what factors play a role in this learning, and what you can do to influence them. Standardized achievement testing can be a friend or an enemy in this process. All interpretations and uses of test results are subject to a rigorous test: Does validity evidence support this interpretation or use? If the answer is yes, then you should proceed with the interpretation or use. If the answer is no, you should question why anyone would want to interpret or use a test score for that purpose without supporting validity evidence, and you should also consider the consequences on students of how test scores are interpreted and used.

Acknowledgments

This book has been a long labor that has been aided by many contributors. Foremost among these are my many students who have read earlier drafts of this book, read and analyzed many related essays and research, discussed and argued the issues, and gleefully pointed out flaws in the earlier drafts. Any flaws that remain are my sole responsibility.

Cathy Taylor of the University of Washington has been a very valuable advisor, critic, and friend. My colleague Eva Midobuche here at ASU West provided valuable advice on Chapter 9. Valerie Larrison also provided assistance in this project. Their comments as reviewers proved very helpful in the development of this book. Many essays and research studies contributed to the ideas presented, and although references in the back of this book attest to their influence, the hundreds of educators—among them, testing specialists who study and write about standardized achievement testing—contribute to this continuing debate about its value and direction. Also, Lynda Griffiths of TKM Productions copyedited this book. Her timely, thorough, and competent efforts are appreciated.

Part I

Foundations for Standardized Testing

The first of three parts of this book provides a foundation for understanding the types of standardized tests used and the validity of how test scores are interpreted and implemented. This foundation is perhaps the most important part of the book, because it provides a context for understanding achievement testing.

Chapter 1 introduces a model for student learning that includes cognitive and affective outcomes that students achieve as a result of their schooling and the factors that influence these outcomes. Some of these factors are under the control of schools and educators, whereas other factors exist outside of school. Chapter 1 argues that it is important to understand what the outcomes are and what we, as educators, can do to influence student learning in the context of these external factors.

Chapter 2 provides the basic concepts in testing and statistical ideas that you may find as you read this book and deal with test scores in your educational career. This chapter features an extended discussion about test score scales associated with the normal distribution. Many ideas from this chapter are applied in subsequent chapters.

Chapter 3 discusses the most important idea in the book: validity. As you will see, validity is a rich, complex subject. What you should realize is that validity teaches us all to ask the right questions about any test score interpretation and use.

These three chapters provide a core of information that you will find useful in learning about the types of standardized tests and the issues that you will face when interpreting and using their scores.

1

A Model for Student Learning

This chapter's purpose is to have you think about creating your own working model for student learning that will guide you in your teaching. Although your model may include ideas presented in this chapter, the foundation of your model will build naturally from your own beliefs about what students should learn and what factors influence learning. As a teacher or teaching-in-training, you probably have thought about this model and have an idea about what this framework looks like. Now is the time to think more seriously about this model, before you begin your study of standardized achievement testing.

A model for student learning is likely to have three parts. The first part includes many outcomes of education, such as how students develop as a result of their 12-year experience in school. The second part of this model includes all factors over which we teachers have control and are believed to cause these outcomes. Certainly the quality and amount of our teaching are two important factors in this second element. The third part includes all factors outside school over which we have *no* control. For example, family stability and socioeconomic status have a strong influence on student learning.

To focus on the content of this chapter, consider your answers to two fundamental questions:

1. What are the desired outcomes of schooling?
2. What factors cause these outcomes?

The basic structure of this model for student learning looks like this:

Outcomes	Causes of These Outcomes
Student Learning	Factors Internal to School + Factors External to School

Build your own working model that identifies the learning outcomes that you think are crucial to one's education. Then identify the forces existing inside and outside schools that influence these outcomes. As you do this, you will realize that we teachers have an important role in determining our students' success, but we are not alone in having an influence on student learning. Factors existing both inside and outside school that are not under our control also have great influences on student learning. As you more clearly identify these outcomes of education, standardized achievement testing will enter this model, as a potential friend or foe, depending on how we interpret or use test results, validly or invalidly. This chapter is loosely based on the important work of Carroll (1963, 1985).

What Are the Desired Outcomes of Education?

Let us start with the idea that there are many outcomes of a good education. No test will ever be an adequate measure of these outcomes. In fact, most standardized achievement tests are merely small surveys of knowledge and skills sampled from a broad domain of student-learned behaviors.

Generally, these outcomes can conveniently be categorized into three human behavior domains: cognitive, affective, and psychomotor.

- The *cognitive domain* involves intellectual behavior, including knowledge, skills, developing abilities, and intelligence.
- The *affective domain* involves emotions as well as emotional tendencies and emotional intelligence, such as attitude, locus of control, perseverance, personality, self-confidence, self-concept, self-esteem, and motivation.
- The *psychomotor domain* includes physical actions that involve mental behavior.

The cognitive domain is the main concern of educators. Although many educators support the affective domain, there are pockets of resistance about its importance in American education that reflect a legitimate argument. The psychomotor domain is probably the least important of these three (and will not be discussed in this chapter), but the psychomotor domain does play an important role in our daily lives.

Cognitive Outcomes of Schooling

The desired cognitive outcomes of schooling differ considerably from simple knowledge to very complex forms of behavior, such as highly intricate mathematical or scientific problem solving. Diverse values and beliefs also affect a person's choice of these outcomes. Cognitive outcomes of schooling are determined through a complex, long process of deliberation that involves a variety of constituencies, usually at the state level. The outcomes are often called *content standards*. Zwick (2000) reported that nearly all 50 states have or are developing content standards. These standards define the content that the state legislature or the state's school board believes should be implemented in its state. Normally, when content standards are adopted, the state mandates an achievement test that reflects these content standards.

Knowledge

The most fundamental kernel of the cognitive domain is knowledge. All knowledge consists of facts, concepts, principles, and procedures. A *fact* is a declarative truth that most people agree is true. A *concept* is a term that requires a definition, is distinguished by characteristics, and can be tested by providing novel examples and nonexamples (Roid & Haladyna, 1982). The word *novel* is used in this explanation because if the examples and nonexamples were not novel, one would be testing only memory as opposed to understanding of knowledge. Generally, we educators like to teach and test for understanding instead of rote memory. A *principle* is a lawful relationship. And last, a *procedure* is a set of activities one follows that has a purpose. Table 1.1 shows the four types of knowledge with examples of test questions for each.

Logical analysis and research point to using multiple-choice tests to measure knowledge (Haladyna, 1999). Essay tests can also be used to measure knowledge too, but this item format requires expensive scoring and human judgment that can be inconsistent and biased. Therefore, most standardized achievement tests use the multiple-choice format. Knowledge is at the core of most standardized achievement tests. This is an important idea that you should keep in mind as you read other chapters. Too often, school curricula are filled student outcomes that require knowledge and not enough outcomes and test items that measure more complex mental behavior (Frederiksen, 1984). Moreover, we teachers tend to overemphasize the memorization of knowledge and give less attention to the understanding or the application of knowledge to solve problems and to think creatively or critically.

Skills

Knowledge involves knowing or understanding facts, concepts, principles, and procedures. Skills are complementary to knowledge because skills involve *doing*. A *skill* is an application of knowledge; it is a singular, learned behavior performed by a person. There are mental skills and physical skills in the school curriculum. Each type of skill requires performance. With the automotive example, some skills in changing the tire

TABLE 1.1   *Four Types of Knowledge*

Knowledge	Example in Terms of a Test Question
Fact	What is the composition of an automobile tire? (There is only one correct answer.)
Concept	What is "balancing a tire"?
Principle	Which type of tire inflation strategy will make for a comfortable car ride? (Based on a principle)
Procedure	Which is the correct way to change a tire? (Checking students' knowledge of a procedure)

are (1) setting the hand brake, (2) loosening the lug nuts, (3) jacking up the car, (4) removing the tire, (5) putting on the spare, and (6) tightening the lug nuts. Other procedures are needed as well. These involve securing a safe area to change the tire (off the road, not on a hill), getting tools and the spare tire ready, and perhaps putting on some music to listen to while you work. Most skills are directly observable and have a tangible result. The connection between knowledge and skill is indisputable; one can argue sensibly that knowing comes before doing.

Skills require observation. Multiple-choice tests measure only the knowledge of a skill, not the skill itself. Test developers economically substitute a measure of knowledge of a skill for the measurement of the actual skill, because to measure a skill requires performance and observation by a trained judge. Thus, many standardized achievement tests, though referring to skills, usually emphasize knowledge. Teachers often try to measure skills by using skill tests in reading, writing, and mathematics. Table 1.2 gives examples of typical skills learned by students in the elementary grades.

Like knowledge, the school curriculum and state content standards have many references to skills. Instructional (behavioral) objectives are used to describe these skills. One dilemma facing educators and the public who want students to learn is the emphasis placed on the learning of skills versus the application of skills.

Fluid Abilities

Many cognitive psychologists are increasingly researching and writing about fluid learned or developing abilities (Lohman, 1993; Messick, 1984; Sternberg, 1998). These abilities have complex compositions that are very familiar, such as reading, writing, mathematical and scientific problem solving, critical thinking, and creative thinking. Each ability can be well described and measured. The best way to measure an ability is a performance test that emphasizes novel behavior that generalizes to the fluid ability instead of referring to a domain of specific knowledge and skills. Because each fluid ability is complex, it is also very slow growing. All fluid abilities consist of a foundation of knowledge, a large set of skills, and even affective traits. Psychomotor behavior is often found in a fluid ability. At the core of any fluid ability is the student's tendency to apply this knowledge and these skills to create, to think critically, and to solve a problem

TABLE 1.2   *Typical Skills in the Elementary School Curriculum*

Skills	*Student Learning Objectives Emphasizing Skills*
Reading	Identify facts from nonfiction material. Derive meaning from picture clues. Differentiate fiction from nonfiction.
Writing	Use correct spelling, punctuation, capitalization, grammar and word usage, and good penmanship to complete effectively a variety of writing tasks.
Mathematics	Add, subtract, multiply, and divide whole numbers, fractions, and decimals.

that the test or test item has required. Table 1.3 gives examples of fluid abilities you might encounter in school and in life. In actuality, there are thousands of fluid abilities, many of which seem very interrelated.

One of the many manifestations of educational reform is in teaching students fluid abilities instead of teaching students to memorize facts, concepts, principles, and procedures. Wiggins (1989, 1993) has popularized *authentic assessment*, where school testing seems realistic and important to students. Despite criticisms about what "authenticity" might be, this type of teaching and standardized achievement testing has increased. Authentic assessment is founded on performance-based, not multiple-choice, tests (Frederiksen, 1984). Wiggins and fellow test reformers support the teaching and assessing of these fluid abilities as superior to traditional knowledge and skills teaching and testing. Learning a fluid ability is more demanding because knowledge and skills are only part of the ability. Applying knowledge and skills in complex ways is the essence of a good test item measuring a fluid ability.

Writing, the most commonly known fluid ability, dominates state standardized testing programs. It consists of modes (e.g., narrative, imaginative, persuasive) and analytic traits (e.g., organization, voice, conventions). Schools and school districts have a writing curriculum and feature instruction that emphasizes writing. Knowledge about writing and writing skills is important, but the act of writing is the focus of the writing assessment.

The problem with any fluid ability is that each is difficult to define and test, and the cost of scoring the test is very high. Another problem is that judges who score student writing can be inconsistent and biased. Thus, elected and appointed officials are not as eager to support the measurement of fluid abilities as they are for knowledge.

TABLE 1.3   *Examples of Fluid Abilities*

Category	Examples of Fluid Abilities
School	Reading, writing, speaking, listening, mathematical problem solving, scientific problem solving, social interaction and social systems
Creative abilities	All visual and performing arts, including painting, sculpture, poetry, fiction, plays, photography, furniture design, dance Creative writing (essays, books, poems)
Professions	Physician, architect, nurse, teacher, accountant, electrician, lawyer, social worker, financial planner, dietician, pharmacist, plumber, comedian, stock broker, electrician, interior designer
Sports	Golf, baseball, football, basketball, tennis, boxing, sky diving, volleyball, wrestling, swimming, bowling, archery, horse racing, soccer
Recreation	Crocheting, gardening, automobile restoration, stamp collecting, humor, karaoke, billiards, orienteering, hiking, equestrian, pitching pennies, card games, computer games, skateboarding

Nonetheless, many states and school districts are increasing their interest in fluid abilities, particularly writing.

Intelligence

Intelligence is usually thought of as a general capacity for learning. Three mental abilities commonly associated with intelligence are verbal, quantitative, and analytical. Traditionally, intelligence is regarded as a relatively stable trait that is not affected by a rich or poor intellectual life. Although there is evidence that people inherit the capacity for intelligence from their birth parents, intelligence may also be influenced in prenatal life and in the first five to seven years of life (Bloom, 1976). A study by Husen and Tuijnman (1991) done in the Netherlands showed that environmental factors have an influence on intelligence. In fact, the author cited home background as a strong factor on intellectual growth. One might argue that since schooling is an intellectual activity occupying about 900 hours a year of a student's time, plus homework, schools probably provide a basis for intellectual growth that increases one's intelligence. The amount of intelligence increase caused by schooling, however, is an issue of considerable importance to educators and the public supporting education.

Educators and the general public would like to think that all students can learn equally well if each was provided with the same rich experience in the home and in the school (thus, all students would achieve to a high level). This idea has not been proven by experience or research, however. Instead, most psychologists think that intelligence strongly affects learning, explaining the consistently high correlation between intelligence and achievement measures.

Standardized intelligence testing is not pervasive in school, partly because of frequent, historical misinterpretation and misuse of intelligence test scores (Gould, 1996; Jensen, 1980). These intelligence tests have not helped teachers, because intelligence test scores have not benefited us in planning our students' education. Chapter 4 discusses intelligence and valid and invalid interpretations and uses of intelligence test scores.

Affective Outcomes of Schooling

Up to this point, the emotional side of schooling has not been mentioned. Most states and school districts have content standards or curricula that are cognitive in nature. Seldom do these states and school districts mention the affective domain, except in the vaguest terms. But to what extent are you interested in adding an emotional component to your model for student learning? This section briefly describes what some of these outcomes might be. Some educators might want to include these affective traits in the right-hand column as factors that may influence learning, and this also may be true.

Each affective outcome listed in this section has received considerable attention from researchers. However, very little formal assessment of affective outcomes of schooling has been reported. Standardized achievement tests typically do not assess these affective traits. The set of traits presented do not exhaust the affective domain but are certainly worth considering in your working model of student learning.

Attitude

Attitude is an emotional tendency for or against an object. Attitude toward school and subject matters has been the object of long-term investigation. Haladyna and Thomas (1979) examined attitudes toward school and seven subject matters in grades 2 through 8, and determined that students have a generally declining attitude toward school but a sustaining attitude toward certain subject matters. They discovered that some subject matters were more highly regarded, such as physical education, art, and music. They also found that social studies was universally disliked. Moreover, older students disliked social studies more than younger students. Low-cost surveys of attitude are possible and provide easy-to-obtain outcome measures of student attitude. To what extent should educators and the public value student attitude toward school and its subject matters?

Motivation

Motivation is another emotional disposition that reflects the degree to which students are willing to commit to achieving a goal. We educators like to think that motivation is learned, and one of our jobs is to increase it. Educational psychologists distinguish between two kinds of motivation: intrinsic and extrinsic. *Intrinsic motivation* requires that a student sets a goal for learning but that the student does so because he or she wants to set this goal for personal satisfaction. This is motivation for its own sake. *Extrinsic motivation* is setting a goal because by achieving that goal, the student will get a tangible reward, such as points in a course or subject, a higher grade, praise, or a parent's financial gift. Goals set by students can be influenced by many factors, coming from the home or the teacher or even classmates. Thus, complex factors are working on motivation. *Self-efficacy* is one aspect of motivation where the student assesses whether he or she has the ability to achieve a goal.

Perseverance

Perseverance, a very desirable human trait, is seen when a student keeps trying despite setbacks. Some learning environments promote perseverance. Thus, we teachers, perhaps through the environment created in our classrooms, can influence this affective trait. We can motivate students to set realistic goals, to make plans of action to achieve these goals, and to persevere in attempting to attain the goals. As you can see, perseverance is a very desirable outcome of schooling.

Self-Concept

Self-concept concerns self-awareness and the value a person attaches to himself or herself. Shavelson, Bolus, and Keesling (1980) posited four divisions of self-concept: academic, social, emotional, and physical. Academic self-concept is probably the one that is of most concern for educators. We teachers want confident learners who believe in their ability to learn. However, academic self-concept varies at times in life in different classrooms with different teachers and with different subject matters. There is some evidence to link self-concept with achievement, so self-concept becomes more than an outcome of school—it is one cause of student learning.

Certainly, teachers are in the business of improving student self-concept, because we teachers want our students to be confident learners. Will self-concept be added to your model as a valued outcome of a good education? As a cause of learning?

Anxiety

Anxiety is generalized fear. Some anxiety can be good, as in just before a major event, such as an athletic contest, a speech, or a test. If anxiety is too high, however, it can prove disabling to a student. One can generally link anxiety to school or specifically link anxiety to a certain aspect of school. Mathematics anxiety, for example, is well documented, specific to a subject matter that can make some students avoid mathematics courses and any mathematics assignments, especially problem solving.

Test anxiety affects about 25 percent of the general population. It increases throughout the grades and is related to performance on tests, as you might expect. Test anxiety and general anxiety are treatable. As a teacher, you might want to monitor anxiety and test anxiety to see if you can reduce it at the individual level as well as at the classroom level.

Limitations of Wanting and Using Affective Learner Outcomes

Public and legislative support for promoting affective student outcomes is lacking in U.S. schools. Standardized tests of affective outcomes of schooling are not popular and initiative for collecting student affective measures is inadequate. Still, few teachers would claim that the emotional side of student learning is unimportant. Attitude, motivation, perseverance, and self-concept are several concepts from a larger collection of terms that reflect the affective domain. You may decide to build your model of student learning based on these affective components, but the assessment of student measures of these traits is not likely to be appreciated or used by the public or its representatives, legislators and school boards.

Summary

So what are the ideal outcomes of schooling? Table 1.4 suggests several outcomes that may be logical extensions of modern learning theory and reform-oriented leaders in education. Research expounds on the various ways that intelligence is important in society. The idea of including fluid abilities in your working model is well grounded in personal experience. Cognitive learning theories have focused on the development of abilities and provided a scientific basis for the development of these abilities. The idea of knowledge and skills is also well grounded in the history of education and personal experience. The notion that knowledge and skills is an integral part of fluid abilities is a newer idea but one that should have permanence in pedagogy.

TABLE 1.4 *Idealized Outcomes of Schooling*

Outcome	Measure
Intellectual development that seems captured by the term *intelligence*	Any intelligence test
Fluid abilities, including reading, writing, speaking, listening, mathematical and scientific problem solving, and critical and creative thinking	A test of fluid abilities, usually performance based; writing assessments are the most common type
Supporting knowledge	Tests of essential knowledge that foster the development of fluid abilities; published standardized achievement tests seem to capture this knowledge very well
Supporting skills	Tests of essential skills that foster the development of fluid abilities; published standardized achievement tests seem to capture the knowledge of skills very well
Affective component of fluid abilities— namely, motivation, attitude, self-concept, self-esteem, academic self-confidence, perse- verance, internal locus of control, and other qualities existing within emotional intelli- gence	Test developers are beginning to recognize this component, but there are no standardized tests of this aspect of fluid ability or of the concept *emotional intelligence*

What Factors Outside of Schools Influence These Outcomes?

Now that we have identified potential outcomes of schooling, we can speculate about those factors that cause these outcomes. As a teacher, you will develop your personal learning theory that not only tells you what the important outcomes are but also how you hope to help students attain these outcomes.

Intelligence

Earlier in this chapter, intelligence was treated as an outcome of schooling. Intelligence is nurtured in school and developed to the fullest extent possible. In this section of the chapter, we deal with intelligence as a cause of student learning.

Chapter 4 discusses the many aspects of intelligence. Knowing one's intelligence level helps educators understand student learning. Certainly, teachers know that highly intelligent students often learn more quickly and thoroughly and that students of lower intelligence generally struggle in school, learn slowly, and fail to learn as much as highly intelligent students. High intelligence does not guarantee or ensure a high degree of learning, however. The human equation for student learning that you are building in this chapter has an emotional component that influences one's success in learning.

Given that some students will have below-average intelligence, we teachers try to help all students learn so that they can develop the abilities they need to thrive in society. We cannot ignore intelligence as a factor in learning, and we should not expect all students to learn at the same level or at the same speed, because intelligence seems to govern the quality and speed of learning.

Social Capital

The late, highly esteemed sociologist, James Coleman (1987), coined the phrase *social capital* to suggest that all people have a social heritage that strongly affects learning. Social capital refers to the character and values a student carries into school. Coleman attributed social capital to family and home influences and even to neighborhood values. This powerful idea is strongly supported in research and is so pervasive in its strength that it can hardly be questioned. Strong family support for education is incredibly important. Without social capital, students have little chance for academic success. Coleman argued that with very low social capital, no amount of schooling will matter. This chilling conclusion suggests that schools and teachers have virtually no chance of helping students learn when social capital is at a bankrupt level. Indeed, a review of the prison population might support this reasoning. Prisoners have lifelong records of low achievement, poor decision making and judgment, dysfunctional families, and other social problems. The social capital in this population is very low.

A recent study in California reported in *The CRESST Line* (2000) showed that 65 percent of differences among schools on achievement test scores were related to poverty and English-speaking ability. Cohn (2000) reported several significant studies where from 64 to 91 percent of the differences among children, schools, and states could be linked to social factors—namely, number of parents in the home, parents' education, type of community, and economic status. One might draw the conclusion that it is not what the schools teach but the students' social capital that determines their achievement level. Let us examine aspects of social capital to see if any of these fit into your developing model for student learning.

Prenatal Factors.   New research on nutrition suggests that prenatal nutrition contributes to intellectual development. Not surprisingly, mothers spend time nurturing themselves before giving birth in hopes of producing a healthy child; in contrast, evidence proves that alcoholic and drug-addicted mothers affect their newborns in a negative way. Recent research has also uncovered significant cognitive impairment in children with low birth weight. These children, by the fact that their birth weight is low, are predicted to be more likely to have lower intelligence, lower achievement, and more behavior problems than average-weight newborns (Taylor, Klein, Minich, & Hack, 2000). As researchers continue to conduct studies on factors that impair children before they are born, it is likely that they will discover other categories of prenatal factors that will cause students to be at risk.

Single Parents and the Changing Family Structure. According to Whitehead (1993), the phenomena of divorce and out-of-wedlock childbirth are producing a generation of children who live in poverty, often lack a father, and consequently do very poorly in school. The changing family structure is a late-twentieth-century phenomenon that is painfully harming children. For instance, in 1990, close to 57 percent of births were nonmarital. Thus, the reporting of the low status of children's achievement by Herrnstein and Murray (1994) reflects two pernicious causes: lack of family structure and poverty arising from a single parent who is often a mother and is often not prepared to support her family. The *Arizona Republic* (December 9, 1990) reported that 20 percent of students have an emotional, learning, behavioral, or developmental problem traceable to the dissolution of the family. Even worse, 25 percent of these troubled youths suffer more than one of these disabilities. Whitehead reported that even after controlling for race, income, and religion, scholars find significant differences between children's achievement in intact families versus single-parent families.

A recent study by Caldas and Bankston (1999) involving 42,000 graduates in Louisiana who were given a curriculum-relevant achievement test led these researchers to conclude that family structure was three times more effective than poverty as a predictor of achievement. Single-parent families was the most potent predictor of lack of success in schools. In fact, the proportion of two-parent families, which fluctuates from state to state, is nearly perfectly correlated with state achievement levels. Thus, state comparisons seem to be nothing more than comparisons of the family structures found in each state. That is how powerful the family influence is for a child's education. The disrupted family does not have to lead to low achievement and other problems in and out of school, but research is showing that it often does lead to these problems. No one should tacitly assume that schools can easily address this problem.

Student Mobility. One indicator of social capital is student mobility. Itinerant students who are not in the same school year after year typically do not have good records for learning. It is easy to see why. Lack of continuity and social context will hurt even the most able students. Some students move in and out of school regularly during the school year. Their learning suffers and their achievement is well below the national average. These children also suffer from many of the other limitations of low social capital listed in this section.

Alspaugh (1999) reported in a study done in the Midwest that students who move to a larger middle school or high school had lower achievement records than students who do not move. His study argues for family stability, especially in the elementary school. Rumberger and Larson (1988) pointed out that it is easy to link mobility to low achievement, but they caution that there may be other contributing factors, such as poverty or family dysfunction. Their research, however, does show that highly mobile students tend to have both social and academic problems.

Parental Education. One of the best predictors of student learning is parental education. Does it make sense that educated parents will promote educational values that lead to a better educated student? Indeed, this consistent correlation between the most influential parent, the mother, and standardized test scores is easy to understand.

Parenting Ability.   Interest in parenting ability has been increasing since the appearance of the popular book by Dr. Spock more than 50 years ago. To what extent does parenting influence the mental development of children? Parents would like to think that their influence on their children is considerable. Otherwise, they would not use all the resources they do in raising their children. Another article in the *Arizona Republic* (December 8, 1991) reported that a Carnegie Foundation study found that 1.5 million students come to school unprepared. It is not surprising to trace this lack of preparation to parents.

One of the most extensive and pernicious manifestations of low parenting ability is child abuse, which is "nonaccidental use of physical force or the nonaccidental act of omission by a parent or other custodian responsible for the care of a child" (http:// my.webmd.com/content/asset/miller_keane_6793). Although the extensiveness of child abuse and its effects on student learning is not easy to measure, it must be considered a factor affecting student learning that comes from outside the schools. Early childhood programs are seldom adequately supported to overcome the problems presented by children with parents who have low parenting ability.

Neighborhood (Social Fabric).   Sociologist James Coleman went so far as to assert that social capital includes neighborhood values that carry into the home. Perhaps this is why many large cities have color-coded maps showing neighborhoods with high standardized test scores, helping parents find areas in which to live where the educational values in neighbors' homes are highest. Coleman showed that in neighborhoods that have strong religious mores, students tend to do better in school. Examples include Jewish, Mormon, and Catholic communities, where synagogues, temples, churches, community centers, and other social gathering places provide positive influences for students, including an appreciation for a good education. Caldas and Bankston (1999) also found that the neighborhood influence was more powerful than the structure of an individual family.

Poverty.   One of the most troubled groups of people in the United States, and in the world for that matter, are those living in poverty. The number of children living in poverty in the United States is large and growing. A Harris poll, reported by Berliner and Biddle (1995), concluded that one in five children live in poverty, and for infants, the ratio is one in four. A survey from the National Center for Educational Statistics (1996) reported that the poverty rate was at 21.2 percent for children under the age of 18.

This increase in poverty is also supplanted with considerable variability in school funding, which further affects the poor. A report from the *New York Times* said that social well-being is at a 25-year low. Four of six indicators for troubled children have increased: child abuse, teenage suicide, drug abuse, and dropping out of school. These statistics and our own observations of students with low social capital confirm why the problem of low social capital is so powerful.

Bracey (1998) reported that 89 percent of the variation in national achievement test scores for states can be explained by knowing the number of parents in the home, the type of community in which the child lives, the education level of the parents, and the poverty rate. The relationship between any set of intelligence or achievement test scores and poverty is remarkably strong. Table 1.5 shows the correlation of family

TABLE 1.5   *Correlation of SES to Achievement*

Annual Household Income	ACT Composite Score, 1998/2000
Less than $18,000	18.5/18.3
$18,000 to $24,000	19.3/19.1
$24,000 to $30,000	20.1/19.8
$30,000 to $40,000	20.6/20.4
$40,000 to $50,000	21.3/21.1
$50,000 to $60,000	21.7/21.6
$60,000 to $80,000	22.2/22.1
$80,000 to $100,000	22.8/22.6
More than $100,000	23.5/23.4
ALL TEST TAKERS	21.0/21.0

Source: Adapted from National Center for Fair and Open Testing (Fall 2000g).

income to achievement test scores. This Educational Testing Service (ETS) report cited other research current to 1980 that provides similar links to family income. It concluded, "Students from middle and upper-class families have home and community environments that provide more support for educational attainment, and attend better schools, to name a few relevant factors" (ETS, 1980, p. 8).

Summary

This section suggests that two powerful factors exist outside of school that affect student learning and performance on standardized achievement tests: intelligence and social capital. These two factors should not serve as excuses for not teaching students who have low intelligence or negative social capital. We teachers are in a profession that recognizes the need for *all* students to learn. Our efforts to educate the most problematic students may not show up on test scores but we are obligated to provide the richest and best experience possible for these students so that they will be able to live as productive members of society.

What Factors Inside Schools Influence These Outcomes?

This section discusses factors that exist in schools that are known or have been shown through research and theory to have an influence on student learning or affective outcomes of learning. These factors should not surprise you.

School Effects

Does schooling make a difference in a student's life? This question cannot be answered through experimental studies, because to deny schooling to anyone would not be a logical alternative. However, there are descriptive and comparative studies that suggest that schooling does make a difference.

Prekindergarten schooling makes a difference in a student's academic performance. In studies where students are assigned to prekindergarten or no prekindergarten, those with the school experience later do better on tests of academic knowledge and skills and also have better attendance records (Bland, 2001). California and Texas are leaders in prekindergarten education; the other states seem woefully behind, however. Georgia has just initiated prekindergarten education for all of its students funded by a lottery and voter referendum.

A study by Lee and Loeb (2000) in the Chicago Public Schools suggests that school size makes a difference in learning. Smaller elementary schools seem to provide better education according to teacher surveys. Interaction with students is greater and the learning environment in these smaller schools is more positive. Studies like this one give credence to the idea that schools make a difference in student achievement.

Effective Teaching

Good teaching has many known, coordinated elements, including the following:

- Clearly stated, important learning outcomes presented to students at the beginning of the school year, preferably based on the state's content standards and/or the school district's curricula
- Clear expectations to your students about what they are supposed to learn
- Getting parents involved as partners in helping students learn
- Instruction that is developmentally appropriate for each student
- Effective classroom management
- Frequent, nongraded feedback to students to guide their learning
- Appropriate assessment of student learning using a variety of assessment formats, including performance tests and portfolios
- Summative evaluations of student learning, which may include classroom assessments and standardized achievement tests
- Recognition for the emotional side of learning that includes many qualities discussed earlier in this chapter, such as motivation and attitude toward school and subject matters
- Frequent chances to become successful and establish a positive history of learning, which implies that students will have continuing opportunities for success in learning, as opposed to a more traditional approach where failure is tolerated

This list is not the definitive be-all and end-all of teaching. Indeed, the third edition of the *Handbook of Research on Teaching* (Wittrock, 1986) represents teaching in its full complexity. No list can do justice to this complex profession.

Quantity of Instructional Time

The amount of time spent learning is an issue that has received considerable attention with researchers. Stallings (1980) observed, "Teachers need to be told more than just to allocate additional time to academic activities and to keep students on task. They need to know how to use time effectively in a variety of activities, how to vary time with different groups, and how to support students to keep them on task" (p. 11). Stallings presented compelling evidence that the amount of time allocated to student learning is less important than the quality of instructional time. She discussed *allocated time* as the time scheduled by the teacher for instruction on a subject and *engaged time* as the time spent by students actually engaged in active learning. The best instruction gets students on task for longer periods than the worst instruction. She reported differences in engaged time as much as 45 minutes in a typical 60-minute class period. Stallings further argued that the quality of instruction interacts with the quantity of instruction.

Fisher and Berliner (1985) presented a variety of perspectives on the idea of time well spent in the classroom as a powerful factor in learning. Their edited book contains a variety of essays citing research supporting this idea about time and learning. Studies such as those by Fisher and Berliner show that it is how teachers spend time in the classroom that counts. Engaged, active learning time is better than wasted time. If a teacher spends 45 minutes doing nothing important with students, then that time does not count. But if that time is spent learning, then test scores should show more learning.

One way to extend learning time is homework, but this, too, has to be well invested in useful homework, not busywork. One of the most extensive treatments on homework was done by Cooper (1989). For the most part, homework is beneficial to older students—junior high and beyond. Below the junior high age, homework does not seem to have much effect on standardized achievement measures. Cooper (pp. 188–191) provided guidelines for homework that are based on his extensive research. Homework should *extend* what is being learned in class and not simply be more of the same or drill and practice. Teachers should prepare the homework assignments carefully and make them clear to the students. Also, the students must see the value of homework as extending or improving their learning. Having consequences for doing homework is one way to create motivation, even if it is the less desirable extrinsic motivation. However, Cooper believes that homework should have a diagnostic value. There is little doubt that when teachers assign homework, when students are conscientious about using it, and when the homework is evaluated by the teacher in a meaningful way, students will learn more (U.S. Department of Education, 1987).

Learning Environment (School and Classroom Climate)

The social composition of the classroom and the school has been the object of considerable interest of researchers and has emerged slowly as a factor to consider in helping students learn (Brookover et al., 1978). Thus, one can hypothesize that the learning environment is a valuable factor in developing your model for student learning. We teachers can shape and improve the learning environment, because we believe that a positive learning environment will help students learn.

The learning environment is hardly a single, holistic concept. In fact, quite the opposite is true. The learning environment exists at two levels: school and class. The school climate reflects leadership in the school, within its faculty and staff, the facilities themselves—factors such as safety, discipline, and rules; opportunities and rewards for student participation; level of expectations for students; administration/faculty/student collegiality; and home support, cooperation, and participation.

At the classroom level, each teacher has the ability to create a class learning environment that uniquely reflects his or her leadership and teaching ability. Whether the class meets once a day for an hour or continuously, as in a self-contained classroom, the learning environment is a powerful factor in student learning.

The classroom learning environment can be considered in two dimensions: social/psychological and management/organization (see Table 1.6). These two dimensions speak to separate and complementary ideas about classrooms and student learning. The social/psychological dimension is seen as facilitating good instruction and student learning and has many other outcomes of an effective nature, whereas the management/organization dimension probably resembles what is called "good teaching."

Three standardized tests of class climate are (1) the Classroom Environment Scale (CES); (2) the Learning Environment Inventory (LEI); and (3) the My Class Inventory (MCI). Moos (1979) described in detail the usage of the CES instruments. A good reference for all three of these instruments is Impara and Plake's (1998) *Mental Measurements Yearbook* (13th edition). However, teachers can design their own "home-grown" surveys that address specific concerns they have (Haladyna, 1997). The classroom climate can be surveyed to determine the status of the class regarding the conditions for learning.

School Leadership

Research on effective schools shows that leadership is critical (U.S. Department of Education, 1987). The principal must be a strong leader with a clear sense what is valued in schooling and the will and way to lead teachers and students actively involved in learn-

TABLE 1.6 *Two Dimensions of the Learning Environment*

Social/Psychological	Management/Organization
Class cohesiveness	Formality of rules
Physical environment	Pace of instruction
Friction between teacher and students	Goal direction and clarity
Favoritism for certain students	Satisfaction with school work
Cliques (student subgroups)	Organization of class activities
Apathy (disinterest)	Difficulty of class work

ing. Thus, academic goals should be the paramount emphasis. The school must be an orderly place with clear discipline policies, routines, rewards for success, and safe access for all students. High teacher morale is also an important criterion. A school with effective leadership will earn a solid reputation with students, parents, and staff.

Funding for Schools

An argument often heard is "If we had more money in the budget, we could buy the things that are needed to improve schooling." Payne and Biddle (1999) echoed this argument by reporting that there is a strong link between school funding and achievement. Certainly there is considerable disparity among schools and school districts in terms of funding. Their study involved the added problem of child poverty, which many educators believe is a strong causal link to achievement (see Terenzini, Cabrera, & Bernal, 2001). Most children living in poverty are very low achievers. Attending poorly funded schools in poverty areas of the United States does not logically seem to forecast average or high achievement. Would added funding in these areas break the cycle of poverty and low achievement that is seen over and over again? Although the study by Payne and Biddle shows that students living in poverty in underfunded schools suffer in terms of mathematics achievement, critics of this research are hesitant to draw the obvious conclusion that funding matters. But the most convincing argument Payne and Biddle give is that children living in poverty have inadequate nutrition, housing, clothing, health care, and life experiences. There is also reason to believe that family units are less positive in these environments than those seen with more affluent families. Thus, one might argue that if schools provided the social services that the home does not provide, the playing field for these children might be improved and therefore their performance might improve. But can schools overcome the handicap of low social capital? Although the role of school funding may not be as well researched as one would like, this appraisal of children living in poverty who attend underfunded schools provides a compelling argument that begs for further study to support funding as a critical agent in improving achievement.

Using Your Model Effectively in Teaching

At this point, you should have a pretty good idea about your model for student learning. You have identified the outcomes you want students to achieve, and you have identified the external and internal causes that fit your particular ideas about school and student learning. Now it is time to address some important issues and questions that involve standardized achievement testing.

What Does Your Model Indicate That Each Student Should Learn?

The first thing you might do is to flesh out the student outcomes. The outcomes you select will more than likely be cognitive, and they should come directly from state content standards and the school district curriculum. Will any outcomes be affective? Is there a connection between the two? What about psychomotor outcomes? With respect to cognitive outcomes, are you expressly interested in knowledge, or are skills also important? Are you concerned about using knowledge and skills in problem solving, critical thinking, and creative thinking? What about subject-matter disciplines? Does your state or your school district have specific content standards and a curriculum? Will you emphasize knowledge and skills or abilities?

What Is the Best Assessment of Student Learning?

The most appropriate measure of what you teach is likely to be classroom assessments, which are nonstandardized measures of student learning. However, we teachers are held accountable for developing student abilities in reading, writing, and mathematics, and for helping students learn the knowledge and skills that support these abilities. Standardized achievement tests measure this knowledge and these skills. As you understand your model better, you will develop strategies to enable you to serve your students better. Standardized achievement test scores may help you understand how much your students are learning as well as help you develop strategies for improving their learning. However, as you will learn in this book, there are many pitfalls in the way of this lofty goal.

As you work you way through these important questions, you will reach the point where you match what you have in your student learning outcome column against what the standardized achievement test measures. The degree of match will help you decide what value the standardized test has in your instructional planning and evaluation.

There are two major threats to valid interpretation of student achievement measures. First, the test might underrepresent what you are teaching. The test scores will not reflect adequately what students have learned, because too little content on the test is matched to your teaching. You may change what you teach to match the test, or convince school leaders that what you are doing is more valuable. Second, the test might not be a sufficient sample of the content that you believe you were expected to cover in your teaching. This insufficiency would minimize or discredit the test as a good measure of student learning in your class, school, or school district.

Chapters 5 and 6 will help you better frame your thinking about the role of achievement testing in your teaching. Chapters 7, 8, 9, and 10 raise serious issues that must be faced when using standardized achievement test scores.

Summary

This chapter has given you some important background about schooling. You have been encouraged to think about and develop your own model of student learning. This model will likely have three components: student outcomes and external and internal causes of these student outcomes. The next two chapters continue to build the foundation you will need for studying and evaluating standardized achievement testing and for using information from these tests effectively in helping students learn.

2

Basic Concepts and Principles of Standardized Achievement Testing

This chapter discusses the basic concepts and principles of standardized achievement testing. Definitions for common terms in testing are given, examples are provided, and some major standardized achievement tests are briefly identified. Since testing involves statistics, this chapter presents a brief primer on statistics that you might find useful for interpreting standardized achievement test scores or evaluating validity evidence.

Common Terms: Definitions and Examples

This first section defines terms used throughout this book and provides examples. A *test* is a standardized way to obtain information about student learning. It may consist of one or many test items. A multiple-choice test usually has many items. A performance test can contain a single item, a writing prompt, and the student response is scored in several dimensions using rating scales. Two types of tests are used for assessing student learning: classroom and standardized. The *classroom test* measures specific learning that occurs in the classroom, hopefully connected to the school district's curriculum. Classroom tests help teachers assess student learning over a specific time, such as during a lesson, a thematic unit, or a grading period. These tests are so named because teachers design these tests. For assessing classroom learning, accept no substitute. The fairest way to assess a student for something he or she was supposed to learn in class is a *teacher-made classroom test.* Of course, we teachers have available to us a variety of other criteria to assess students, such as portfolios (Haladyna, 1997). Nonetheless, the test (or a quiz) remains a major criterion in assessing student learning. Unfortunately, research has consistently shown that many teachers lack the necessary skills to construct good tests (Stiggins, Griswold, & Wikelund, 1989). Teacher-made tests may be keyed to our teaching and to district curriculum objectives or state or school district content standards. However, these tests may also be flawed in other ways to the extent that they prevent us from getting really good assessments of student learning.

The *standardized achievement test* broadly surveys learning. This kind of test has a low degree of association with the learning that occurs in a classroom during a grading period (usually nine weeks). Standardized achievement tests are given under standardized conditions: Everyone gets the same or equivalent test items, pencils and paper, average room temperature, a time limit or sufficient time to answer all items, a quiet room, and no interruptions. An assumption is made that the students have received relevant instruction and adequate preparation to take the standardized achievement test. Such tests also provide you with norms—tables that show relative performance of any student compared with other students for any grade level covered by the test. Table 2.1 shows comparisons between the standardized achievement test and the teacher-made classroom achievement test. As Chapter 5 shows, there are many types of standardized achievement tests, including publishers' achievement tests, school district curriculum-based tests, state-mandated tests based on a state's content standards, and national tests based on a hypothetical national curriculum.

TABLE 2.1   *Comparisons between Standardized Achievement and Teacher-Made Tests*

Criterion	*Standardized Achievement Test*	*Teacher-Made Test*
Content	General survey of student learning usually based on an idealized curriculum, state content standards, or a school district curriculum	Specific to a classroom for a time period; should be related to the school district curriculum and/or state content standards
Reliability	Generally high	Generally low
Grading	Not useful for student grading	Valid for student grading if the tests are linked to district curriculum or the state content standards
Teacher evaluation	Not valid for teacher evaluation unless evidence is produced showing a strong linkage of the test content to state or school district content standards and controls exist for external factors	Valid for teacher evaluation if the content of the test is matched to the content for the class
Norms	A basis for comparison among students or groups of students	No norms exist
Length	Usually very long	Usually less than one hour
Source	Produced by a testing company, school district, or state	Produced by a teacher
Administration conditions	Very standardized	Can be very flexible to meet student needs or accommodate learning styles or disabilities

When students respond to a test, a set of rules is used for scoring the results to arrive at a test score. This *test score* is the descriptive number that characterizes the amount of student learning measured by the test. Generally, the teacher adds the points assigned to correct answers to multiple-choice test items, or uses rating scales and adds up the ratings on each important trait that is being evaluated.

Evaluation generally refers to a subjective judgment about a student, instructional program, teaching, or issue. When evaluating, the evaluator usually considers relevant information before making a judgment. For instance, when teachers are evaluated, the result is further employment, merit pay, or dismissal, among other alternatives. Or a teacher may decide that a certain reading program works or needs improvement or may favor one reading program over another. The teacher may evaluate student learning, deciding that the student is making satisfactory progress or needs an improvement plan. Grading is an evaluation based on classroom performance. Any testing program should be evaluated to determine if its good outweighs the bad consequences, and a program can be retained, revised, or retired. Every evaluation is simply a judgment based on everything known about the program, student, teacher, or testing program that is being evaluated.

Assessment is a very important activity. It is a systematic method for getting and using test scores and other information to draw inferences about student learning, teaching, or instructional program effectiveness. Dependable and reliable information will provide dependable and reliable assessments. Both teacher-made and standardized achievement tests are useful for assessing student learning.

It is important to distinguish between evaluation and assessment. *Evaluation* is the larger, more inclusive activity that leads to an action (e.g., promote the student, provide an improvement plan for the student, keep a reading program, change your curriculum, etc). *Assessment* is a more specific activity, usually focusing on student learning. The thought processes for evaluation and assessment, however, are the same.

Three Types of Test Score Interpretations

When we teachers see a test score, we potentially have three ways to interpret that test score and characterize student learning.

A *criterion-referenced interpretation* allows us to look at a test score concerning what we think a student has learned or should learn. One criterion-referenced interpretation is that a score of 40 on a 50-item test reflects about 80 percent of what was to be learned. Criterion-referenced test score interpretations are very specific about the instructional objectives we have used to develop the test and how we can interpret student learning in reference to these objectives. Criterion-referenced interpretations are beneficial because they tell us how much a student has learned of a specific topic. (Sometimes, the term *domain referenced* is used to denote the same idea, but *criterion referenced* is the more popular term.)

A *norm-referenced interpretation* is useful for comparing students with other students. Parents and other laypersons like to know how they compare with others and how their children compare with other children. A variety of scales or statistics are used to calculate norms. Nevertheless, the intent of norm-referenced interpretations is to decide how much higher or lower one score is compared with another score. We will get more deeply into this topic in the next section. Norm-referenced test score interpretations are used when it is important to select or assign someone to a group or to give an award or honor.

A *standards-based interpretation* is a newer idea and one that has considerable merit. It is similar in character to the criterion-referenced interpretation, but there are some qualities to make a distinction. A set of content standards gives teachers an organized set of student learning objectives that are very specific about knowledge, skills, and abilities tested. Most states now have their own content standards (e.g., Arizona, Florida, Michigan, Ohio, Oregon, Virginia, and Washington, to mention a few). For example, Florida, like most other states, has a well-developed set of content standards (http://www.firn.edu/doe/sas/fcat.htm). From a test score scale, Florida's content experts will use a standard-setting process to divide the scale into five categories that very much may resemble grades A, B C, D, and E, but are called levels 5, 4, 3, 2, and 1. Pennsylvania is setting standards on its tests using four categories: advanced, proficient, basic, and below basic (http://www.pde.psu.edu/regs/chapter4Q&A.html). This gives parents and other citizens convenient ways to track the progress of a school, school district, or state. For instance:

Reading Comprehension for the Big Rainbow School District				
Year	*Advanced*	*Proficient*	*Basic*	*Below Basic*
2000	32%	31%	22%	15%
2001	34%	32%	20%	14%

Peter scored 22 on a 25-item math test. The test was supposed to sample some content he and his classmates had been learning the last two weeks. His performance (88 percent correct) tells Peter that he is pretty good, but there is room for improvement. This is a criterion-referenced interpretation. Peter learned that this was the highest score in the class. Using a norm-referenced interpretation, Peter was top scorer in the class, but he knew he could do better, for 88 percent shows room for improvement. If this test were derived from state content standards, we would relate Peter's score to those standards, such as advanced, proficient, basic, and below basic.

The process for developing tests that provide this kind of interpretation is more involved and systematic and usually consults educators, parents, business leaders, and other citizens in the state or school district. Standards-based reporting is growing increasingly more popular with the public.

The Unit of Analysis for Interpreting Test Scores

A recurring theme with the use of any test scores is the unit of analysis. In other words, when you obtain a representative test score for a student, class, school, school district, or state, you want to tell others what that score means. A student's score may mean something to that student, his or her parent, or the teacher, but a group of student scores may have another, related meaning.

So when you think about the learning outcomes and measures you want in your model for student learning, you need to think about scores for each student, for the class, for the school, or for the state. You also need to consider the meaning of scores. As larger units of analysis are used, their meaning covers up the diversity that might exist in the data. Only the individual score speaks to a more basic, fundamental unit—the student. No unit of analysis is better or worse than another, but the unit you choose makes a difference in how you interpret a test score. If a teacher is concerned about his or her class, then the class is the unit of analysis. The teacher looks for growth or positive change for the class, and worries less about the growth or change of each student. Sometimes, the composition of a group of students is significant. Take, for example, a class mean that is well below average. If the class consists of only five students who are mentally retarded, this low average score is expected. But if the class consists of five students who are gifted, the teacher will justifiably wonder what caused them to score so low on this test.

A good rule of thumb is that if the unit of analysis is large—say a class, school, school district, or state—the score is likely to be very reliable (less error). However, larger units of analysis cover up important information. Testing specialists like to disaggregate (break down) data to show patterns and trends that are not visible when data are lumped together for a larger unit of analysis. When the unit of analysis is a student, the reliability may not be as high as desired, but the student, as well as his or her parents and teachers, like the information provided, especially if diagnostic scores are linked to the school's curriculum.

What Statistics Do You Need to Know to Interpret Standardized Achievement Test Scores?

Although this chapter is not devoted to a great deal of statistics, a little bit of statistical information is helpful in understanding the technical ideas behind test score scales and norms, which are useful for norm-referenced test score interpretations. This section introduces some descriptive statistics as an introduction to the section on test score scales and norms for norm-referenced interpretations.

Mean (Average), Median, and Mode

On a 50-item math test, Luke got 40 items right, Maria got 43 items correct, and Lin Sue got 25. To arrive at the *mean (average),* you add their three scores (40 + 43 + 25 = 108) and divide this sum by 3 ($108 \div 3 = 36$). The mean score is 36 (72 percent correct). The mean is a descriptive statistic. It is a measure of central tendency. The median and the mode are also measures of central tendency. For a large set of test scores and for many reasons, the mean is preferred. Test score means generally vary between 50 and 90 percent correct of total points possible, because test designers know that such tests generally do a good job of measuring the breadth of student learning. It is important to interpret test score means validly. If you see a test with a mean of 90 percent correct, you might conclude that the test is too easy or the students who took the test really know their stuff. If you see a test with a mean of 45 percent correct, you might conclude that the test was really difficult or the students who took the test didn't have a clue. As you can see, knowing the mean of a test can be useful, but knowing the mean also raises important questions about student learning.

The *median* is the middle score in a set of scores. If there is an even number of scores, calculate the mean of the two middle scores to find the median. Is it really necessary to have a median *and* a mean? Aren't they about the same? In most cases, the mean will do. However, when you have a very small sample, the median is fairer than the mean for talking about the central tendency of data. For instance, take the average price of homes in my neighborhood:

Home 1	*Home 2*	*Home 3*	*My Home*	*Mean*	*Median*
500,000	500,000	500,000	100,000	400,000	500,000

Which statistic is the one that best tells the truth about the typical cost of homes in my small neighborhood? Mean or median? Since the median represents three of four homes, and the mean is not very much like any home in the neighborhood, the median is a good measure of central tendency.

The *mode* is the most frequently appearing score in a distribution of scores. For instance, in the distribution of numbers 1, 4, 6, 6, 8, 8, 8, the mode is 8, and the median is 6. In the previous example on prices of homes, the median and the mode are the same. Sometimes, when a distribution of scores has two or more modes, the mode is the appropriate measure of central tendency. Bimodality indicates two groups being represented in the sample. Disaggregating this set of scores may tell more about what is happening to each group.

Range and the Standard Deviation

To interpret a mean validly, one needs to know more about the distribution of test scores. Did anyone score far above the mean? Far below the mean? To help you understand this, Table 2.2 shows the highest scores, 50 out of 50, or 100 percent for Carol, and the lowest score, 20 out of 50, for Tommie. The difference between the highest and lowest score is the *range,* which is Carol's score minus Tommie's score ($50 - 20 = 30$). So the range is 30. The range is a good statistic—easy to calculate and understand. A wide range of scores on a standardized achievement test is considered good by test developers, because the students vary greatly in achievement, and the wide range of

TABLE 2.2 *A Set of Student Achievement Test Scores with a Mean of 36 and a Standard Deviation of 10*

Name	Score	Deviation from the Mean
Carol	50	$50 - 36 = 14$
Maria	45	$45 - 36 = 9$
Luke	40	$40 - 36 = 4$
Chance	25	$25 - 36 = -11$
Tommie	20	$20 - 36 = -16$

Range: Carol's 50 – Tommie's 20 = 30

scores confirms that fact. In other words, a wide range of scores indicates that some students have learned more than other students. A test should show this fact. In the classroom, having a large range in test scores is probably a bad thing, because teachers want their range to be very small and the mean of the test scores to be very high, showing effective teaching and high student learning.

The *standard deviation* is difficult to compute. Fortunately, computers calculate this useful statistic. The standard deviation is computed from an average of squared test score deviations from the mean. The standard deviation has some good properties that are very useful for interpreting test scores. For the set of scores in Table 2.2, the computer calculated a standard deviation of 10. Carol's score is more than one standard deviation above the mean—1.4 standard deviations to be exact. Maria's score is a little more than one standard deviation above the mean—0.9 to be exact. Luke is very close to the mean—0.4 standard deviations above the mean. Chance is 1.1 standard deviations below the mean. And Tommie is 1.6 standard deviations below the mean. We will see that the standard deviation is very important for making norm-referenced test score interpretations.

More about Norm-Referenced Test Score Interpretations

A raw test score is based on the number right in a multiple-choice test or the sum of ratings in a performance test. You now know how to calculate the mean and the standard deviation of these scores. With a basic understanding of the mean and the standard deviation, you can now learn about norm-referenced test score interpretations. We can begin with an understanding that student test scores are very likely to be normally distributed, as Figure 2.1 shows. Standard deviation units help you locate any test score in the normal distribution. When you locate a score, you can then make many different kinds of norm-referenced interpretations.

The Relation of Percentages of Student Scores to Standard Deviations

Notice in Figure 2.1 that the area between one standard deviation unit above and below the mean in the normal distribution includes about 68 percent (or two-thirds) of all student scores. Two standard deviation units above and below the mean includes about 95 percent of all student scores. Three standard deviation units above and below the mean includes about 99 percent of all student scores. By knowing the student score in standard deviation units, you can determine the percentage of students scoring above or below that score. This is the most fundamental type of norm-referenced interpretation.

The Relation of Cumulative Percentages to Standard Deviations

Again referring to Figure 2.1, notice that the percentages of students scoring at certain standard deviation units can be added up cumulatively. For instance, at the middle mark (0) we have 50 percent of student scores above that point and 50 percent of student scores below that point. Below −1.00 standard deviation from the center, we have 15.9 percent of all students. At three standard deviations above the mean, notice that we have accounted for 99.9 percent of all student scores. If you have a student who scores above 3.0, then this student is very rare, indeed. Only 1 in 1,000 students score that high or higher. Thus, the cumulative percentage is a useful index for locating the status of student scores relative to other student scores.

The Relation of Cumulative Percentages to Percentile Rank

A very useful scale for norm-referenced interpretation is the *percentile rank*. This scale is directly related to the idea of cumulative percentages shown in Figure 2.1. Percentile rank is an ordinal scale. It shows the percentage of students scoring at or below the percentile rank. Looking at Figure 2.1, notice that at one standard deviation above the mean, the percentile rank and the cumulative percentage is about 84, referred to as the 84th percentile. That means that whatever that test score is, about 84 percent of all students tested score below that percentile rank.

Percentile ranks are often used with parents and other laypersons to communicate rank or status relative to other students. The higher the percentile rank, the higher the standing among students. A percentile rank of 1 is the lowest rank; a percentile rank of 99 is the highest percentile rank. Although percentile rank is good for norm-referenced interpretations, you should never perform arithmetic on percentile ranks to measure growth or differences. Why? Because the differences between ranks is not uniform throughout the normal distribution. Notice the distance between the 50th percentile and

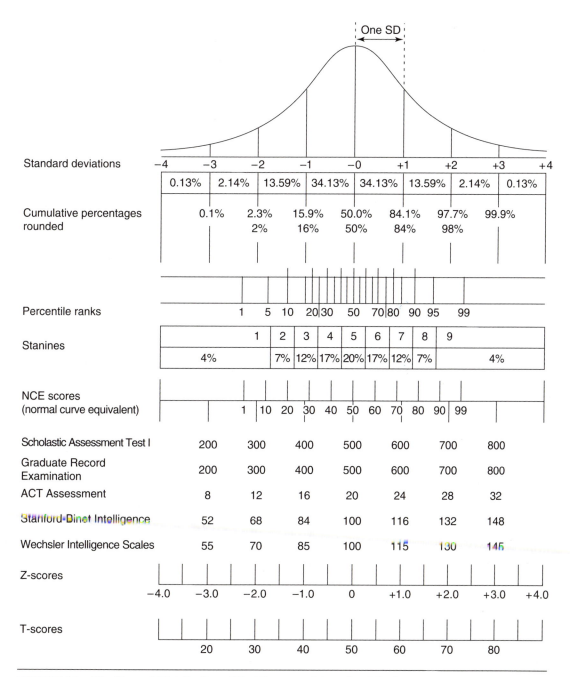

FIGURE 2.1 *The Normal Distribution of Test Scores and Associated Scales*

the 60th percentile. Then notice the difference between the 80th percentile and the 90th percentile. These intervals may be the same as to percentile ranks, but the score differences in standard deviation units is different. The difference between the 80th percentile and the 90th percentile is actually more than the difference between the 50th percentile and the 60th percentile. Don't confuse percentile rank with percentage. *Percentage correct* refers to the number you get when you divide the number right on the test (e.g., 7) by number of items on the test (e.g., 10), which, in this example, is 70 percent. Percentage correct is useful for criterion-referenced interpretations but not for norm-referenced interpretations.

In summary, percentile ranks may be used for norm-referenced interpretations of differences among students or groups of students. However, it would be inaccurate to use the percentile rank to estimate the amount of difference between students or groups or growth over time.

Stanines

When reporting scores to parents, media, and public, percentile equivalents may be too challenging, so stanines were invented to simplify percentile ranks. Stanines of 1, 2, and 3 are distinctly below average; stanines of 4, 5, and 6 are considered to be in the normal range; and stanines of 7, 8, and 9 are above average. Stanines are like percentile ranks; therefore, you should never use arithmetic on stanines to show differences or growth. These scales are elastic, like percentile ranks, and they stretch at the high and low ends. Stanines can be found in Figure 2.1 below percentile ranks.

Normal Curve Equivalents (NCEs)

Because percentiles have this limitation due to their ordinal nature, the normal curve equivalent (NCE) was invented by the United States government to help in program evaluation where different achievement measures may have been used. Basically, the NCE scale is nothing more than the normal distribution divided into 99 equal intervals, resembling the percentile rank scale shown in Figure 2.1. Notice that the NCE scale has equal intervals, and therefore group comparisons or growth comparisons are valid, whereas with percentile rank, such comparisons are not valid.

Scale Scores

So far, we have discussed norm-referenced interpretations involving ordinal scales and percentages. Now we look at more precise norm-referenced interpretations using scale scores. Most standardized achievement tests use scale scores because such scores provide the convenient norm-referenced interpretation.

Z-Scores

The name for units of standard deviations in the normal distribution is *z-scores*. Figure 2.1 shows z-scores for the normal distribution. A z-score of zero places a student at the mean of the normal distribution: 50 percent score higher; 50 percent score lower. A z-score of zero has a percentile rank at the 50th percentile. A z-score of 1.00 is the point in the normal distribution where 84 percent of all students score lower and 16 percent of the students score higher. So a z-score of 1.00 would be at the 84th percentile. A z-score of 1.00 is pretty high; even higher is a z-score of 2.00 About 5 percent of all students score higher, and 95 percent of all students score lower. The approximate percentile rank for a z-score of 2.00 is 95th percentile. A z-score of –1.00 is symmetrically lower. About 16 percent score lower than –1.00 and 84 percent score higher than –1.00. The percentile rank for a z-score of –1.00 is the 5th percentile. About 5 percent score lower than –2.00 and 95 percent score higher than –2.00. Z-score is the fundamental metric used with the standard deviation to place every student score in the framework of the normal distribution.

T-Scores

T-scores were invented by an Englishman at tea time or was it a golfer at tee time? No matter, t-scores are not used all that much anymore. The value of a t-score is to illustrate that you can transform any z-score into any norm-referenced scale you want by multiplying the z-score by a constant number and adding an arbitrary mean. The t-score has a constant multiplier of 10 and an arbitrary mean of 50. So t-scores have a mean of 50 and a standard deviation of 10. An 80 is a very high t-score, and a 20 is a very low t-score. A t-score of 20 is three standard deviations below the mean. A t-score of 80 is three standard deviations above the mean. All scale scores involve the same mathematical operation, as you will see.

College Admission Test Score Scales

The *Scholastic Assessment Test I (SATI)* and the *Graduate Record Examination (GRE)* produce standardized test scores that are on the same test score scale: a mean of 500 and a standard deviation of 100. Can you determine what a score of 600 represents? About 84 percent of the students taking this test score lower. The makers of these two tests decided on a scale that ranges from 200 to 800. The first test (SATI) is mainly used as a college admissions criterion along with student grades and other factors. The second test (GRE) is often used along with student grades and other criteria for admissions to a graduate school program.

　　ACT Assessment scores are on a different test score scale: a mean of 20 and a standard deviation of 4. Thus, a 28 is a very high score, two standard deviations above average, where 97.7 percent of students score at that point or lower. This test is also used as a college admission criterion along with student grades.

Intelligence Test Score Scales

Intelligence tests have been traditionally set on a scale where the average score is 100 and the standard deviation is 15 or 16. *The Stanford-Binet Intelligence Test* uses 16 as a standard deviation, whereas the *Wechsler Adult Intelligence Scale (WAIS)* and the

Wechsler Intelligence Scale for Children (WISC) uses 15. A WISC score of 145 is very high, with a z-score of 3.0, which means three standard deviations above average. What percentage of students score at or below this point? 99.9 percent.

Grade-Equivalent Scale. The grade-equivalent scale is more popular than the previous scales but has many limitations, according to Mehrens and Lehman (1987). Basically, the median score for a grade level on a standardized achievement test receives a grade equivalent for the grade that took the test. Since the school year has 10 months, the grade equivalent comes in tenths. If a student gets a grade-equivalent score of 4.1, this means that the student scored at the same level as fourth-graders in their first month of school. A grade-equivalent score of 6.7 indicates that the student scored at the same level as a sixth-grader in the seventh month of school. Grade equivalents may seem like a handy and useful way to obtain a norm-referenced interpretation, but these grade-equivalent scores are very misleading. Parents and others are likely to think that a grade-equivalent score suggests that the student is working in the curriculum at that grade level. A grade equivalent is nothing more than a level of performance that is normed to represent students at different points in their educational careers. Because of this serious limitation, the grade-equivalent scale not recommended for use.

Summary

All teachers and other educators need to be familiar with Figure 2.1 and be able to make norm-referenced interpretations based on information presented in that figure. Norm-referenced interpretations are useful for ranking students, classes, schools, or school districts, for selection, placement, or admission to programs. One caveat, however, to norm-referenced interpretations is that any interpretation is subject to certain rules involving validity. The argument for the interpretation must be logical and evidence should exist for making this kind of interpretation. Generally, test publishers are careful about the kinds of interpretations made from their test scores.

Reliability

Test scores have random error built into them. So when you see a test score, say 75 percent, a part of that score is true and another part is random error. Random error is regarded as large or small, positive or negative. What is really frustrating is that one never actually knows how much error there is in a test score. A reliability estimate offers a way to understand random error in test scores. It defines about how much confidence one can have in a group of test scores. The reliability index can be computed in a number of ways, but all indexes range from 0.000 to 1.000. We will not concern ourselves with the computation of reliability because these indexes are supplied to teachers for their interpretation. Rather, we will concentrate on interpreting reliability coefficients. Table 2.3 gives you a simple way to evaluate these indexes.

Multiple-choice test scores can have very high reliability if the test is long enough and if it contains many discriminating items of a similar nature. On the other hand, per-

TABLE 2.3 *Interpreting Reliability Indexes*

Index	Discussion
Above .90	Very reliable; about as high as it gets
Between .80 and .90	Good but not great
Below .80	Not very good; not much confidence can be placed in these scores

formance test scores have difficulty achieving high reliability because human judgment is involved in scoring, which adds random error. The merits of a multiple-choice or performance test should never be judged solely on its reliability. Multiple-choice tests usually measure knowledge and skills, and performance tests usually measure complex skills or abilities. As you can see, both have their purpose. Each type can give you a different, yet complementary, interpretation.

Interrater Consistency and Reliability.   A very common type of performance test requires student work to be evaluated by a judge. The scoring guide, sometimes called a *rubric,* is a descriptive rating scale that is used by the judge. The problem with ratings is that judges using the same scoring guide and looking at the same student work may not agree. This error is blended into the total score and contributes negatively to reliability. Thus, performance tests tend to have lower reliability than desirable due in part to the fact that judges must rate student performance using these scoring guides.

Standard Error of Measurement and Reliability.   When you know the reliability estimate, you can figure out the standard error of measurement. This index is a standard deviation of error. It defines how much confidence one can have in a test score if that score were true. For example, assume that a passing score is 70 percent and a student scored 68 percent. The standard error is 5. One generally constructs a two-standard deviation error interval around that score. That means that if the true score is 68 percent, the test score will randomly fluctuate between 58 and 78 percent. Given this range of error, how confident can you be that you are making a correct pass/fail decision? Not very. Thus, standard errors of measurement are used by testing specialists to provide a zone of confidence for test scores that one might apply in decision making. In public surveys, this is often called *sampling error* or the *margin of error.*

Implications of the Standard Error of Measurement.   What can you learn from this discussion of reliability? Teachers should never be too confident or overconfident about any test score, because the margin of error may be larger than desired. If you are talking about a graduation or licensing test, then the consequences of making a decision can be considerable. Teachers must have great confidence in their decision-making accuracy. If a reliability coefficient is above .90, this is very good for decision making, because the standard error of measurement is small and one's confidence in the score is greater. If the coefficient is lower, then more caution should be exercised in making pass/fail decisions. If the coefficient is really low, say below .80, one should have grave doubts about the accuracy of decision making, because the standard error of measurement is too large. For students near the cutoff for the pass/fail decision, it is impossible to know on which side the true score resides.

Correlation

Correlation is a descriptive statistic showing the relationship between two sets of numbers. In this case, these numbers are usually test scores. Computer programs compute correlations and provide probability statements to help teachers decide whether the correlation is a chance observation or a nonzero. Computing correlations is not an issue for teachers. If you want to learn about computing correlations, consult any of many excellent books on descriptive statistics. Most computer programs spit out correlations in seconds. For our purpose, we will concentrate on interpreting correlation coefficients produced by a computer program. Let's say we have two sets of reading test scores: the state reading test and a publisher's reading test. Do the tests measure about the same thing (reading comprehension) or do they measure different aspects of reading? As we try to answer this question, we will find out if students who score high in one reading test also score high in another reading test, and if students who score low in one reading test also score low in the other reading test. This is the question that correlation answers. The correlation coefficient is a descriptive statistic that measures the relationship between two variables. The coefficient is a number that ranges from -1.00 to 1.00. All correlations are subject to two simple rules:

- *Rule 1:* A correlation has to be statistically significant in order for us to assume that it is not zero. This test for statistical significance shows us if the true correlation is zero or something else other than zero. If the correlation coefficient is statistically significant, then we can assume it is not zero. Once we have established that a correlation is statistically significant and not equal to zero, we can go to Rule 2. (If, for some reason, you have to decide if a correlation coefficient is statistically significant, then you have to know what the probability of getting that correlation coefficient or higher by pure chance is. A statistical computer program usually provides that probability. Typically, you may set up a criterion, usually .05, for deciding. If the probability is equal or less than .05, you may conclude that the correlation is not really zero. If the probability is more than .05, you may conclude that the correlation coefficient is zero.)
- *Rule 2:* If a correlation is statistically significant, we also want to know if it is practically significant. For practical significance, we want to know if the correlation is high enough to get excited about it, to make an interpretation, to use it in prediction, or to make a causal inference. The way we answer the question about practical significance is to square the correlation coefficient. That result shows us the percentage of variance explained in the first test score by the second test score.

Table 2.4 provides a simple guide to help you interpret correlations. The first correlation is statistically significant, so we know that the true correlation is not zero. We also know that the true correlation is probably .05, which is very small. Is this practically significant? No. We square the correlation coefficient and see that it accounts for very little variation in achievement scores. Therefore, this first correlation has statistical significance but very little practical significance.

The second correlation is not statistically significant. Because it is not statistically significant, we will assume that the real correlation is zero and that the practical significance is also zero.

The third correlation is statistically significant. The test for practical significance shows that 9 percent of the variation of achievement test scores is explained. Although 9 percent is not large, it does tell us something about the importance of the learning environment. If you knew that the learning environment contributed positively to student learning, might you be interested in providing a positive learning environment in your classroom? This assumes that in your model for student learning, you think that the learning environment has a small positive effect on student learning.

The fourth correlation is not statistically or practically significant. Does this seem contradictory, given that the third and fourth correlations have the same coefficient of correlation? Statistical significance is strongly affected by sample size. With a large sample, virtually any correlation coefficient is statistically significant. In the fourth correlation, the sample size was not very large, so we must reluctantly conclude that both statistical and practical significance is zero. This might motivate you to get a better size sample in a future study, but you must hold the line here and conclude that there is no correlation. What a disappointment, because we all know that love for lima beans has a profound effect on student learning.

The fifth correlation is both statistically and practically significant. How practical is this result? Well, 36 percent of the variation in achievement can be explained by intel-

TABLE 2.4 *Understanding Correlation Coefficients*

Correlation Coefficient	One Variable	Other Variable	Statistical Significance	Practical Significance
.05	Achievement	Mom's height	Yes	.0025
.02	Achievement	Dad's height	No	.00
.30	Achievement	Learning environment	Yes	.09
.30	Achievement	Love for lima beans	No	.00
.60	Achievement	Intelligence	Yes	.36
−.60	Achievement	Television viewing	Yes	.36

ligence. We could say, then, that there is a moderate tendency for high-scoring students to have high intelligence scores.

The last correlation in Table 2.4 shows a negative correlation of the same size as the previous correlation. The correlation is still statistically and practically significant, except the interpretation of trends is opposite of the interpretation of trends for a positive correlation. In this last example, we could surmise that the more one watches television, the more likely one is to have low achievement test scores.

Uses of Correlation

Correlations are used for many purposes in testing, among them are prediction, cause-and-effect reasoning, and equivalence.

Prediction.   Some tests are used for prediction purposes. For example, a college admissions test like the SATI or the ACT Assessment are well-known tests used because of their hoped-for predictive power for college grades. The GRE is used to predict graduate school grades. Tests of this type generally have good prediction ability, therefore results can influence a decision about admitting a student to a program. Correlation is the basis for making predictions. However, no correlation is perfect and no prediction system based on correlation is perfect. Thus, one should not overrely on correlation for making predictions. On the other hand, the higher the correlation, the better the prediction.

Cause-and-Effect Reasoning.   The best way to verify cause-and-effect reasoning is to perform highly controlled experiments where groups receive differing treatments and are observed after the treatment. This practice is seldom done in education, however, as it may be unethical or harmful to students to give them the treatment that is believed to be less effective. Science has developed a method of reasoning whereby correlations are used to build an argument that something *(X)* is the cause of something else *(Y)*. Correlation is not by itself proof of a cause-effect relationship. One needs a logical argument and a collection of evidence, one piece of which may be correlation. There may be many naturally high correlations, say between height and weight, but one would not want to argue that height causes weight or that weight causes height. The emphasis on cause-and-effect reasoning comes from having well-conceived hypotheses and evidence surrounding the hypothesis that supports this thinking. Here is a good example: Children living in poverty tend to do poorly in school. The correlation between family income and achievement is positive and very high. Thus, through personal experience, reading, research, and discussions with others, you are likely to evolve a theory that poverty is a cause of low achievement. Would you argue that low achievement causes poverty? Maybe. But for students born in poverty, the former hypothesis seems defensible.

Chapter 1 dealt with cause-and-effect reasoning built on research that mostly includes correlations. Although this is never direct evidence of causes, the correlations help us, as teachers, to understand the various factors that may be influencing student learning and the strength of these factors. For instance, family and home influences and intelligence have very high correlations with measures of student learning. We can build an argument that these two factors are causes of student learning. You also learned in Chapter 1 that teachers who use student time well have students who learn more than students with teachers who use student time poorly. Maybe this will be a causal factor in your model for student learning. Maybe you will concentrate on using student time productively, or extending student learning time with an effective homework program.

Equivalence.   Let's say we have two tests that measure the extent to which students like lima bean soup. One test takes three hours to administer, and the other test takes three minutes to administer. We correlate a set of scores for a representative sample of students to see if the two tests seem to measure the same construct: love of lima beans. We get a correlation of .80. By our probability test, it is statistically significant. We know that both tests have imperfect reliability. If reliability had been higher, the correlation would be higher, so we might conclude that indeed the two tests must measure the same thing. In the future, we will use the three-minute test, which includes serving lima bean soup and having the students give us their opinion in the form of a rating.

As you can see, correlation is a statistical science that helps teachers understand some things about testing. You will probably not use correlation in your teaching career, but if you are around standardized tests and are using these test scores for prediction, for causal reasoning, or for test score interpretation, you will want to know what correlations mean and how to interpret them.

Bias in Testing

Investigating bias is very important in standardized achievement testing. In fact, Chapter 7 is devoted to this topic. As much as we want students' achievement test scores to reflect their learning, bias often gets in the teacher's way. The term *bias* has two connotations in testing. The first connotation is that bias is a policy or action that works systematically against certain individuals. In this context, the term *test bias* is loosely used to describe how a test is used to make unfair pass/fail decisions or is used to evaluate unfairly a student, class, school, school district, or state. A more accurate description of this kind of bias involves validity, which is the main topic of Chapter 3. You may hear comments that standardized achievement tests are biased against certain religious, racial, or ethnic groups. Any interpretation or use of test scores might be unfair because of this bias. Test makers are therefore always concerned about this kind of bias, but proving such bias is difficult. Nonetheless, we teachers are ethically bound to study it and eliminate it.

The second connotation for bias is a formal, statistical concept, which goes by several names. This bias is a *directional error* that is introduced into test scores that affects some test takers (and their scores) but not others. For example, imagine that when you step on a scale, you get your weight (plus or minus a little random error). When I step on the same scale, I lean against the wall and my recorded weight is about 10 pounds less than my actual weight. This difference of 10 pounds is bias in measurement. In other words, leaning against the wall made me weigh 10 pounds lighter. Testing experts call this *construct-irrelevant variance,* because variation is introduced into test scores that distorts the meaning of the score for some test takers. Recently, testing experts have been interested in test score bias brought by raters in a performance test. Some raters are harsh and some are lenient. If your work was assigned to two harsh raters, a bias would be introduced in the scoring that would lower your score below its true level, and if your work was assigned to two lenient raters, the bias would be in the other direction.

Those involved in intelligence and achievement testing are very concerned about bias and want to eliminate it. The *Standards for Educational and Psychological Testing* (American Educational Research Association, American Psychological Association, & National Council on Measurement in Education, 1999) call for the elimination of bias in testing.

For quite some time, students classified by social class, ethnic background, race, and gender have achieved different results in tests. Test reformers and concerned citizens have often expressed the idea that such tests are biased because of these consistent differences. For instance, immigrant students do poorly on many intelligence or achievement tests. Are the results biased or do the low results reflect a true level of mental ability or student learning? Through the study of other test scores and conditions, one might find evidence of bias that shows that immigrant students lack language proficiency; thus, it is unlikely that their actual achievement or intelligence is being measured. The achievement or intelligence test merely reflects something we already know: The immigrant students have not mastered reading and speaking in the English language.

Standard Setting

Another significant technical topic is standard setting. For tests with important consequences, such as promotion or graduation or standard-based interpretations, points on a test score scale must be established that will separate students into categories. For standards-based interpretation, it might look like this:

Categories→	Advanced	Proficient	Basic	Below Basic
Range in scores→	100%–90%	<90%–80%	<80%–70%	<70%

For a graduation test, perhaps the passing score is established at 75 percent. How this score is set is a very important issue. Obviously, testing standards should be set in fair and defensible ways; in fact, there are testing standards governing how test scores are set (American Educational Research Association, American Psychological Association, & National Council on Measurement in Education, 1999). Here are some desirable and defensible and undesirable and indefensible ways to set standards. (For those interested in addressing this issue more deeply, consult a recent book on this topic by Cizek [2001].)

Desirable and Defensible	Undesirable and Indefensible
Item Judging. Content experts make judgments on an item-by-item basis about how students should perform on each item. This is a very popular method.	*Quota.* About 20 percent of those tested will fail. Wherever that point is on the test score scale will be the cut score. Quotas disregard the effort of students and fail a predetermined number of students. This is a very unfair method.
Contrasting Groups. Students are identified who are novices and masters. The point in the test score distribution that divides these two groups is where the cut score is set.	*Arbitrary.* Some states and jurisdictions arbitrarily set a cut score at a convenient level, such as 70 or 75 percent, without regard for the technical issues or what the meaning of the score is.
	Statistical. Some standard setters will set a standard based on the normal distribution (see Figure 2.1). Although this may seem mathematical or statistical, it is very much like the quota method.

Conjunctive versus Compensatory

Another important issue that arises in standard setting is which strategy to use: conjunctive or compensatory. Take, for example, a standard writing performance assessment where a pass/fail decision is to be made. Should a student pass each of the six traits being assessed or is a total score sufficient? The *conjunctive strategy* requires that the student would pass each of the six scores that make up the total score. The argument is that one must meet a minimal standard in each of the six content areas that makes up writing. Low performance in any one content area will not be tolerated. The *compensatory strategy* considers only the total score. Low performance in one content area can be compensated by high performance in another content area. Refer to Tommie's score in the following chart.

Trait	A	B	C	D	E	F
Cut Score	3	3	3	3	3	3
Tommie	4	2	3	2	4	3

Tommie's total score is 18. Using a *conjunctive* model, and a cut score of 3 for each of the six content areas, what decision would be made? Tommie would pass A, C, E, and F, but he would fail B and D. Using a *compensatory* strategy, Tommie's total score of 18 would be used as the cut point for the total score. Using the conjunctive strategy, Tommie failed B and D because the cut score is 3. As you can see, the conjunctive compensatory strategy is more demanding and rigorous. When compared with the compensatory strategy, the conjunctive strategy will fail more students than the compensatory model. The compensatory model is more forgiving.

As a teacher who is part of a standard setting team, this is a crucial issue you will have to help decide: conjunctive or compensatory. When the public welfare and safety is at stake—such as careers in law enforcement, nursing, or medicine—the standard setters often choose the more rigorous conjunctive model. When students are considered in pass/fail testing situations, compensatory standard setting may be more forgiving. The issue is never easy to resolve, and no strategy is recommended over the other. The choice is a matter of values of the standard setters and an acceptance of the consequences of their decision. For more information about the conjunctive and compensatory decision-making strategies, see Haladyna and Hess (1999).

What Are Technical Standards and Why Are They Important?

There are a number of professional organizations in the United States that promote good testing practices. These organizations have developed standards that they encourage their members to use in their testing programs. Since these members also include employees of testing companies, the standards are codes of behavior about testing that involve just about everyone in testing. Chapter 10 deals with many of the principles to live by in testing. The majority of these technical standards have to do with validity and responsible test interpretation. The next chapter deals with validity. Although the technical standards are not featured in Chapter 3, validity is very much connected to these technical standards

Summary

This chapter has surveyed basic concepts and principles of standardized achievement testing. Definitions and examples have been given to explain these concepts and principles better. These definitions and examples provide the foundation for many technical issues in testing, but testing, unfortunately, is a very technical science with several competing theories and a large body of research that ranges from highly mathematical work to very practical things. This chapter, then, represents just a beginning understanding of a very complex, technical field. Throughout this chapter, references have been made to more substantial treatments for readers who are seeking more information.

3

Validity

Validity is the most important consideration in testing. What one evaluates in standardized achievement testing is the validity of an interpretation or the use of that test score for a certain purpose. Test score validation is a complex, reasoning process that involves both logic and empirical evidence. This chapter introduces you to this logical reasoning process, and then asks you to apply this process to various uses found in standardized achievement testing.

The chapter begins with discussions of interpretations we teachers want from standardized achievement test scores and typical uses to which we put these test scores. Next, the complex idea of validity is addressed. A major issue with validity is the consequence of one's interpretation and use of test scores. Interpretations and uses of test scores that may vary in validity will be examined. As you will see, tests are not inherently flawed or destructive. However, in some circumstances, we need to question seriously the way we interpret and use standardized achievement test scores.

What Is the Meaning of an Achievement Test Score?

When discussing test score interpretation, we refer to the *meaning* of a test score. That is, a test score should always be interpreted as to its (1) intended meaning (i.e., what the test developers intended or claimed) and (2) context (i.e., conditions that surround the obtaining of the test score).

In this book, the main focus is on standardized achievement tests, but this idea may be extended to teacher-made classroom tests as well. As stated in Chapter 2, any test score can provide three kinds of meaning: criterion referenced, norm referenced, and standards based. For the classroom test, the test score reveals how much the student has learned compared with some curriculum or content standards, which is a criterion-referenced interpretation. Generally, teachers do not or should not make norm-referenced interpretations of their classroom test scores. Since we want all students to learn as much as they can, norm referencing does not really tell us how much they have learned.

Nevertheless, we teachers are very likely to make norm-referenced comparisons on standardized achievement tests because we generally intend these standardized achievement tests to give its consumers useful information on how our students are doing compared with others school abilities such as reading, writing, mathematics, social studies, and science. Some of these standardized achievement tests offer information about speaking and listening and even study skills. Each test is only a small sample of knowledge and skills from a larger domain. Because the sampling is done very carefully, the test provides a good estimate of performance on the entire domain of knowledge and skill that each test represents. Norms are provided that allow us to compare performances among students, classes, schools, and even states. Some tests, such as the most recent Stanford Achievement Test (Ninth Edition), or SAT-9, provide teacher-made standards of performance indicating advanced, proficient, basic, and below-basic performance levels for students at appropriate grade levels.

Serious concern exists concerning the validity of interpreting and using these test scores, and these concerns are discussed in Chapters 7 and 8. Certain influences that we do not want can artificially boost or lower test scores but are nonetheless introduced. Some of these unwanted influences are (1) cheating, (2) inappropriate curriculum realignment to a mandated test, (3) excessive test preparation, (4) excessive motivation, (5) test anxiety, (6) disinterest, and (7) misinterpretation (going beyond claims of the publisher). Another criticism is that the tests tap knowledge and skills but fail to measure the more important application of knowledge and skills to problem solving and to critical and creative thinking. Yet another criticism is that the imposition of these tests into the classroom robs teachers and students of instructional time and has a documented negative influence on both students and teachers (Cannell, 1989; Haladyna, Nolen, & Haas, 1991; Herman & Golan, 1993; Heubert & Hauser, 1999; Linn, 2000; Mehrens & Kaminski, 1989; Paris, Lawton, Turner, & Roth, 1991; Smith, 1991a, 1991b).

In fairness, these negative influences are not caused by test publishers. Users of test results are the perpetrators. Their inexpertise with invalid test score interpretation and uses leads one to conclude that standardized achievement testing is not a healthy influence in the schools. Chapter 7 will review some practices promoting invalid interpretations and what motivates these practices. Chapter 8 examines the effects of these practices on students, teachers, and the general public.

Standardized achievement tests come in many forms. Two commonly used general standardized achievement test series are the Iowa Test of Basic Skills (ITBS) and the SAT-9. Educators generally think the content of these tests represents the basic knowledge and skills that students should possess as they go through their school experience. These tests have been carefully developed to correlate will well-known textbook series through the participation of literally hundreds of teachers and other educators working as advisers. In many respects, the ITBS and SAT-9 reflect a national curriculum, although such a curriculum does not really exist. However, if it did, we educators and the public would likely think that these tests are adequate in reflecting this large collection of knowledge and skills that our students should learn.

The knowledge we test may consist of thousands of facts, concepts, principles, and procedures that we expect students either to memorize or to understand. Skills are also numerous. Any test is merely a small sample from this domain of thousands of identifiable facts, concepts, principles, and procedures that are taught in school. Before interpreting any standardized achievement test score, however, it is a good idea to know about how the tests from which the scores come match up to what we teachers are actually teaching. A prevailing theme throughout this book, as well as in U.S. education, is this strong link between content standards or curriculum, the instructional program, and the classroom and standardized tests that are used to evaluate student learning.

Match or Mismatch to the Curriculum

Following up on this idea about test content and its relation to curriculum and instruction, a key idea in the valid interpretation of standardized achievement tests scores is matched or mismatched tests and curriculum. The test used in a school or a school district should have specific, explicit links to the state content standards or to the school district curriculum. Any discussion of validity must address this match/mismatch issue. For example, you may find yourself in any of the scenarios shown in Table 3.1.

When interpreting or using standardized achievement test scores, knowing which of the conditions is present is important before you attempt to interpret or use a set of standardized achievement test scores. Validity in this context has to do with how meaningful any interpretation of a test score is for a student, a class, a school, a school district, or an entire state. Obviously, tests that match your content standards have high relevance to educators and the public, because you should be teaching exactly what the test is measuring. In this situation, one might argue that interpreting test scores as measures of student learning is very valid. Partially matched tests provide a rough indicator of how students are learning, but these tests lack precision in giving the kind of interpretation wanted. Another problem with a partially matched test is that the part that matches up is easy to measure but the part not matched to the content standards is the hardest to test. Thus, the partially matched test would give a biased view of student learning. Mismatched tests provide information about student learning, but the mis-

TABLE 3.1 *Levels of Test/Curriculum Match*

Condition	Description of Content Match with Test
Match	The content standards of the state or school district match this test by design. In other words, the test was designed to reflect the content standards.
Partial match	The content standards of the state or school district partially match the content of this test. Overlap may be very high to very low.
	A test might be exported from an outside source that has some degree of match to these content standards.
Mismatch	The content standards of the state or school district do not match the content of the test.

match creates confusion about what is being taught, how much students have learned, and how various instructional programs are working.

Interpretation 1: Test Scores Reflect the Amount of Learning during a Child's Lifetime.   If you have found an achievement test that matches the content that you want, the most valid interpretation of a test score is that it reflects learning that a student has experienced from birth to the time of the test. As Chapter 1 argues, many factors influence student learning over this time. Factors existing outside school have a strong influence on student learning, including intelligence, economic status, and parents. Most educators would argue that a combination of these factors plays an important role in shaping student learning. A test score obtained under ideal conditions with a matched test can provide a good snapshot of a student's reading comprehension, writing ability, mathematics ability, or social studies and science knowledge and skills. A teacher values such scores, especially when reporting them with respect to the normal distribution discussed in Chapter 2. The teacher can see a child's score compared with thousands of other students who are about the same age or grade level. Such test scores give a sense of how much learning has occurred as well as predict future test performance and suggest the potential for furthering the student's education.

Interpretation 2: Test Scores Are Often Broken Down into Categories of Scores Showing a Profile of Learning by More Specific Aspects of Student Learning.
Standardized achievement tests can be reported by subscores showing how students did in certain areas. Although these subscores may not be based on many test items, we teachers like the information it provides, so we tend to use it. However, the reliability of these subscores is extremely low. As was briefly mentioned under the topic of standards-based test score interpretation in the previous chapter, many testing organizations are beginning to report scores in large categories that reflect developmental levels. For instance, the National Assessment of Educational Progress (http://nces.ed.gov/nationsreportcard/civics/civ_assess_achieve.asp) uses the following distinctions in student performance for all subjects and grade levels:

Basic: Partial mastery of prerequisite knowledge and skills that are fundamental for proficient work at each grade.

Proficient: Solid academic performance for each grade assessed. Students reaching this level have demonstrated competency over challenging subject matter, including subject-matter knowledge, application of such knowledge to real-world situations, and analytical skills appropriate to the subject matter.

Advanced: Superior performance.

These standards-based interpretations require that teachers are basing their instruction on the content standards that the test measures. In other words, there is a good match between the content standards and the test.

What Type of Interpretation Is Desired and Why?

In Chapter 2, you learned about three types of test score interpretations: criterion referenced, norm referenced, and standards based. As you think about the meaning of a test score, you can make reference to each type of interpretation in the context of whether you think or know that the test is relevant, with regard to content and instruction, for the students being tested. You need to assure yourself that there is a match between the content of the test and the content standards, and the content of the test and instruction. Without such assurances, the validity of any test score interpretation is low regarding the assessment of student learning.

What Are Some Common Uses of Test Scores?

One guiding principle that seems to prevail across time and with most educators and the public is that test scores should be helpful to teachers, parents, and students in guiding the student to learn (Cooley, 1991). By adopting this principle, you will be in a position to better evaluate the validity of many uses of test scores. You can ask: How is this use of test scores helping my students learn?

Standardized achievement test scores can be put to many other uses (good or bad). Figure 3.1 lists some of these uses without any statement about how valid it is to use a test score in that way. But as you consider each use, you might get in the habit of asking yourself if a logical argument can be given to support that use and if there is evidence to support that argument. With many uses, it is difficult to argue that a test score use is logical, and it is difficult to find empirical support in the way of validity evidence. The uses listed in Figure 3.1 provide the basis for lively discussions among educators, parents, policymakers, and elected officials, and the issue of validity plays importantly in each of these uses.

Several testing experts have noted that in the middle of the last century, standardized test interpretations and uses were benign (Cooley, 1991; Smith 1991a). Mainly, students took tests so teachers and principals could adjust the curriculum to balance achievement in the many areas of knowledge and skills that comprise the school curricula. Test scores were also used to evaluate the school curriculum. The mismatch between the curriculum and the standardized test might cause educators to question their curriculum or criticize the test because it failed to reflect their curriculum. The mismatch between teaching and the standardized tests might also cause teachers to question what they were teaching or how effectively they were teaching. Few teachers would ever have used test scores to evaluate their teaching, because the outcomes of student learning are very complex and because so many other factors outside school have an influence over these scores.

As the importance of test score uses increases, the issue of curriculum match/mismatch is seldom considered. As you wonder about different uses of achievement test scores, you should always ask the crucial question: Does the test measure what you want it to measure?

FIGURE 3.1   *Uses of Standardized Test Scores*

- More states are passing legislation requiring students to meet high standards through pass/fail graduation or certification tests.

- Making comparisons among states, school districts, schools, classes, and students using test scores is a way to evaluate states, school districts, schools, classes, and students.

- The academic achievement of a state, school district, school, class, or student is monitored over time.

- A strength or weakness in the curriculum or an instructional program is identified based on test subscores.

- Students are placed in certain instructional levels based on test scores.

- Students are selected for special programs based on test scores.

- Test scores indicate a good place to buy a house.

- A school is closed based on chronic low performance on tests over time.

- Accountability is based on test scores. Accountability generally has two meanings. The first is providing information to policymakers so that they can make wise decisions about programs and resources allocated. The second is holding someone responsible for a set of test scores.

- Test results are used to make changes in curriculum or to initiate curricular reform.

- Test results are used to shape or inform policy in a state, school district, or school regarding the education of students.

- Test scores are used to retain a teacher or give a teacher a pay raise (also applies to principals and superintendents).

What Is Validity and What Has It to Do with Interpretations and Uses of Standardized Achievement Test Scores?

As noted at the beginning of this chapter, validity should be your paramount concern when interpreting or using standardized achievement tests. This chapter has suggested that validity involves interpretation and uses of test scores and ensuring that the content of any achievement test is exactly what you want it to be. Is it matched to state or school district content standards?

What Is Validity?

Validity refers to how accurately test results are interpreted or used. This idea can be posed in two questions:

1. How valid is it to interpret a test score in this way?
2. How valid is it to use a test score in this way?

The two questions should imply that validity exists in degrees, from low to high, not in absolute ways, such as valid or invalid. Also, *validity* refers to how you interpret or use test scores, not to the validity of a test. Any test score can be validly or invalidly interpreted or used depending on the circumstances. Take a non-English-speaking student from Saudi Arabia who takes the SAT-9 achievement test on her first day in the United States. Is it valid to interpret the resulting test score for this person who does not speak English? In some settings, a low test score for this student would result in failure. Is this valid, if the student has not yet received instruction or has not mastered the language sufficiently to display her achievement? This is the vital issue with validity. Chapter 7 contains a comprehensive discussion of factors that undermine or weaken validity of interpreting or using achievement test scores. These factors are not excuses for low achievement but, rather, valid explanations for why students score lower or higher than you expected.

What Is a Validity Argument?

For any test we teachers give, we build a logical argument that says a specific test score interpretation or use is valid. The argument might be based on a learning theory or drawn from our experiences in the classroom. It might be an old argument or a new one. It is usually a question or declarative statement regarding whether a specific test score meaning or use is valid—for instance, How valid is it to use a set of test scores for making pass/fail decisions for high school graduation? The argument will be more complex and may also state that all students have had an opportunity to learn the content upon which the tests are based. There will be multiple opportunities for students to be tested. Students with special needs receive special education. As you can see, the validity argument requires many conditions.

What Is Validity Evidence?

As noted earlier in this chapter, the way test score validation works is that evidence is collected to build the argument that it is valid to interpret or use a test score in a certain way. Validity evidence can be found with a set of procedures, a research study, a statistical analysis, or a logical argument. If evidence exists, you evaluate the evidence and make a judgment that it is valid to interpret or use a test score in a certain way. If evidence is lacking or contrary to your beliefs, then you argue that it is wrong to interpret or use the test score in a certain way. Since this evidence is evaluated subjectively, validity reflects a degree of willingness to interpret or use a test score.

Similar to the way an attorney presents a case in a court based on arguments and supporting evidence, validation is the process of collecting and organizing this evidence supporting an argument that a specific interpretation or use of a set of test scores is valid. Selecting the first test score use in Figure 3.1, you might ask how valid it is to make a pass/fail decision based on a set of test scores. This decision might affect a student's high school graduation. The test sponsor, usually a state, then has to build a solid case consisting of an argument and supporting evidence that says it is highly valid to use test scores to make a pass/fail decision. What are some conditions in the classroom that need to exist to establish validity for an achievement test score with a specific interpretation or use? Usually these conditions in the classroom include the following:

- We identified content that we wanted the students to learn. Perhaps we presented this as instructional objectives or textbook material. This content is matched to our state content standards or a school district curriculum.
- We provided instruction aligned to these objectives. This instruction is usually planned to be sequential and developmentally appropriate with cycles for review and extension or application of what is learned to complex tasks, often involving problem solving or critical thinking.
- We decided to use a multiple-choice test based on prior research and analysis because it is best suited to measure knowledge and some skills, or we decided to use a performance test because it seems more appropriate to test the complex ability we are teaching.
- We constructed test items following a set of guidelines.
- We reviewed our items and checked for bias, clarity, correctness, and linkage to these objectives.
- We made sure that all aspects of the content were tested at appropriate cognitive complexity, such as recall, understanding, and application of knowledge.
- Our test scores were fairly reliable because we had at least 50 good items on the test.
- We sampled the content very thoroughly, based on our test blueprint (specifications).
- We allowed students to review the results, raise questions about items, and challenge answers, to ensure that student scores accurately reflect their learning,

Up to this point, the focus has been on test content, but there are other types of validity evidence. The primary type of validity evidence is reliability, which was discussed in Chapter 2. If reliability is low, it does not make sense to interpret or use a test score, because the margin of error is too great to get a clear indication of the amount of student learning.

Those involved in technical evaluations of large-scale standardized achievement testing have even stiffer requirements for validity evidence. The *Standards for Educational and Psychological Testing* (American Educational Research Association, American Psychological Association, & National Council on Measurement in Education, 1999) contains one of the best accounts of the kinds of validity evidence large-scale achievement testing programs need. To add to this, the American Educational Research Association (2000) has provided some guidelines. Haladyna (2002) gives a comprehensive discussion of how validity evidence might ideally be organized and presented to support a test score interpretation and use. Validating test score interpretations and uses is a very extensive and long process.

So, in addition to the content concerns stated previously, what are some of the other types of validity evidence that teachers' standards expect test developers to assemble in support of interpreting and using test scores?

1. We can talk to students about what they are thinking when they answer a question, what mental process they are using, and how they arrive at the answer.
2. We can look at the internal structure of test item responses. One of the primary pieces of validity evidence is reliability, but consistency among judges in performance testing and the dependability of pass/fail decisions are other concerns.
3. We can examine the correlation of test scores from our test with other test scores and measures to see if patterns of relationship are predictable and meaningful.
4. We can study differences among groups or growth over time to see if curriculum, instructional programs, and teaching make a difference.
5. We can examine the consequences of our test score use on students and the constituency that the testing program serves. (The idea of consequences is briefly discussed later in this chapter, and Chapter 8 is exclusively devoted to this important topic.)

As you can see, validity evidence can be quite substantial for large-scale and important testing programs (Downing & Haladyna, 1997). Test companies spend considerable time and money in compiling validity evidence. For example, SAT-9 has extensive validity evidence (Haladyna, 1998), but this validity evidence is directed at specific interpretations and uses, not all or any interpretations and uses. The public and its elected officials are often tempted to use tests in ways that the publishers of the test did not intend.

Who Makes the Judgment about Validity?

Since test score validation is a logical process involving an argument and validity evidence supporting this argument, you might wonder exactly who makes judgment calls regarding validity.

Group 1: Elected Officials.   As you might guess, people responsible for making policies and allocating resources come to mind as judges of test validity. They want to know that tax dollars are being wisely spent to educate students, because they recognize the importance of education in a democratic society. Another important reason for making legislators responsible for judging validity is that they are responsible for raising and allocating resources to education. These individuals need information to help their decision making. A second group of elected officials are school board members, who also make policies and allocate resources to schools. Although these elected officials may not have testing acumen to make such judgments, they have the fundamental responsibility for making this judgment due to their elected status.

Group 2: Educators.   The second group of validity judges includes school district administrators who may want to evaluate the curriculum, the instructional program, and the teachers. Another group of educators are those who specialize in testing and contribute the expertise regarding the argument and related validity evidence bearing on test score use. This group includes those in the testing industry, those working within testing programs for states and school districts, and faculty from universities who specialize in testing. The role of this second group is usually advisory to the first group.

Group 3: The Public, Including Especially the Media, the Business Community, and Parents.   One kind of of accountability is providing information to policymakers so that they can make wise decisions about programs and allocating resources. Not only does the public *want* information about student achievement, this group *demands* such information. The public has a right to know how its tax dollars are being spent. If student achievement declined over years, the public would rightfully ask why and want appropriate changes. If achievement improves, the public may turn its attention to other problems or concerns in society. Because we always have a lower 15 percent of our students not performing at the level of the upper 85 percent, the public continues to keep an interest in test scores.

Since testing is such a public enterprise in which we all participate, test interpretation and use is an inclusive activity. It behooves all of us to be literate in the idea of validity and the ideas discussed in this chapter regarding the validity argument and validity evidence. With this background, let us have a closer look at how standardized achievement test scores are used in U.S. education.

High-Stakes Test Score Uses

The next two sections deal with an important distinction in standardized achievement testing: high-stakes and low-stakes test score use. These two terms actually refer to a continuum that represents the seriousness of consequences of using a test score for a certain purpose. The purposes in this section seem very important to people in general, especially students and educators. One of the best treatments of high-stakes testing is *High Stakes: Testing for Tracking, Promotion, and Graduation* (Heubert & Hauser, 1999). This volume was sponsored by the National Research Council and represents an effort by leaders in the field of testing and education to complete a comprehensive and scientific study of high-stakes testing. Recommendations they make are echoed in the last chapter of this book.

In the next major section, Low-Stakes Test Score Uses, the consequences of using a test score for a certain purpose seems less important and consequential. There is no line of demarcation between high-stakes and low-stakes test scores. Your judgment will be your best guide. But let us examine some purposes and evaluate the validity of each purpose using reasoning and what evidence we can gather.

Pass/Fail Testing

The use of test scores to make pass/fail decisions is very common in U.S. society, especially in professional certification and licensing. Indeed, teachers, nurses, police officers, physicians, dentists, lawyers, and architects must pass tests before they are allowed to practice in most states. But pass/fail testing is now prevalent in many states at both elementary and secondary levels. In these situations, it is very important for the test sponsors to have ample validity evidence supporting the use of test scores to award or deny a professional license or high school diploma. Chapter 6 addresses this important category of test score use and the validity challenges.

State-to-State Comparisons

Policymakers, media, and the public want to use standardized achievement test scores to make comparisons among states to find out how well their state is doing compared with other states. This practice of making state-to-state comparisons based on achievement test scores is invalid for many reasons.

First, few tests are designed to sample student learning that is common in all states. As basic as reading, writing, and mathematics are, no test could claim to be the common denominator when states and their school districts continue to develop their own content standards that drive what is to be learned in that state. Certainly, there is common knowledge that the public might agree all students should know, and these tests probably measure that. But as test reform critics point out, elementary knowledge or basic skills are not enough. It is important to ascertain if students can use their knowledge to solve problems and to think critically and creatively. Therefore, there is no commonly accepted achievement measure to make state-to-state comparisons of student achievement.

Second, as Bracey (1998) pointed out so persuasively, most of the variation in state scores may be linked to the number of parents living at home, the type of community in which the child lives, the parents' education, and poverty. Thus, states with the highest proportion of parents living at home, superior community types, highest parent education, and lowest poverty rate have the highest scores. Therefore, state-by-state comparisons seem to reflect prevailing social conditions in the state instead of the education program.

Third, state-by-state comparisons cannot prove that one state provides a better education than another state. Can any state distinguish itself as having a unique curriculum, instructional paradigm, or other influence that may have caused its test score status? Most states vary considerably in school district organizations, resources, teachers, and students. Drawing an inference at the level of a state would be indefensible. Take the state of Illinois as an example. It has Chicago—a state unto itself, with its enormous cultural diversity, its significant inner city with social problems and a century-long record of low achievement, and its affluent high-achieving suburbs. How should Illinois be evaluated with other states, such as neighbors Indiana, Wisconsin, and Iowa? Does one report Illinois in terms of an average or does one separate Illinois into geographic units: Chicago, suburbs, everywhere else?

When making comparisons among school districts and schools, it is easy to fall prey to the very same problem. Such comparisons can be valid only if there is a common ground (content standards), well-designed tests are administered under optimal conditions, instruction is intended to match these content standards, and analysis takes into consideration factors that exist outside school that influence test scores. Finally, no single test or test battery can cover the wide spectrum of outcomes desirable in all school-age children. Consider the model you built for yourself referred to in Chapter 1. It is very likely that the outcomes are more numerous than any test can identify and measure adequately.

State-by-state comparisons should not be done. If they are done, however, they reflect the general makeup of the state concerning social conditions and other demographics. In states where the highest proportion of the population is most educated, has the most resources, has the most school funding, and has a high proportion of two-parent families, test scores are highest. One does not have to administer achievement tests to students to know this.

Year-to-Year Comparisons in States, School Districts, and Schools

Policymakers, including legislators and school board members, want handy, incisive summaries of student learning each year so they can make judgments about how well the state or school district or school is doing. This makes sense to the public, and, in fact, is a primary need of the public: Are the schools teaching our children?

Evaluating a Teacher, a School, or a School District

Perhaps the most detrimental and misguided attempt at improving schooling is the use of test scores for evaluating teaching. Experts in evaluation and testing have provided strong arguments against this practice (Berk, 1988; Haertel, 1986). The main reason that any evaluation of teachers, schools, and school districts is usually invalid is that it is very difficult to separate the influence of the school from the influence of powerful nonschool factors, such as intelligence, socioeconomic status, and family.

Here's a story on state comparisons that is repeated too often. It shows how test scores can be misused. In Arizona one year, a small decline in Scholastic Aptitude Test scores from one year to the next was reported in the local newspaper as a sign that teachers in the state were failing. The chain of reasoning seemed to be that if test scores averaged 450 in one year and fell to 446 the next year, this can be attributed to poor teaching. Such faulty reasoning can be criticized in a number of ways.

The Scholastic Aptitude Test was designed to predict college grades; it does not reflect student learning. Most psychologists think this test measures intelligence. The sample of students taking the test are college bound and therefore not representative of the entire student body of the state. So, this is a biased sample. The amount of test score decline reported is minuscule. You learned in Chapter 2 about scales and norms. Statistically speaking, some differences are very small. The above cited drop is .04 of a standard deviation. Such a drop in scores is comparable to going to a weight-loss clinic and finding that the one-year program helped you lose 3 ounces of unwanted fat!

What conditions would have to be present to make such comparisons valid?

1. A test or battery of tests would have to validly sample from the large domain of knowledge and skills represented by the curriculum. Because most standardized achievement tests reflect a small sample from a large domain of knowledge, these nationally normed survey tests cannot provide a good sample of exactly what teachers teach during a school year. This mismatch between what is taught and what is tested makes the standardized test score a poor measure of student learning for a specific year. State-produced tests have a greater likelihood of providing good achievement measures, and a school district test should be finely tuned with its curriculum.

2. Classrooms at every grade level also vary tremendously in the composition of students, including their needs, abilities, interests, backgrounds, and previous educational experience. How can these differences be accounted for in evaluating teachers, schools, and school districts? These factors play an important role in determining student achievement.

3. If tests reflected multiple indicators of achievement and if the model suggested in Chapter 1 was used, could tests account for the fact that students in classes differ and teachers do not have the same resources that other teachers do? Teachers have very little control of the content of what they teach and the methods they use. Not all teachers enjoy the same level of resources available and other personnel to assist them. They have no control over parents, and certainly parents play a very strong role in student learning. Thus, holding teachers accountable for student learning seems unfair.

As you can see, the use of a set of test scores from one of these nationally normed standardized achievement tests for evaluating teachers, schools, and school districts is invalid from several perspectives. Validity evidence for this practice is not claimed by the publishers of these tests. Those proposing to use test scores to evaluate teaching have no validity evidence to support this practice. Although the match of test content to curriculum and instruction can be improved, other problems remain. Thus, one must conclude that teachers should *not* be evaluated using test scores as a criterion.

Identifying a Good Place to Buy a House

Some cities have maps showing the typical test scores of students in neighborhoods. These maps inform newcomers where the "best schools" are, which is really saying in another way that here is a neighborhood where the homes have parents with high levels of education and high income. Obviously, no test publisher would claim that test scores should be used to identify the best schools in this way, but ask real estate agents in any city if they know about the map and how they use it. Chances are they will tell you where to buy the map and help you use it to pinpoint the right neighborhood for that new home that has the "best schools."

Closing a School Based on Low Test Scores

Test scores have been used to identify schools where test scores are extremely low. The profile of such a school is familiar to educators: poverty, a high percentage of single parents, a low education level of parent(s), high unemployment, a large percentage of limited English-speaking parents and students, and a high level of domestic violence, to mention a few conditions. Based on low achievement test scores, some policymakers have threatened school takeover or closure. Such policies should be not carried out without a model that considers nonschool influences on student achievement. The schools that house these children have the greatest challenge to educate the most difficult students with disabilities. These schools or school districts may not be funded adequately to overcome the problems these learners have. Is it fair to hold schools and teachers accountable for poor performance? To make this test score use valid would require many conditions, including adequate resources to overcome the disabilities of these students and extensive educational programs to make up for the deficits of their environment. Also, information should be obtained about school leadership, curriculum, and instructional programs at the school before making a hasty decision to take over or close a school.

Accountability

Earlier in this chapter, in Figure 3.1, two meanings of accountability were given. The first involved shared information about school achievement to improve education. The second involved assigning responsibility or blame for low achievement. We will now examine accountability more thoroughly.

Reform is a constant theme in education. Accountability and assessment have been working hand in hand in reform movements for more than 50 years (Linn, 2000). These relatively inexpensive achievement tests are mandated by legislators or school boards to pinpoint how much learning is achieved in this nation's schools. However, most testing specialists have pointed out that if tests are used as a beacon of student learning, this beacon can be corrupted (e.g., Haladyna, Nolen, & Haas, 1991; Smith, 1991a, 1991b). Using the same test forms, using old norms, focusing on the content or items that appear on the old test, and good old-fashioned cheating will produce score gains that hardly qualify as indications of real learning. The pressure to produce high test scores is seen as the heart of the problem in high-stakes testing. As Linn and others have frequently stated, the most important outcomes of education cannot be summarized by a single test or a single set of scores from a test. The alternative is to use a variety of indicators—multiple measures of student learning that sample student behavior more comprehensively.

These critical conditions of high-stakes accountability systems emerge from Linn's analysis:

- High-quality achievement tests should reflect exactly what the content standards expect (e.g., writing tests to measure writing ability).

- Student progress should be tracked in absolute rather than normative ways, making comparisons over time instead of pitting classes, schools, and school districts in competition.
- Standards should be set high, as befitting our reputation as a world leader.
- Performance levels should be established, such as advanced, proficient, basic, and needs improving.
- Growth in achievement should be measured over time instead of making comparisons among classes, schools, or schools districts.
- Legitimate sources of invalidity should be reported in the context of accountability. (Threats to valid test score interpretation and use are discussed in Chapter 7.)
- Positive and negative consequences should be included in this accountability system, as suggested in Chapter 8.
- The assessment should be comprised of all students, including those in special education, students living in poverty, and students learning to speak English. Given that these three latter groups typically perform poorly on such tests, special programs are needed to help them achieve.

Part of the problem of accountability is responsibility: Who is responsible for the success or failure of students? In some settings, teachers are awarded merit pay or tenure and public accolade for having their students score high. Others quickly point out that intelligence and home factors usually account for this high performance, not teaching. Another approach is to hold legislators and school board members accountable, because they control resources and often dictate policy and mandate testing programs.

This section has discussed high-stakes test score use and some conditions that are necessary to validate these uses. For the most part, researchers are discovering that the consequences of high-stakes testing may not be positive. As we continue to study high-stakes testing, perhaps, like Linn, others will observe the consequences of high-stakes student testing and conclude that the bad outweighs the good.

Low-Stakes Test Score Uses

This section examines the uses of test scores that seem less consequential to most people. For the most part, the validity evidence applied here is some indication that students are being served well—that is, that the use of test scores somehow helps students learn and causes little or no harm.

Identifying a Weakness in the Curriculum or in an Instructional Program

Using test scores to reveal a weakness in your curriculum or your instructional program is a good idea only if the test validly measures something that you believe your students should learn or should have learned. Such tests should be very well matched to your state's content standards and your school district curriculum.

Curriculum always needs to be studied and evaluated. Are teachers teaching the "right stuff"? For nearly a century, a common complaint has been that we teachers teach facts and force students to memorize these facts. The value of such teaching is consistently questioned. Tests of memory of facts and disassociated knowledge have been recently criticized as having little bearing on the more important objective of using knowledge and skills to solve problems and to think critically and creatively in life. Tests can be used to study and evaluate curriculum. The links between curriculum and tests can inform educators about interpretations. But the importance of curriculum analysis is to ensure that our students are learning what we want them to learn. Sometimes, the issue may become one emphasizing basic knowledge and skills versus emphasizing higher-level thinking. The public always supports basic knowledge and skills, but to what extent is there a commitment to teaching and testing for the application of this knowledge and skills? The implication is that such teaching and testing is more involved and expensive. For instance, writing assessments involve student performance where the cost of scoring increases greatly because well-trained judges have to be used. Many states and school districts are committed to this more expensive form of testing, but the cost is a major deterrent.

The *instructional program* should be evaluated. Usually, tests have a diagnostic capability that allows teachers to see the overall benefit of instruction as well as the aspects of the curriculum over which they have not been very successful. Adjustments are made to improve the program. In some circumstances, new programs have to be developed or adopted.

These uses of test scores are fundamental to good education. The kind of validity evidence educators seek are changes in test scores that can be linked to changes in curriculum, curriculum emphasis, and instruction.

Placing Students in Certain Instructional Levels Based on Test Scores and Other Information

The logic of placement testing is to find an appropriate level for a student to receive instruction. Placing a student in a group where instruction is developmentally too advanced or below that functioning level does not serve the student well. This practice has been ongoing for many years and will continue. Validity evidence of such placements using test scores can include gains in test scores that seem related to instruction. The important condition present in any placement decision of a student is the total picture provided by the test score and other information. The test score alone should not be a deciding factor.

Selecting Students for Special Programs

Achievement test scores can be used to identify gifted students for selection to a gifted program. However, the use of such tests limits the definition of giftedness and ignores intelligence, leadership, visual and performing arts, and creativity. Most educators would supplement this information with other information before making such an important decision. As with other low-stakes test uses, the use of a test score should be validated by showing some positive benefit to students as a consequence of the test use. Students selected for special programs based on test scores would be doing well in these classes and subsequently test out positively in the future.

Threats to Valid Interpretation

A persistent danger for any test score interpretation and use is invalidity. Tests are flawed measuring instruments. Chapter 7 shows that many threats to valid interpretation exist that are not always considered when making a selection or using test scores in other ways. As testing increases in U.S. education, more and more observers are questioning the validity of test score interpretation and use, especially if the test score is omnipotent. Testing specialists have begun to identify categories of factors that undermine validity. These effects are "construct-irrelevant variance," but a more practical term is *test score pollution.* Any factor that interferes with an accurate interpretation can be viewed as polluting the interpretation of the test score. Some major polluting threats are mismatched tests, cheating on the test, inappropriate test preparation, inappropriate or unfair test administration, and failing to consider the context for a student's or a group of students' performances. Chapter 7 is devoted entirely to the problem of test score pollution.

What Are Intended and Unintended Consequences of Interpretations and Uses?

Messick (1989) is credited by his colleagues as introducing an important dimension to testing—namely, that educators should be aware of the social context in which tests are administered, scored, interpreted, and used. If we decide through study that the consequences of testing are generally positive, we can maintain the testing program, but if most evidence shows negative consequences, then we might question the reason for the testing program. As Mehrens (1998), another noted testing authority, pointed out recently in an essay, there are potential values and dangers to any testing program. Thus, educators must collect validity evidence attesting to the consequences of a testing program, both positive and negative, and weigh this evidence against the purposes of testing.

The recent emphasis on consequences calls to attention the fact that the bad consequences may outweigh good consequences. By surveying, interviewing, and collecting other information, we teachers can begin to assess the consequences of test interpretations and uses and determine the value of a testing program. Although collecting this kind of information has a tremendous cost, it is part of the burden of the testing sponsor and users of test information to learn that the harmful effects of testing are reduced or eliminated. Chapter 8 is devoted to a fuller discussion of this issue.

Summary

This chapter has explained that validity is not a property of a test; rather, validity refers to how one interprets or uses test scores. We must have some evidence supporting any test interpretation and use. Without validity evidence, our interpretation or use is false or questionable at best. Further, we must assess the consequences of testing on the public: good or bad. By applying these criteria to each desired test score interpretation or use, we will lead ourselves to more sensible testing and more valid interpretations and uses of test scores.

Standardized achievement tests as featured throughout this book have many purposes, which vary in evidence for validity. Overall, testing experts for quite some time have reminded us that these test scores grossly oversimplify student learning and are not qualified for or suited to the many uses we would like them to have.

Fundamentally, test scores should help teachers do a better job of teaching, to find better methods or reform curriculum. Test scores should help policymakers study education and make wise decisions about what programs to keep and discard, and allocate enough resources to help teachers teach. This chapter has shown that some interpretations and uses can help educators accomplish the worthwhile goal of improving student learning, but other interpretations and uses are simply too invalid.

Part II

Standardized Testing

The next three chapters discuss three distinctly different types of standardized tests. Chapter 4 focuses on standardized intelligence testing, which is a primary factor in student learning. Chapters 5 and 6 address various types of standardized achievement tests. Intelligence and achievement are intertwined concepts that seem hard to separate or distinguish. Part II gives you a comprehensive look at intelligence and achievement tests and how they interplay in U.S. education.

Intelligence is a familiar, well-researched human characteristic. Not surprisingly, there are many intelligence tests. Most of these tests are used for (1) admissions decisions to colleges and universities as well as graduate and professional training programs, (2) selection to gifted programs, and (3) assignment to classes for students with mental disabilities, such as retardation. Chapter 4 examines different ideas about intelligence. Then several prominent intelligence tests are discussed and evaluated in terms of the validity of some proposed test score interpretations and uses.

Chapter 5 discusses many types of standardized achievement tests and provides some ideas that are useful for various purposes. The chapter also presents some shortcomings or pitfalls in measuring and using achievement test scores. Because there are so many achievement tests in the world, the chapter discusses only a small sample of these tests. Validity of various test score uses is also discussed.

Chapter 6 addresses the growing, important world of high-stakes standardized testing, where pass/fail decisions are made. High school students and, to some extent, elementary school students are increasingly being forced to take a graduation or promotion test to advance in their educational careers. Those among us vying to get professionally licensed have to pass a licensing test to practice in a state or U.S. jurisdiction. Many professional people are trying to get certified through specialized training and meeting criteria for certification, which often includes a certification test.

These three chapters comprise an important core of information about standardized testing in the United States today.

4

Intelligence and Intelligence Testing

Intelligence is the primary distinguishing trait of human beings. In Chapter 1, intelligence was described as one of the most powerful influences on school learning. A sustaining hypothesis in this book is that although intelligence is a somewhat stable human trait, resistant to dramatic change, intelligence is developed and nurtured in the school setting.

This chapter is also about intelligence and intelligence tests. These tests have many useful purposes in education—for example, to serve as one of several criteria in admissions decisions to colleges, universities, and graduate and professional schools, and to identify students with special learning needs for assignment to appropriate classes or educational programs.

By knowing more about the intelligence of students, we teachers can develop strategies for helping each of our students learn. We may also want to consider the role that intelligence testing can or should play in our lives, because such tests may have positive or negative social consequences depending on how we interpret or use intelligence test scores.

This chapter is divided into two sections. The first explores intelligence and discusses two views. One is that intelligence is unitary in nature and the other is that intelligence is multifaceted. Emerging theories of intelligence that seem promising to educators and the public are also explored. The second section focuses on intelligence testing and the validity of various interpretations and uses of intelligence test scores in school settings.

Section One: What Is Intelligence?

That which distinguishes us from animals is intelligence. Marilyn vos Savant (1988), who is reputed to be the smartest person in the world, stated that if you took your dog to a class you were attending, the dog might sit there attentively and not bark, but your dog would not learn or do particularly well in the class. Your dog might not even understand the subtleties of *The Brady Bunch*.

Intelligence is a very general mental capability. In 1923, psychologist E. G. Boring defined *intelligence* to be "what the intelligence tests test." Noted educational psychologist Arthur Jensen (1969, 1986) observed, as many others have, that when one studies the statistical relationships among all cognitive tests, one finds a common element, which Jensen and other educational psychologists consider to be intelligence. These educational psychologists refer to general intelligence as *g*. Intelligence involves figuring things out, catching on to things, and making sense of things. It is not limited to book learning or memorization alone.

Within any culture, there is considerable variation in intelligence. There are people who are mentally retarded who are barely able to speak and dress or feed themselves. They lack the most elementary knowledge and skills to sustain life. These individuals learn very slowly and have difficulty adapting to new situations. Their intellectual inability is not due to cultural deprivation, English language deficiency, or inadequate social capital. At the other extreme, there are people with incredibly high verbal, quantitative, and analytical abilities. Their adaptive abilities are superior to those of most others. These people with exceptional intellectual abilities may be aided by exposure to the mainstream U.S. culture, their language facility, and superior social capital, but there is something else that distinguishes them as superior intellectually: intelligence. This contrast between mentally retarded and highly intelligent individuals gives validation to the idea that intelligence is real and profoundly affects lives.

Distinguishing between Intelligence and Achievement

Distinguishing between intelligence and achievement is difficult because the two concepts intertwine. Intelligence and achievement test scores are highly correlated. Arthur Jensen (1986) estimated this correlation to be about .85 across many intelligence and achievement tests. For our purposes, intelligence represents the capacity or potential to learn. Most intelligence tests seem to focus on three related mental abilities: verbal, quantitative, and reasoning/analytical. When you see a test that measures these three abilities and that is the interpretation you want to make, you are looking at an intelligence test.

Achievement tests are supposed to reflect learned cognitive behavior. The interpretation of an achievement test score answers the question: How much did you learn? Unfortunately, all cognitive tests reflect both intelligence and achievement. Thus, we might consider that any cognitively oriented test is a mixed measure. In other words, a continuum exists that looks like this:

Intelligence   Achievement

Every test will reflect some degree of intelligence and achievement, but to tease out the exact amount of each will be very difficult, if not impossible. The key to distinguishing between the two is the kind of interpretation intended and the logical argument and validity evidence brought to bear to support that argument.

One should be mindful that English language learners, students with emotional and physical disabilities, students who live in cultural deprivation or isolation, and students who live in poverty may not have sufficient opportunity to develop or demonstrate their intelligence via test performance. Chapters 7 and 9 discuss some of these problems associated with students and the factors that may unfairly cause students to get lower scores than deserved.

Finally, there is some evidence that intelligence develops slowly over a lifetime under optimal conditions, and that intelligence declines later in life as part of the aging process. However, this growth can be very slow. Thus, we educators like to think that a good education will stimulate the growth of intelligence. A study by Husen and Tuijnman (1991) suggests that a rich history of education does influence intellectual development. Although the study's result is hardly surprising, what is surprising is that there is a lack of studies supporting this logical idea. Schooling and intellectual activities seem to stimulate intelligence, and isolation and deprivation seem to diminish intelligence.

Data and research presented in the book by Herrnstein and Murray (1994) also provide extensive evidence of these differences between people with high or low intelligence. Having high intelligence is not a guarantee of success in life, but the patterns of people with high and low intelligence are very clear and do not seem caused by social and cultural factors.

Other Names for Intelligence. Intelligence has many names; some synonymous terms include *ability, aptitude, cognitive ability, mental ability, learning ability,* and *scholastic aptitude.* This last term is the most curious because of its obvious link to schools. As Linn and Gronlund (2001) pointed out, intelligence is the more traditional term. The other terms generally came into use to get away from the stigma of intelligence and intelligence testing.

The three components of intelligence—verbal, quantitative, and analytical—might arguably be considered subabilities of intelligence. As discussed later in this chapter, some psychologists think that these three components comprise unique mental abilities that tend to stand alone. They reject the idea of general intelligence and favor a multiple intelligence theory. This multiple intelligence theory has grown very popular. One should always ask about the validity of claims in support or against any theory of intelligence. Such a view of intelligence should be based on theories and supporting research, including tests that claim to measure intelligence. At the heart of claims about multiple intelligence is validity evidence. And having tests that measure a definition of multiple intelligence is helpful. The dominant view in the United States is that intelligence is unitary in nature (general intelligence); research supporting this view spans most of the twentieth century (Jensen, 1980). But each generation of scholars and the public like the idea of multiple intelligence. There is enormous appeal in this idea that each individual can be highly talented in one or more abilities. Later in this chapter, this idea is expanded.

Why Should Educators Be Concerned about Intelligence?

Educators should be concerned about intelligence because it is a significant influence in society, it is an important factor in student learning, and, to the extent possible, teachers want to nurture and develop each student's intelligence.

Importance of Intelligence.   For most purposes in life, having moderate to high degrees of intelligence seems to be advantageous. As one gets older, high intelligence seems more beneficial. Complex societies, such as that of the United States, demand and reward high intelligence. As work tasks become more complex, those with adequate or higher levels of intelligence can master these tasks, while those with little intelligence have difficulty performing even the most elementary tasks and simple jobs. People with high intelligence tend to make better decisions and are better problem solvers and critical thinkers. People with low intelligence tend to have less ability in making good decisions, solving problems, and thinking critically. Those lacking intelligence seem to have the majority of problems in society. These people are most likely to be uneducated, unemployed or employed in minimal paying jobs, drug addicts, criminals, welfare recipients, single parents usually in a home without a father, alcoholics, and domestic abusers. They also tend to have poor health and hygiene, have trouble with temper and rage, be less able to regulate themselves, be less able to make plans and achieve long-term goals, and generally make poor decisions that make their lives miserable. Certainly any of these problems can exist for anyone, without relationship to intelligence, but the main idea is that those with severe deficits in intelligence seem to have a multitude of problems.

Role of Intelligence in Student Learning.   As educators, we need to know the role that intelligence plays in student learning. We know from personal experience as well as theory and research that intelligence is a condition that affects how much a person learns and how well he or she learns. Low intelligence suggests slow learning, inadequate learning, inability to make wise choices, difficulty in solving problems, inability to think critically, and low adaptive ability. We also know that low intelligence too often leads to failure in schools. Students who fail to achieve a high school education are often relegated to underemployment, few choices of occupations, and generally unproductive lives.

Goal of Education and Educators.   With any class of students for whom we are responsible for teaching, intelligence plays an influential role in the strategies we use in teaching and the results we get. As a teacher, the realization is that students with low intelligence have to be given ample opportunities and careful guidance to help them succeed, even if their goals may be modest compared with higher-ability students. The learning curve may be less steep for low-intelligence students, the road to success in school will be longer and slower, but the trip down the road is very important if each student is to achieve success in school and thereby live a productive and satisfying life.

Students with high intelligence have many roads to success. Our goal is to provide them with guidance to grow both intellectually and emotionally. We also know that our success in helping them is more likely, compared to our success in helping students with low intelligence. Nonetheless, the challenge to educate low-intelligent students should continue to receive high priority.

What Do We Know about Intelligence?

Psychologists have reached some consensus about intelligence and the tests purported to measure it. The following assertions summarize the general knowledge about this complex human trait:

- Intelligence can be measured. Some psychologists think that any cognitive test is either directly or indirectly a measure of intelligence. A type of statistical analysis called *factor analysis* typically shows a single factor emerging from a battery of cognitive test scores, leading these psychologists to conclude that the common factor is intelligence. However, some experts will argue the opposite (e.g., Gould, 1996); therefore, this topic is controversial.
- The variation of measured intelligence is distributed as a normal curve (bell-shaped), as shown in Figure 2.1 in Chapter 2.
- Intelligence tests often reflect the culture for which they were designed and are therefore applicable only within that culture. According to Thomas Sowell (1994), virtually all cultures have intelligence tests. These tests seem to have the same three common components (verbal, quantitative, and analytical) that are highly valued in advanced societies. All societies in the world value intelligent behavior.
- The brain's physiology with respect to intelligence is not well understood, but this is a continuing and active area for research. Interestingly, an emerging field of research is the influence of prenatal care and nutrition on intelligence.
- Members of all racial and ethnic groups range tremendously in terms of intelligence. In other words, intellectually gifted people can be found in all racial and ethnic groups.
- Racial and ethnic differences in test performance in the United States are well documented. These differences are not necessarily due to bias in the testing process. However, it is noteworthy that some racial and ethnic groups have very low socioeconomic status and low social capital that may contribute to their plight. Communities that are comprised solely of a single racial or ethnic group tend to be isolated from society. Thomas Sowell (1994) is a strong proponent for cultural diversity as an enriching experience for all people. He uses examples worldwide to make his point. Sowell argues that monocultural societies are less successful than multicultural societies. Those who live in these monocultural societies tend to do poorly on tests based on a culture in which they have little or no experience. Teachers who work on Native American reservations, for example, point out the worthlessness of standardized achievement tests (Haas, Haladyna, & Nolen, 1990). The tests are designed for mainstream U.S. culture, but Native Americans living on reservations have difficulty identifying with a culture they hardly know, so motivation to perform and test performance are both very low (Estrin & Nel-

son-Barber, 1995). Related to this assertion is the fact that English language learners may not be adequately proficient in the English language to take an intelligence test. Also, one should cautiously interpret intelligence test scores for students with emotional and physical disabilities.

- The causes of high and low test scores are not clearly inherited or the result of one's environment. It is easy to attribute intelligence to parents, and certainly strong, positive correlations exist, but separating genetic inheritance from environmental factors is very difficult. Few experts in this field take extreme positions that one or the other is the primary cause of intelligence. As more is learned about this complex problem, researchers are seeing that intelligence, environment, and interactions between the two contribute to one's intelligence level.

- Intelligence is required in many types of work and occupations but not all. The more complex the environment, the more likely that intelligence is required. There is a growing realization that changes in the world, especially involving technology, require more intelligent people who are also more educated.

- Other human traits are very important in many types of work and occupations. *Emotional intelligence* captures the union of emotions and intelligence that affects our lives. People with moderate and low levels of intelligence can be highly successful in advanced societies because they have developed abilities that their society values. The most obvious examples are entertainers and athletes. Although many entertainers and athletes may have high intelligence, it is not their intelligence that earns them national or worldwide recognition and success. Their success comes from their specialized developed abilities. There are numerous examples of successful people in the world whose good fortune is not linked to intelligence alone.

- Intelligence test scores have increased by about 15 points in the last 50 years worldwide (Flynn, 1998), which, as pointed out in Chapter 2, is one standard deviation. This is a very significant amount of growth. Something is happening in the world to increase intelligence. Psychologists have hypothesized about the cause of this gain: Might education be contributing to this overall growth? What about nutrition? What about urbanization and socioeconomic status? Also, is it not illogical to think that an intelligent species evolves into a more intelligent species over time? Research that clearly shows the causes is lacking, but the increase seems to be real.

- Intelligence tends to grow, stabilize, and decline over a lifetime. Schooling appears to make a difference. In other words, those actively involved in learning tend to sustain their measured intelligence, whereas those discontinuing their education note a small but progressive decline. For this reason, educators and others have hopes that schooling and a lifelong devotion to learning stimulates intelligence. This idea alone is an endorsement for the value of education in the life of each individual and in all societies throughout the world.

- Boys and girls do not differ in overall intelligence. However, when looking at sub-abilities, differences do exist. Boys tend to score higher in spatial abilities tests; girls do better in verbal tests. The range of variation *within* boys and *within* girls is quite large compared with any differences *between* boys and girls.

Literally thousands of studies of intelligence were conducted during the twentieth century. Nonetheless, many unanswered questions will continue to motivate more research. Intelligence is and will continue to be a research topic of great interest to educators and psychologists. As noted previously in this chapter, intelligence test scores tend to predict school achievement moderately well (the correlation is about .85). However, other factors seem to be causally related to achievement. These factors include the amount of formal schooling (opportunity to learn), family income, parents' education, motivation, persistence or perseverance, and self-confidence. Thus, achievement seems to be influenced by a combinations of factors. The quest for a weighted formula that links achievement to a student's life history continues to be a fundamental issue in human learning and research about the causes of student learning.

A Brief History of the Study of Human Intelligence

As noted previously, the study of human intelligence has been dominated by two opposing views: one that intelligence is a single factor (*g* for *general intelligence*) and the other that intelligence is multifacted (*s* for *specific*). The single-factor view has a longer history and appears to be the dominant theory. The multifactor view appears periodically in this history as a challenger to *g*. Charles Spearman (1904) observed the possibility that both *g* and *s* might be defensible views of intelligence. Can researchers understand intelligence as a single entity, and, at the same time, recognize multiple intelligence? This brief history cannot possibly do justice to those named who have contributed so greatly to the study of intelligence; therefore, references are sprinkled throughout this section to give interested readers access to more complete discussions of each person's contributions.

The study of intelligence comes from a natural curiosity of humans to describe themselves. What distinguishes humans from plants and other animals is intelligent behavior. Language and mathematics come to mind as two distinguishing qualities of human intelligence. Also, the way people adapt to situations through critical thinking, reasoning, and problem solving seems to make humans unique among other living things. Psychologists have shown an interest in intelligence since psychology's inception. This natural curiosity has evolved into a highly refined science that is active, growing, and controversial.

Single-factor theory received its impetus from the work of Spearman (1904) early in the twentieth century, but many researchers and scientists have actively participated in this continuing study of the single-factor paradigm. Lewis Terman's adaptation of the Frenchman Alfred Binet's intelligence test has become a U.S. standard for testing intelligence: the Stanford-Binet Intelligence Test. Terman's longitudinal study of a cohort of gifted children for more than 60 years provides living testimony about the advantages of being intellectually gifted (Terman & Oden, 1959). The Wechsler Intelligence Scale for Children (WISC) and the Wechsler Adult Intelligence Scale (WAIS) are very trustworthy and highly respected tests used for measuring intelligence. These intelligence tests are individually administered by trained examiners.

Group-administered tests followed Terman's and Wechsler's tests. These group tests were widely used in the middle of the twentieth century, but frequent misinterpretation and misuse of intelligence test scores caused many organizations and states to end intelligence testing. Nonetheless, college and graduate admissions tests, such as the old Scholastic Aptitude Test (SAT) and the current Graduate Record Examination (GRE), appear to be intelligence tests, although the euphemisms of *aptitude, ability,* and *scholastic aptitude* are often used in place of the term *intelligence.*

Louis Thurstone was a brilliant psychologist who took the opposing view to Spearman's unitary view of intelligence. An intellectual rival of Spearman, Thurstone developed the Chicago Tests of Primary Mental Abilities Test in 1941 and it included seven measures: verbal comprehension, word fluency, number facility, spatial visualization, associative memory, perceptual speed, and reasoning. Employing the statistical method of factor analysis in precomputer days where armies of workers grinded out calculations using mechanical calculators, Thurstone provided evidence of these primary mental abilities. He enjoyed some success with this theory, but as World War II approached, his theory waned, and the use of his test has diminished as the test was last published in 1974.

Another brilliant psychologist, J. P. Guilford, took up the gauntlet for multiabilities and, through considerable research, developed a model of the human intellect that he called the *structure-of-the-intellect.* The representation was a cube consisting of 120 specific mental abilities, many of which were represented by tests. Guilford's research is captured in several influential books of the time (e.g., Guilford, 1967). On the popular front, his tests were used to identify students for gifted educational programs. Guilford's impressive research has virtually been abandoned since his death, but his tests and his model are still used in gifted education to some extent.

Robert Sternberg continued the tradition of multiple abilities theory with a three-pronged theory of human intellect that evolved in a program of research. Sternberg's studies and books continue to popularize the multiple intelligence movement. However, recently Sternberg (1998) appeared to be wavering in his approach to intelligence. In this recent essay, he acknowledged the powerful evidence of single intelligence and began to outline an approach that he calls *learned abilities* that appears very similar to *fluid abilities* discussed in Chapter 1.

Howard Gardner's influential writings brought new life to the multiple intelligence theory (Gardner, 1986). His orientation to intelligence, which is very practical, engages the public and has won popular support (Gardner & Hatch, 1989). However, the lack of specific tests of these abilities and empirical research make it difficult for mainstream psychologists to support this recent effort.

A renowned educational psychologist from the University of California at Berkeley, Arthur Jensen's extensive research and essays have strongly supported single-factor intelligence. His *Harvard Educational Review* article (Jensen, 1969) produced a firestorm of controversy, because he argued that compensatory education, which intended to boost the scores of chronically low-scoring minorities, failed and that heredity is causally linked to intelligence. This essay contradicts strong opinions held by many social scientists that environment plays the most important role in human development. His *Bias in Mental Testing* (Jensen, 1980) is perhaps one of the most definitive texts on intelligence written to date.

Richard Herrnstein and Charles Murray (1994) revived this century-long controversy about the definition of intelligence, its origins in nature, its importance, and the plight of people who traditionally score low on these tests. Their book contains mostly the results of research studies and government surveys supplemented by some speculation about the origins of intelligence and what society might do to solve the problems associated with low-scoring people. The authors leave no doubt that people with low intelligence scores (and low intelligence) have records of low achievement and undesirable social behavior. We educators are dedicated to increasing student learning and eliminating undesirable social behaviors associated with low intelligence. But this kind of social change does not occur in schools or in society easily. Herrnstein and Murray's gloomy analysis of the underclass in the United States is similar to Jensen's descriptions in his earlier works (Jensen, 1969, 1980).

Although many essays have been generated by the bell curve controversy, the continued discussion of intelligence spurs more studies as well as policies and programs designed to improve thinking and eliminate antisocial behavior. The increased awareness contributes to society's growing collective awareness about the importance of intelligence in today's schooling.

Some Conclusions about Intelligence

General intelligence seems well established in theory and in testing as a primary human trait. Research shows that general intelligence strongly affects student achievement and is a factor to consider when planning instruction for any student. Teaching students with low intelligence is challenging, but, as educators, we must help all students learn to their fullest capability. The consequences of having this low-intelligence population not achieve is too great not to succeed in their education.

Emotional Intelligence

There are three spheres of human behavior—cognitive, emotional, and motivational—according to Mayer and Salovey (1997). The cognitive sphere is thus far considered to be intelligence. Motivation is goal-oriented behavior that can be developed in students, and it is very important. The third sphere has existed for most of the last century but has lacked a clear-cut identity. That identity is now known to be emotional intelligence. Mayer and Salovey define *emotional intelligence* as

> the ability to perceive emotions, to access and generate emotions so as to assist thought, to understand emotions and emotional knowledge, and to reflectively regulate emotions so as to promote emotional and intellectual growth. This definition combines the ideas that emotion makes thinking more intelligent and that one thinks intelligently about emotions. (p. 5)

Mayer and Salovey provide impressive theory and research to demonstrate that the study of emotional intelligence has a scientific basis and may generate serious study in this new century. Daniel Goleman (1995) popularized this idea in his book, *Emotional Intelligence.* Goleman, who thinks of emotional intelligence as a key to success in life, describes five dimensions of emotional intelligence:

- *Self-awareness:* The premise is that understanding one's own emotions is crucial in succeeding in life in all ways. Recognizing one's emotions helps one make better decisions in life.
- *Managing emotions:* Being able to understand one's own emotions is important, but, more important is the need to control one's emotions, especially in times of great stress or gloom. Having the ability to control emotions means one is able to overcome emotional problems quickly and move on with one's life.
- *Motivating oneself:* A person who is self-motivated controls impulses and delays gratification. Motivated people word hard. They have high productivity, and they tend to succeed at most things they try.
- *Being able to recognize one's own emotions and deal with feelings:* The highly emotionally intelligent person is also good at sensing other people's feelings. Having empathy and understanding for others is an essential people skill.
- *Handling relationships effectively:* This ability involves recognizing other people's emotions and dealing with them through effective communication.

Goleman argued that people with high intelligence will not succeed if they also have low emotional intelligence. On the other hand, a person with high emotional intelligence might overcome the disability of low intelligence. For example, one might compare two people with identical measured intelligence, and these two people may differ in their lifetime achievement and overall happiness. What accounts for these differences? Motivation? Emotional intelligence? Or some combination of the two?

Emotional intelligence is a new idea that appears to have an emerging scientific basis. As this sphere of human behavior is studied more, researchers hope to find that it can be measured, that it can be developed, and that this development positively affects students' lives. In this emerging idea that fluid abilities are an important outcome of education, Snow and Lohman (1989) clearly identified emotion as a vital component. Thus, emotional intelligence seems to have a strong link to the development of fluid abilities. Mayer and Salovey (1997) agreed. Despite diversity among cognitive psychologists, they seem to have some common themes. One of these themes is the emotional sphere of cognitive behavior.

Fluid Abilities

Fluid abilities were identified and discussed in Chapter 1. These fluid abilities are highly desired outcomes of schooling. The concept of fluid abilities is both old and new. Horn (1985) held that the intellect consisted of fluid and crystallized abilities. The latter is much of what is called intelligence, and the former is something that grows slowly over a lifetime and seems affected by instruction and other life experiences.

In the context of school and learning, fluid abilities have been characterized in this book as the main objectives of schooling. These fluid abilities include reading, writing, speaking, listening, mathematical and scientific problem solving, creative thinking, and critical thinking. Cognitive psychologists such as Lohman (1993) and Snow (1989) think that fluid abilities grow slowly and unevenly over a lifetime. Each person can recognize the fluid abilities within himself or herself and how they develop. All people have a profile of fluid abilities, but some are more developed than others. Personal experience reveals that these fluid abilities are very complex, consisting of basic knowledge and skills, but also an emotional component, and the use of all of these to perform in some complex way.

There are literally thousands of fluid abilities. An individual can personally master or reach excellence in only a few of these abilities. By developing one ability, a person has to make sacrifices in the development of other abilities. Developing school-based abilities (reading, writing, mathematical problem solving, etc.) will help all students because these abilities will be needed and used throughout their lives.

In conclusion, high intelligence certainly enables the learning of many fluid abilities, but those with average or low intelligence can assuredly attain high levels of fluid ability. And many fluid abilities do not make high demands on intelligence.

Emerging Fusion of Ideas about Human Intelligence

This section attempts to weave the themes presented in this chapter into an emerging fusion of ideas about human intelligence that may be useful in helping you think about the role of intelligence and intelligence testing in student learning (see Figure 4.1).

Emotional intelligence appears to be a promising concept that may be a useful complement to intelligence. High intelligence is not a guarantee of success in life and

FIGURE 4.1 *Fusion of Related Ideas*

Cogntive Intelligence (Cognitive Ability)		
Verbal Ability	Quantitative Ability	Reasoning (Analytical) Ability

↑   ↓

Fluid (Learned, Developing) Abilities						
Reading	Writing	Speaking	Listening	Critical Thinking	Creative Thinking	Many More

↑   ↓

Knowing One's Emotions	Controlling One's Emotions	Recognizing Other's Emotions	Controlling and Using This Recognition	Self-Motivation
Emotional Intelligence				

low intelligence is not a death sentence. People with high emotional intelligence can function well in society and those with low emotional intelligence may have social maladjustment problems that hinder their success. There is a definite need for more theory and research in this area.

The development of fluid abilities seems worthwhile and connects strongly to cognitive and emotional intelligence. Virtually all fluid abilities require intelligent behavior and social interaction. An emotional aspect of any fluid ability is unmistakable. The fluid abilities linked most closely to schools are reading, writing, speaking, listening, mathematical and scientific problem solving, creative thinking, and critical thinking. These fluid abilities are interrelated and interdependent. They comprise school curricula and state content standards. Figure 4.1 summarizes this working hypothesis about the fusion of related ideas called *intelligence.*

Conclusion

As you can see, intelligence is hardly a simple topic that enjoys a large degree of consensus. It continues to be one of the most active and interesting fields of research and development in psychology and education. Practically speaking, the debate continues regarding the structure of intelligence, the causes of intelligence, and the usefulness of intelligence testing. Table 4.1 provides a reading list of recent discussions of intelligence, not all necessarily agreeable with each other.

Section Two: Uses of Intelligence and Special Ability Tests

In a field so controversial as intelligence, it is surprising that the tests discussed in this section have endured so long. This fact is testimony to the collective belief that intelligence is real and that knowing about one's intelligence is useful. For the most part, the trend of defining intelligence in a unitary way will probably continue, and the tests that measure this unitary definition of intelligence will also persist, mainly because these tests are found useful for some purposes.

Oddly, many test publishers have taken traditional intelligence tests that seem to reflect a single factor (intelligence) and created subscales reflecting important cognitive processes. So, despite the strong evidence for single-factor intelligence, the publishers and test authors are letting educators know that they support the idea that intelligence has verbal, quantitative, and analytical subabilities that can be measured.

What Are Some Typical Uses of Intelligence Tests?

Although intelligence tests have declined in popularity in recent years, the authors and publishers of these tests have offered many potentially valid uses for these test scores, such as the following:

- Help teachers assess the readiness of students for learning to read, write, speak, listen, and solve mathematical problems.

TABLE 4.1   *A Reader's Guide to Studying Intelligence*

Author and Title	*Brief Summary*
Gardner (1986) *The Mind's New Science*	This provocative book has stimulated the rebirth of multi-intelligence theories.
Gould (1996) *The Mismeasure of Man*	This book could be described as the "dark history" of the theory of intelligence, showing how intelligence was mismeasured and misused historically.
Herrnstein & Murray (1994) *The Bell Curve*	This book starts off discussing very systematic patterns in human behavior associated with intelligence and then segues into essays on how to make the world a better place.
Jensen (1980) *Bias in Mental Testing*	This classic, singular work describes the impressive research basis for single-factor intelligence.
Neisser (1988) *The Rising Curve*	This book, which is the product of a conference by the American Psychological Association, gives readers information about intelligence and its controversies. In particular, contributors examine the increase in intelligence test scores worldwide.
Sternberg (2000) *Handbook of Intelligence*	This valuable volume contains the most up-to-date information about intelligence from a variety of highly respected scholars. This book comes closest to being a comprehensive textbook on intelligence and intelligence testing.
Sternberg & Grigorenko (1997) *Intelligence, Heredity, and Environment*	This updated set of essays on intelligence from leading scholars represents a diversity of views about the nature of intelligence and its origins.

- Group students for instruction according to their subabilities.
- Diagnose learning difficulties.
- Help students and their parents make plans for future education.
- Counsel students toward occupations that better fit their potential for learning.
- Help make admissions decisions for undergraduate and graduate educational programs.
- Select students for special programs, such as for mentally retarded or for gifted.
- Make employment decisions.
- Study human behavior through research.

Any intelligence test score used for any of the preceding purposes requires validity evidence supporting that use. Is it valid to use an intelligence test score to assess the readiness of a student for learning to read? The test publisher would have to answer that question by making a claim and supporting it by logical argumentation and validity evidence. Thus, the preceding list should be not taken as an approved or validated list of uses of intelligence test scores. The rest of this chapter will examine some tests and investigate the validity of their uses. But the point of this section is to help you understand that each and every use of an intelligence test score should be put to the test of validation. What's the logic behind the use and what's the evidence supporting this logic?

The Range of Intelligence Tests

Table 4.2 contains a list of several intelligence tests widely used in the twentieth century. The next sections will discuss these tests by categories: (1) individually administered, (2) group administered, (3) college and university admissions tests, and (4) graduate program and school, or professional training admissions tests. However, the tests named and briefly described in this chapter are hardly comprehensive of published intelligence tests. For more information about any test represented or not represented here, consult *The Fourteenth Mental Measurements Yearbook* (Plake & Impara, 2001) or any of the webpages offered throughout this chapter.

Individually Administered Intelligence Tests

Two mainstream intelligence tests that are given by a trained examiner to an individual student are examined here. Other tests exist that fall into this category, but these two stand out as the oldest and most often used and cited. Also, each test has extensive validity evidence supporting test score interpretation and use.

TABLE 4.2   *Types of Intelligence Tests*

Name	Description
Individually Administered	Stanford-Binet Intelligence Tests
	Wechsler Intelligence Preschool and Primary Scales for Youth (WIPPSY)
	Wechsler Intelligence Scale for Children (WISC)
	Wechsler Adult Intelligence Scale (WAIS)
	Kaufman Assessment Battery for Children (K-ABC)
Group Administered	Otis-Lennon School Ability Test (OLSAT)
	Cognitive Abilities Test (CogAT)
	Armed Services Vocational Aptitude Battery (ASVAB)
College Admissions Test	Scholastic Assessment Test I (SATI)*
Graduate or Professional School Admissions Tests	Graduate Record Examination (GRE)
	General Management Admissions Test (GMAT)
	Law School Admissions Test (LSAT)

*A specific discussion of the ACT Assessment is found briefly in this chapter and clarifies an ambiguity the reader might have about the distinction between an intelligence test and an achievement test. The ACT Assessment is considered an achievement test. The SATII is very much like the ACT Assessment, more designed to measure the outcomes of a rigorous and high-quality high school education. Thus, both the SATII and the ACT Assessment may be considered achievement tests.

Stanford-Binet Intelligence Test.   Near the end of the nineteenth century, Alfred Binet, Minister of Public Instruction in Paris, France, and his colleagues designed an intelligence test to identify children with mental retardation for the purpose of providing special education. The test tested verbal skills. The person's score on the test could therefore be expressed as a *mental* age—a score that corresponds to the average age of so-called normal children who perform as well as the individual being scored. The basis for Binet's evaluation was the assumption that people who performed below their age level were retarded, those who performed at it were normal, and those who performed above it were gifted.

In 1916, Lewis Terman revised Binet's test for use in the United States. The new test became the Stanford-Binet Intelligence Scale. This test was the first to use Binet's idea of the intelligence quotient (IQ), which is simply the mental age from the test divided by a chronological age. The Stanford-Binet Intelligence Scale now computes a score known as the *standard age.* The Stanford-Binet Intelligence Scale, 4th edition (1986), has many valid uses and some problems.

The current version offers a link to a cognitive learning theory that fits the unitary theory of intelligence but gives credence to a multifaceted theory that includes (1) verbal reasoning ability, (2) quantitative ability, (3) abstract/visual reasoning ability, and (4) short-term memory. The most important use of a test such as this one is its diagnostic potential for spotting conditions that affect a student's learning. Some students have low intelligence and may not be able to learn as well as others. But the diagnostician who administers the test may spot emotional problems, physical disabilities, disruptions in the learning history, lack of opportunity to learn, or domestic/family conditions that interfere in learning. Therefore, the intended use of the test, as a measure of intelligence, is augmented by the skillful use of a trained examiner who can diagnose learning difficulties correlated to this intelligence test score. Students identified as mentally retarded benefit from taking the Stanford-Binet, because the test may result in assignment to special education where the child gets an individual education plan and special education. Finally, the Stanford-Binet also works as a research tool, providing a dependable measure of unitary intelligence. The long history of its existence, coupled with periodic revisions and standardization, provide validity evidence justifying its longevity as an individually administered intelligence test.

The Wechsler Scales.   David Wechsler created several individually administered intelligence tests in the mid-1930s that are individually administered like the Stanford-Binet. Three of his tests are the Wechsler Adult Intelligence Scale (WAIS), the Wechsler Intelligence Scale for Children (WISC), and the Wechsler Preschool and Primary Scale for Intelligence (WPPSI). The three tests, in a complementary way, provide intelligence scores of people from ages 2 to 89! The Wechsler scales are the most commonly used intelligence tests. The test is published by the Psychological Corporation (http://www.psychcorp.com/).

Kaufman Assessment Battery for Children (K-ABC).   Test authors Alan and Nadeen Kaufman have provided a tool for the assessment of children's verbal and nonverbal abilities. This individually administered measure of intelligence can be completed in 35 to 85 minutes. A variety of scales are available, including sequential processing, hand movements, number recall, and word order. Based on research and theory in cognition and neuropsychology, the K-ABC defines intelligence as a child's ability to solve problems using simultaneous and sequential mental processes. Nondiscriminatory assessment was a major consideration in developing the K-ABC. The standardization sample included representative proportions of children based on census data. The publisher is American Guidance Service (http:// www.agsnet.com).

Validity Evidence for Interpreting and Using Scores from These Individually Administered Intelligence Tests.

There are many parallels between the Stanford-Binet and the Wechsler scales. Both are individually administered; both were used for most of the twentieth century; both are well normed, standardized, and often revised; and both have a wealth of validity evidence. A key feature of these tests is that the information is useful if a highly skilled examiner can use results to help the student through some learning problem. Thus, the motive behind both the Stanford-Binet and the Wechsler tests are to help students learn. The K-ABC is a newer entrant into the individually administered intelligence test that has earned wide acceptance.

The creators of these test series and their publishers did not intend that these tests be interpreted and used in ways that are unsupported by validity evidence. These tests are claimed to be useful as a diagnostic tool to (1) identify retarded and gifted students for appropriate assignment to special programs and (2) be used with other information as a diagnostic tool to reveal causes of poor student learning.

To use test scores to make causal attributions by race or gender or to designate students as retarded because they are immigrants and have not yet mastered the English language in which the test is given is clearly invalid. Also, testing students who have lived in a restrictive or culturally isolated society limits their exposure to the mainstream society and may lead to invalid interpretations. Testing students so seriously disabled that they cannot perform will also result in invalid scores. Thus, these intelligence tests are not harmful, but have been used in harmful ways unintended by the authors and the publishers.

Because the predictions people make from intelligence tests are so important, a test administrator is required to be trained in giving these tests and in interpreting results. The casual use of such tests by untrained persons increases the risk of misinterpretation and misuse as well as consequences.

Group-Administered Intelligence Tests

Three tests are discussed that have dominated the small field of group-administered intelligence tests.

Otis-Lennon School Abilities Test–7th edition (OLSAT–7).

Formerly the Otis-Lennon Intelligence Test, the OLSAT–7 assesses students' verbal and nonverbal abilities in grades ranging from kindergarten through high school. Although its name was changed a long time ago, it is still an intelligence test. Administration time is about one hour. The test consists of multiple-choice questions, so no administrator judgment is required. Verbal processes are comprehension and reasoning. Nonverbal processes are pictorial, figural, and quantitative reasoning. The Psychological Corporation publishes this test (http://www.psychcorp.com).

Cognitive Abilities Test (CogAT).   Through nearly 40 years of development, the CogAT (1993 edition) is one of the major group-administered intelligence tests in the United States. Prior to its new name, it was the Lorge Thorndike Intelligence Test. Its purpose is to assess students' abilities in reasoning and problem solving using verbal, quantitative, and spatial (nonverbal) symbols. Concurrently normed with the ITBS, the Tests of Achievement and Proficiency, and the ITED, the CogAT is a completely revised test battery with verbal, quantitative, and nonverbal scores. A Spanish version is available. The test is published by Riverside Publishing (http://www.riverpub.com).

Armed Services Vocational Aptitude Battery (ASVAB).   This multiple aptitude test consists of 10 short individual tests covering word knowledge, paragraph comprehension, arithmetic reasoning, mathematics knowledge, general science, auto and shop information, mechanical comprehension, electronics information, numerical operations, and coding speed. Taking the ASVAB is a part of the AVSAB Career Exploration Program, which can help students with career decisions and entrance into the military services. Test scores are used by all branches of the military for job placements of recruits. As a recruiting tool, the United States Department of Defense uses the ASVAB to test potential recruits to determine their developed abilities and to predict future performance in academic areas. As a guide for high school and postsecondary school students, the ASVAB helps them decide on the career path for which they might best be suited, whether in the military or in another field. Although the ASVAB may seem to be a test of fluid abilities, the test sponsors generally use the 10 subtests to form three major test scores: verbal, mathematical, and academic ability (Ree & Carretta, 1994). Thus, this test meets the criteria established at the onset of this section as an intelligence test.

Validity Evidence from These Group-Administered Intelligence Tests.   Test publishers make claims about the usefulness of their tests. For instance, the first two tests, the OLSAT–7 and the CogAT, intended for use in schools, might provide a list of uses as follows:

- Indicate possible future achievement
- Diagnose learning difficulties by noting discrepancies between intelligence level and achievement level
- Provide information for effective grouping of students for instruction
- Identify strengths and needs of students (verbal, quantitative, analytical)
- Identify students for placement in a gifted program
- Identify students who are mentally retarded for placement in special education

The publishers of these intelligence tests have a long history with intelligence testing. But validity evidence is not always accessible or easy to find. Therefore, you should be cautious about using these tests and test scores until the publishers provide you with validity evidence supporting any of the preceding interpretations or uses.

Factors that contribute to invalid test score interpretation and use are as follows:

1. Any group-administered intelligence test can be compromised if instruction helps a student learn the content of the test. Although such learning may seem appropriate, the interpretation of any intelligence test score is compromised by offering instruction that other students taking the test haven't had. Since an intelligence test is not an achievement test, teaching to an intelligence test undermines the valid interpretation of the test score.

2. Chapter 7 discusses factors that might lead to overestimation or underestimation of a person's true level of functioning due to factors unrelated to the content of the test. Thus, there is a risk of incorrectly interpreting intelligence test scores. Chapter 9 discusses the testing of special populations who typically score low on all cognitive tests. Again, one must ensure that mitigating factors are not accounting for these low test scores.

3. One factor intelligence tests have in common is their unpopularity in schools— and perhaps justifiably so. Widespread misinterpretation and misuse of intelligence test scores historically has resulted in distrust and dislike of these tests. California and other states have abolished intelligence testing in their schools. Studies describing racial or ethnic differences in intelligence contribute to this unpopularity. Consequently, test publishers have avoided the term *intelligence* in renaming intelligence tests. They use euphemisms such as *school abilities, cognitive abilities,* and *scholastic aptitude.*

Group-administered intelligence tests are no longer important in schooling due to many factors. The future of these tests will depend on whether publishers can convince educators that knowing about a student's intelligence will help them better teach the student.

College Admissions Testing

Colleges need selection criteria to choose students for admissions. High school grades come to mind as one criterion that represents school achievement. Research shows correlations of .26 to .38 between high school grades and freshman grade-point average (Bridgeman, McCamley-Jenkins, & Ervin, 2000). These correlations may seem small, but consider the fact that grades are not always assigned objectively or scientifically by teachers. The validity and reliability of grades might be very flimsy. Nonetheless, high school grade-point average (GPA) seems to be a fairly good predictor of success in the freshman year. Thus, if a student achieved highly in high school, he or she will probably achieve highly in college. By adding an intelligence test score to the equation, the prediction of freshman grade-point average might be improved. With this idea in mind, admissions testing had its beginning. Table 4.3 lists several college or graduate school admission tests that seem to reflect this complementary component to grades for college or graduate admissions. One of the most remarkable things about this set of tests is that

TABLE 4.3   *College or Graduate School Admissions Tests*

Test Name	What It Measures	Who Takes It
Scholastic Assessment Test I (SATI) (formerly the Scholastic Aptitude Test)	Intelligence	High school students wanting to enter colleges or universities; these tests are intended for college admissions decisions only
Scholastic Assessment Test II (SATII)	Achievement	
ACT Assessment	Achievement	
Graduate Record Examination	Intelligence	College graduates intending to enter into graduate school
General Management Aptitude Test	Intelligence	College graduates intending to enter into a professional training school
Law School Admissions Test	Intelligence	
Medical College Admissions Test	Achievement	

despite the fact that these tests are used as admission criteria, several of them are arguably achievement tests, as will be discussed later.

Scholastic Aptitude Test (SAT) and the Scholastic Assessment Test I (SATI).   The SAT was originally used to identify men for admissions to elite universities in the eastern United States in the 1940s. The major premise of using a test such as the SAT was to have a powerful two-variable prediction of college grades. Thus, admissions officers could look at high school grades and an SAT score, get a weighted composite, and make the admissions decision on the basis of data that are known to correlate highly to college grades. The SAT served its purpose well. Bridgeman and colleagues (2000) reported in a recent study that when using the SAT and college grades, the correlations improve from a range of .26 to .38 for GPA alone to a range of .38 to .45 with a median of .44 for GPA plus SAT. Thus, adding the intelligence test component increases predictability of freshman GPA for all social/ethnic/racial groups observed.

After World War II, more and more colleges and universities adopted the use of the SAT and it became a widely accepted college admissions test. The test sponsor, the College Board, and the developer of the test, the Educational Testing Service (ETS), have a wealth of validity evidence supporting its use (Educational Testing Service, 1999).

SAT Renamed SATI.   In 1994, the SAT was renamed the Scholastic Assessment Test I (SATI). The name change did not seem to alter what the SAT measured. The term *scholastic aptitude* is another euphemism for *intelligence*. Changing the name of the test does not change the content, which continues to be mainly verbal and quantitative abilities that form the backbone of twentieth-century intelligence tests. Moreover,

Bridgeman and colleagues (2000) reported that the team of high school GPA and the new SATI did not change the predictability of college freshman GPA (College Board, June 1999). The correlation coefficients ranged from .43 to .46 with the old SAT and ranged from .38 to .45 with the new. Interestingly, the only significant change was lower prediction for Hispanic males with the new test (.38).

A blatant misuse of SATI scores is for evaluating schools, school districts, and states. Since the SATI is an intelligence test, comparisons among schools, school districts, and states are not informative about the quality of educational programs.

SATII.   The SATII was created to provide one-hour subject-matter tests in writing, literature, mathematics, biology, chemistry, physics, American history and social studies, world history, French, German, modern Hebrew, Italian, Latin, and Spanish. Thus, the new SATII seems to be an achievement test, designed like the ACT Assessment to reflect the outcomes of the high school curriculum that the student took. This test is a worthy competitor to the ACT Assessment as a admissions criterion and a predictor of college grades. Both the SATII and the ACT Assessment are listed as achievement tests in Table 4.3.

The SATI/SATII is a very successful testing program that serves over one million students a year. Given its long history and high standards for test development and validity, it should continue to serve college-bound students, despite the continued attacks. Consult their webpage for more information about this program (http://www.collegeboard.com/).

ACT Assessment.   According to their webpage (http://www.act.org/aap/index.html), "The ACT Assessment® is designed to assess high school students' general educational development and their ability to complete college-level work." The ACT Assessment is a four-part multiple-choice test: English, mathematics, reading, and science reasoning. It is part of the ACT's Educational Planning and Assessment System (EPAS), developed to serve students preparing for high school transitions after graduation.

Like the SATI and SATII, the ACT Assessment has high standards for test development and validity and also serves over one million students a year who are interested in college. This fine testing program should also continue to thrive in an era where unprecedented numbers of students are college bound. College admissions testing will not be disappearing soon.

Graduate or Professional School Admissions Tests

This group of tests are all used for the same purpose: to provide a graduate or professional school with one of several criteria to use in selecting candidates for their program. As you will see, the four tests selected as representative of this class of intelligence tests are not purely intelligence tests. This points out that the agencies sponsoring these tests have either adopted intelligence as an admissions criteria or have blended intelligence with achievement or focused on achievement. Most of these tests are given in a computer-adaptive environment that offers convenience and economy of administration and scoring, usually at a higher cost.

Graduate Record Examination (GRE). This test is the bane of college students entertaining the thought of going to graduate school, just like the college admissions tests are the bane to high school students. The test measures intelligence. The verbal, quantitative, and analytical scores are used to predict performance in graduate school. Graduate admissions officers use the GRE to assess the intelligence of candidates and thus make appropriate selections of students. Although the GRE is an intelligence test by the this strict definition, other criteria are often employed by graduate schools to augment the GRE score. Some graduate programs refuse to use the GRE. They prefer to employ a variety of other criteria. The test is published by the Educational Testing Service and is offered in a computerized adaptive version nationally (http://www.gre.org/).

The Educational Testing Service also offers the GRE Subject Tests, which include biochemistry, cell and molecular biology, geology, biology, literature in English, chemistry, mathematics, computer science, music, economics, physics, engineering, and psychology. These tests reflect student learning that may have occurred in the undergraduate program. Thus, these subject tests provide supplemental information to the intelligence score obtained from the GRE. This test series is parallel to the SATI and SATII and is also developed by ETS.

Graduate Management Admissions Test (GMAT). According to its webpage (http://www.gmac.com/), the Graduate Managment Admissions Test (GMAT) measures verbal, mathematical, and analytical writing abilities. The verbal section consists of sentence correction, critical reasoning, and reading comprehension, and the quantitative section consists of data sufficiency and problem-solving questions. Compared with other tests in this category, the GMAT appears to be more aimed at measuring intelligence, with heavy emphasis on verbal and quantitative abilities. The inclusion of writing is a learned ability and is an exception to this orientation to intelligence.

The GMAT scores are used by nearly 1,300 graduate management programs throughout the world. The test is given to more than 200,000 people a year at over 600 test sites in more than 170 countries. The test takes about five hours to administer.

The GMAT is designed to help graduate business schools assess the qualifications of those who seek admission to study for an MBA or another advanced business/management program. Test scores are one predictor of academic performance in the first year of graduate management school, but many other factors are considered in the admissions process at most schools. People who take the test can help understand their relative ability and level of preparation they have before applying to any graduate program. The test is developed by ETS (http://www.gmac.com/) for the Graduate Management Admissions Council.

Law School Admissions Test (LSAT). The LSAT is a half-day standardized test required for admission to all 196 law schools that are members of the Law School Admission Council. It provides a standard measure of reading and verbal reasoning skills that law schools can use as one of several factors in assessing applicants. The test is administered four times a year at hundreds of locations around the world. Like other admissions tests, the LSAT focuses on verbal and quantitative abilities, which have been defined as important aspects of general intelligence. The Law School Admission Council sponsors the test (http://www.lsac.org).

Medical College Admissions Test (MCAT).   The MCAT, which is developed by the Association of American Medical Colleges (http://www.aamc.org) in cooperation with medical schools, assesses verbal reasoning, physical sciences, biological sciences, and writing. The content of the MCAT is identified by physicians and medical educators as prerequisite for the practice of medicine. Heavy emphasis is placed on premedical school sciences with prominence on problem solving, critical thinking, and writing. Thus, the MCAT resembles an achievement test more than an intelligence test. Roughly 40,000 people take this test each year for admission to medical schools in the United States. Like the other tests in this group, the MCAT is very heavily researched, and it has a wealth of validity evidence supporting its use.

Bias in Admissions Testing.   Since the influx of middle- and lower-class students and women entering into colleges following World War II, the SAT has been persistently criticized for bias (Crouse & Trusheim, 1988; Owen, 1985). These critics have pointed to research suggesting that the SAT is biased against women, minorities, and athletes. All three groups tend to perform better in college than the test scores predict (Zwick, 1999). Scholastic Assessment Test scores are also used in the awarding of National Merit Scholarships. Since European American and Asian American males tend to score highest on this test compared to other ethnic/gender/racial groups, these former two groups tended to receive the majority of scholarships. Critics correctly pointed out that since females tend to outperform males in high schools, females are likely more deserving of these scholarships (National Center for Fair and Open Testing, 1988). Nairn and associates (1980) issued one of the most scathing attacks on the SAT and the social inequality that seems to manifest when the SAT/SATI is one of the primary admissions criteria. The strong link between family income and SAT scores shows that social conditions in the United States have a stronger effect than one would like. But the developer of this test, the ETS (1980), argued that social conditions, not the test, are the problem. Zwick (1999) summarized the research on this problem and concluded that the SATI indeed does have high predictive validity for all ethnic/racial groups. She stated that eliminating the SATI to increase diversity on college campuses will not work. The real culprit is inadequate high school preparation of many low-scoring students. When that high school education includes more college preparatory courses, SATI scores and college grades of many students from three racial/ethnic groups will improve.

A more recent attack on the SATI was made by Richard Atkinson, highly respected cognitive psychologist and president of the University of California (Kantrowitz, 2001). He proposed to drop the SATI as a college admission criterion. The argument that Atkinson used is that students are spending too much time preparing for the test, treating it as if it was an achievement test, which it clearly is not. Indeed, a feature article in *USA Today* (April 12, 2001, p. 13A) revealed the extensiveness of test preparation for the SATI. A search of the Internet will uncover many test preparation products and services. Apparently, these products and services are intended to earn students higher scores, but do not necessarily increase their intelligence.

A small but growing trend is to deemphasize admissions test scores as admission criteria in favor of a broader set of criteria. College admissions tests such as the SATI and ACT Assessment are being given less weight and more weight is being given to other criteria. According to the National Center for Fair and Open Testing (Spring 2000a), reliance on SATI or ACT Assessment scores narrows the range or diversity of students coming to colleges, universities, graduate schools, and professional schools. Rigid use of these tests favor European American and Asian American males at the expense of other types of students. Many institutions add other criteria for admissions decisions such as achievements, honors, campus and community involvement, and volunteerism. These schools are recognizing the need for a student body that is more broadly based in terms of qualities they like to see in their students. How far this trend will go is difficult to assess.

Despite the criticisms of college admissions testing, the SATI continues to be used by most of the nation's 2,151 colleges and universities (Kantrowitz, 2001). Admissions testing continues to be a large enterprise in U.S. education that seems to rest on tests that appear to measure what is commonly known as intelligence. It's unlikely that these admission tests will diminish greatly in their use, simply because they are very useful in helping administrators sort through student applicants to find those who have the best chances of surviving challenging college or graduate programs.

Corrupting Intelligence Test Scores

Any intelligence test arguably provides a number that is used to describe someone's intelligence. As Chapter 7 points out repeatedly, all test scores are flawed in many ways and should be interpreted cautiously. What are some of these corrupting influences?

Every cognitive task on an intelligence test item can be taught. Such test-specific teaching will improve the student's score but not necessarily improve his or her intelligence. The context for administering an intelligence test assumes that test-specific preparation was not done and that all students have a background that provided opportunities to learn. The normal distribution of test scores obtained from any intelligence test should suggest that people differ in their intelligence. Many validity studies attest to this fact (see Herrnstein & Murray, 1994; Jensen, 1980; or any of the many other references in this chapter). For further validity evidence, consider those students identified as mentally retarded or gifted. Differences in these students are not the by-product of teaching and learning but of some natural phenomenon called *intelligence*.

As noted previously, a search on the Internet will reveal many test preparation organizations. Chapter 10 clarifies what testing experts consider to be appropriate and inappropriate test preparation. In brief, teaching test-taking skills is appropriate, but if the test intends to measure ability and not achievement, preparing candidates by teaching the content of the test lowers the validity of the interpretation.

Test performance can also be corrupted due to the inability to read and comprehend the language of the test; some cognitive, emotional, or physical disability; or poverty. People who live in cultural isolation are also likely to score low on these tests. If intelligence test scores are used for any of the many purposes discussed in this chapter, then validity evidence supporting that use must be required to ensure that each student's score is not corrupted in any of these ways.

Summary

The first section of this chapter discussed the mainstream unitary definition of intelligence as well as the multifaceted approaches to intelligence that have been proposed periodically throughout the last century. The second section examined current intelligence tests and appropriate and inappropriate interpretations and uses of test scores obtained from these tests.

Intelligence is real. It exists in all human cultures and is a referent in that culture. Intelligence can be measured, and invariably it is linked to verbal, quantitative, and analytical reasoning abilities. There is even some evidence that intelligence can grow, if the home and school environment are enriching, but the issue is how much? According to research, intelligence is growing worldwide to a sizable extent.

Intelligence and achievement are inextricably interwoven in our lives. Teasing out the differences is delicate. In concept, intelligence implies capability for learning, whereas achievement stands for actual change in cognitive behavior that comes from learning. Intelligence is a powerful predictor of achievement, and that is why admissions tests rely on it (for the most part) along with achievement.

One can compare and study intelligence as a function of ethnicity, gender, and race, but such arguments are pointless to the purpose of U.S. education. Studying intelligence in various cultures might provide good insight into one's own culture. Intelligence is a potent factor in student learning. Educators are assigned to teach students with varying levels of intelligence. As teachers, we need to figure out ways to help students with low intelligence learn, because, as is obvious, the alternative of failure to learn has very negative consequences in society.

Intelligence testing is a very large part of U.S. school testing, even though the word *intelligence* is not used in conjunction with many of the tests presented in this chapter. Intelligence tests will continue to serve society in many ways. Scores from these tests seem to have several documented valid uses, including grouping students for instruction, diagnosing learning difficulties, making plans for future education, counseling students about future occupations, making admissions decisions, and selecting students for special programs (e.g., mentally retarded and gifted).

Although intelligence testing may play a smaller role in the teaching/learning process, it continues to operate in many valid ways. Educators and others must use this information validly and continue to be vigilant of misinterpretations and misuses of these test scores.

5

Standardized Achievement Testing

This chapter acquaints you with five major categories of standardized achievement tests, discusses several prominent representatives for each type, describes each test's intended uses, and discusses the validity of these uses. Because there are literally hundreds of these tests, many achievement tests are not mentioned in this chapter. More information about these other tests can be found in the *The Fourteenth Mental Measurements Yearbook* (Plake & Impara, 2001). This volume offers the most comprehensive collection of test descriptions and reviews available. A companion volume is the bibliographic reference to all *Mental Measurement Yearbooks*, titled *Test in Print V* (Murphy, Impara, & Plake, 1999). Several textbooks also provide good information about standardized achievement testing of a more limited nature (e.g., Mehrens & Lehman, 1987; Salvia & Ysseldyke, 2001).

A key idea in this chapter is that although test developers create a test for a specific purpose, test users do not necessarily use a test for its intended purpose. Thus, the idea of validity is very important when interpreting and using achievement test scores. The *Standards for Educational and Psychological Testing* (American Educational Research Association, American Psychological Association, & National Council on Measurement in Education, 1999) make it clear that each specific test score interpretation and use should be validated.

Defining Student Achievement

Messick (1989) distinguished between two types of achievement. The first is scholastic achievement, which is an intended outcome of schooling, and the second is a kind of learning that comes from other life experiences outside schooling. Any change in cognitive behavior attributed to learning in a school setting is scholastic achievement. Student scholastic achievement usually consists of knowledge and skills. *Knowledge* refers to memorizing or understanding facts, concepts, principles, or procedures. *Skills* refer to performance that is usually directly observable. Reading skills include identifying consonant sound/symbol relationships in words or deriving meaning from words, picture clues, illustrations, or sounds. Writing skills include organizing ideas, planning, spelling, punctuation, correct grammatical usage, and capitalization. Mathematics skills include adding, subtracting, multiplying, and dividing whole numbers, fractions, and decimals. Some skills are psychomotor, such as keyboarding and skateboarding.

Student achievement also includes the application of knowledge and skills in complex ways, as demonstrated in problem solving, critical thinking, and creative thinking. Throughout this book, heavy emphasis has been placed on the development of fluid abilities that require this application of knowledge and skills in complex ways. Thus, the definition of *achievement* used in this chapter and book includes these slow-growing fluid abilities and knowledge and skills that are needed when developing these fluid abilities.

As noted in Chapter 2, classroom tests are designed to measure specifically what teachers are teaching. Hopefully, this content is directly related to the school district curriculum and/or state content standards. The standardized achievement test is designed to survey a large domain of knowledge and skills that might be representative of this school district curriculum or part of a generic curriculum.

Brief History of Achievement Testing

The need to know about students and teachers is part of the fabric of U.S. education. When the experiment known as *mass education* began in the United States in the mid-1800s, achievement testing was very limited in scope (Haladyna, Haas, & Allison, 1998). Testing involved very simple mechanisms, such as oral examinations or essay examinations, all of which were nonstandardized. In the early 1900s, paper-and-pencil testing came into widespread use. At that time, there was little discussion of what these tests actually measured. In the early 1920s, a major milestone in achievement testing was the introduction of the Stanford Achievement Test (SAT), one of the premier survey standardized achievement tests. Currently, the SAT is in its ninth edition (SAT-9). This test, which is given to millions of students in the United States, covers a broad curriculum for different subject matters and produces norms, tables from which comparisons can be made using the normal curve (see Chapter 2).

Educators have witnessed a lively debate about the merits of multiple-choice and essay format tests for most of the twentieth century (Haladyna, Downing, & Rodriguez, in press; Rodriguez, 2002). The main criticism emerging in the period from 1923 to the present is the focus on testing declarative knowledge at the expense of skills and higher-level thinking, in particularly cognitive abilities, which may be the real objective of education. For the most part, the tests in this chapter are multiple choice in format, and the focus of measurement is declarative knowledge and skills, with some limited emphasis on critical thinking and problem solving.

Monroe (1918) surveyed achievement tests and concluded that textbook content was the focus of these tests. Most standardized tests of that day were school district based and developed by universities. He asserted that these tests were useful to the extent that they reflected teaching objectives. This important idea has survived over time. Ralph Tyler (1950) is credited with advancing this idea in modern education. This idea is reflected in the practice of linking each test item to an objective and classifying each item as to its content and the cognitive behavior that is believed to elicit the item in students. This link between test item and objective shows the crucial nature of ensuring correspondence between a curriculum and teaching, between a curriculum and testing, and between teaching and testing.

The Bloom taxonomy of cognitive behavior (Bloom, Engelhart, Furst, Hill, & Krathwohl, 1956) became the single-most popular book on education, a familiar reference in virtually every educator's library. This cognitive taxonomy promoted the teaching and testing of higher-level thinking, although appreciable evidence exists that educators have had trouble in both teaching and testing higher-level thinking (Seddon, 1978). The cognitive taxonomy promoted the use of objectives to drive both instruction and testing.

In 1969, an influential essay by Popham and Husek (1969), derived from earlier essays on the importance of linking objectives with testing, popularized the phrase *criterion-referenced testing*. After the appearance of this article, more than 600 articles appeared on this topic, spurring new theoretical development and much research. Most testing experts consider criterion-referenced testing as a type of test score interpretation and not a type of test. Nonetheless, many educators erroneously continue to refer to tests based on a coordinated set of instructional objectives as *criterion referenced* and publishers' standardized achievement tests as *norm referenced*. Any test can have a norm-referenced interpretation, if one wishes to compare student scores relatively, but not every test gives a criterion-referenced interpretation.

Criterion-referenced testing is waning in popularity for several reasons. Most instructional objectives seem fragmented and reflect lower-level learning. Since more complex types of learning are needed and the importance in patterns or sequences of behavior is acknowledged, criterion-referenced testing seems primitive by modern standards. About the same time that criterion-referenced testing was at its zenith, cognitive psychology was an infant and began to grow in the ensuing decades. Thus, educators in the last 40 years have been exposed to two opposing learning theories: cognitive and behavioral. Objective-based teaching, mastery learning, and criterion-referenced testing are clearly some by-products of behavioral learning theory. Authentic assessment and complex thinking are by-products of cognitive psychology. Shepard (1991) discussed the dilemma in her study of school personnel who typically take one side of this bipolar view of learning and must make a choice that dictates how they teach and test. Objective-based learning, teaching, and testing focuses on tests that sample from a domain of knowledge and skills, whereas the more modern approach focuses on testing abilities, such as writing or mathematical problem solving. The measurement of these fluid abilities requires a performance format instead of a multiple-choice format.

A persistent theme in the development of large-scale standardized achievement testing programs has been the interplay between curriculum and instruction. Educators have consistently stated the importance of aligning curriculum and instruction to tests given to students. Without this connection, the interpretation of test results does not seem valid. Nonetheless, test scores from publishers' nationally normed standardized achievement tests are routinely published in newspapers for the purpose of comparing schools, school districts, and even states, as if each teacher in each school was responsible for delivering the curriculum on which these tests are based. Although state-to-state, school district-to-school district, and school-to-school comparisons are invalid without tests linked to teaching and without considering out-of-school factors, the practice of publishing test scores and making comparisons is more widespread than ever.

Currently, educators are in conflict over the existence of standardized achievement testing, its appropriate roles, and the frequency of use if adopted. Should standardized achievement tests focus on objectives, to help teachers plan lessons and units more precisely, or should these tests focus on fluid abilities and examine how teachers sequence learning to advance each student's reading, writing, speaking, listening, mathematical and scientific problem-solving abilities, and critical thinking? Most policymakers and the public need to address the issue of the important outcomes of education, as discussed in Chapter 1. The public and its legislative representatives nationally, in each state, and in each school district are not finished with this issue—nor should they be, as this may be an enduring issue for educators and the public.

Remembering the Main Purpose of Achievement Tests

As stated several times throughout this book, the main use of achievement test scores is to help students learn. For every test described in this chapter, an evaluative judgment about the merits or weaknesses of any test has to fall back to this basic, fundamental assertion. The question to be asked is: Will a particular test help us teach better and help students learn? Logical analysis of this situation and validity evidence should guide one's thinking in answering this question.

Types of Achievement Tests and Their Intended Uses

Following is a review of five different types of tests given to millions of students annually. According to Cizek (1998), K–12 pupil enrollment has not increased very much in the last 40 years, but test sales have skyrocketed. The majority of this testing is done in school districts; state-mandated testing is also very large. This section gives you a perspective about the extensiveness of standardized achievement testing. To this point, the most prevalent theme throughout this book (and featured in Chapter 3) has been validity. Mindful of the main purpose of achievement testing, with each test discussed, the desired interpretations and uses of test scores now become the focus. The evidence behind the intended interpretations and uses is presented, misinterpretations and misuses of these tests are described, and the issues affecting each test's future in helping U.S. education are discussed.

Publishers' General Survey Achievement Tests

As the history of achievement test shows, these tests first emerged in the 1920s, with the first edition of the SAT. Other tests soon joined this small group of publishers of large-scale standardized achievement tests, including the Iowa Test of Basic Skills (ITBS) and the high school counterpart, the Iowa Test of Educational Development (ITED); the Metropolitan Achievement Test (MAT); the TerraNova California Achievement Test (CAT); and the TerraNova Comprehensive Test of Basic Skills (CTBS).

Test companies sell their products and services, which include scoring and reporting. Each company invests considerable resources in the development of their products and services. They try to emulate a generic national curriculum, ensuring that their test information captures the important knowledge, skills, and abilities about which the public wants to know. Not surprisingly, these tests appear to test the same curricular areas, as Table 5.1 shows. These test companies survey textbooks and basal series and study curricular trends of national organizations, such as the National Assessment of Educational Progress, the National Council of Teachers of Mathematics, the Writing Process Model, the American Academy for the Advancements of Science, the National Science Education Standards, and the Bradley Commission on History in the Schools.

Iowa Test of Basic Skills (ITBS).   Developed by the University of Iowa test authors and published by Riverside Publishing (http://www.riverpub.com/), the ITBS published parallel forms K and L in 1993, and the current form M tests were designed and developed to measure content standards related to a hypothetical national curriculum.

TABLE 5.1   *Comparisons of Content of Major Publishers' Achievement Tests (Early Elementary)*

	ITBS	**MAT**	**SAT-9**	**TerraNova CAT**	**TerraNova CTBS**
Reading	Vocabulary Comprehension Word analysis	Vocabulary Comprehension Word recognition	Vocabulary Comprehension Word study skills	Vocabulary Comprehension Word analysis	Vocabulary Comprehension Word analysis
Mathematics	Concepts Problems Computation	Concepts and problem solving Procedures	Problem solving Procedures	Concepts and application Computation	Mathematics Computation
Language	Language Listening	Language	Language Spelling Listening	Mechanics Expression	Mechanics Spelling
Other	Science Social studies Sources of information	Science Social studies	Environment	Science Social studies	Science Social studies

Source: Adapted from Cizek (1998).

This achievement test is fully normed from kindergarten through grade 12. Additionally, national performance standards established across grades and content areas may be reported to describe achievement based on expectations determined by a national panel of curriculum experts. The ITBS is available in both complete and survey batteries. The main building block of Riverside's Integrated Assessment System, this battery of tests includes achievement, ability, and career interest. The ITBS reflects more than 50 years of test development experience and research on measuring reading and other language arts content, mathematics, social studies, and science.

Metropolitan Achievement Tests, 7th Edition (MAT–7).   Published by Harcourt Brace Educational Measurement (http://www.hbtpc.com/), this venerable achievement test measures student achievement at 14 different levels, ranging from kindergarten to high school. The MAT–7 is partnered with the OLSAT–6, which was briefly described in Chapter 4 as a group-administered intelligence test. Like the other tests in this category, the range of subjects tested and options for schools and school districts is considerable. Reports are available in a variety of formats. Consult the publisher's webpage for further information.

Stanford Achievement Test, 9th edition (SAT–9).   Also published by Harcourt Brace Educational Measurement (http:// www.hbtpc.com/), the SAT–9 is the oldest and one of the most widely used and respected achievement tests (Kelley, Ruch, & Terman, 1923). It has been revised eight times, attesting to its popularity and longevity. Like these other tests, each edition updates content to align with current curricular trends in the United States. Currently, the SAT–9 has 13 achievement levels, ranging from kindergarten through grade 12. It has multiple-choice tests in reading, mathematics, language, spelling, study skills, listening, science, and social science, and has open-ended tests in reading, mathematics, writing, science, and social science. Like other tests of its kind, the publisher reported that the SAT–9 is aligned with many national organizations. *The Technical Data Report* (Harcourt Brace, 1997) provides a wealth of technical documentation and validity evidence supporting the interpretation of test scores as measures of general school achievement and the use of these scores for the evaluation of a curriculum to the extent that the curriculum is relevant to the school district using the test scores.

TerraNova CAT–6 (formerly California Achievement Test) and the TerraNova CTBS (formerly Comprehensive Test of Basic Skills).   This new series is the sixth edition of the CAT, and is now called TerraNova CAT, published by CTB McGraw-Hill (http://www.ctb.com/). The TerraNova CAT includes an integrated reading/language arts test along with mathematics, science, and social studies. It offers 21 levels spanning kindergarten through high school. Like other publishers' tests, basic and complete test batteries are available.

CTB Mc-Graw Hill also offers SUPERA, which is a Spanish language comprehensive achievement test series, linked to learning objectives in phonics, writing conventions, and mathematics computation, all very basic learning outcomes in schools. The test is said to be designed with native Spanish speakers in mind by using original literature and familiar themes and everyday contexts to measure reading, language arts, and mathematics. One important feature is that of sharing a common scale with parallel English assessments. The Comprehensive Test of Basic Skills (CTBS–5) has been one of the top achievement test series for a long time and has been recently reissued under the TerraNova trademark.

The webpages for these two publishers' achievement tests are not very informative; however, if you are interested in getting more information, you can use the webpage to make contact and request a catalog.

Commonalities among These Tests. Test publishers generally believe that their tests have common qualities that would appeal to most educators—for example:

- Educators are consulted in order to define the content of major curriculum areas.
- Curriculum guides from states and school districts are reviewed.
- National educational goals and national and state content standards are examined.
- The content of widely used textbooks is analyzed.
- High technical standards are maintained that withstand public and professional scrutiny.
- Test scores are provided at a fairly low cost. (When performance measures are added, the cost rapidly escalates and quality of information may not be technically adequate.)

Therefore, these publishers supply products and services that they think the public will like. There is a keen competition for testing dollars in states and in school districts, thus making these tests very competitive in sales and service.

Valid Interpretations and Uses of Test Scores. These tests (and others) are good universal measures of school achievement. Educators would be hard pressed to reject any content from these tests. Publishers are careful to include test content that seems fundamental to U.S. education. The existence of norms provides comparative information to place each student in perspective with analogous students throughout the United States.

The tests may be useful in a general way to evaluate the effectiveness of instructional programs in these subject matters. School districts may want to use such tests to question the value of a specific reading program or an approach to mathematics instruction used in the district. It seems that publishers of these tests intended that their tests be used in this way; therefore, it is likely valid to interpret these tests as general measures of student learning and to use test results to guide changes in curriculum and instruction to match this generic curriculum that the test publishers have conceived.

Thus, to the extent that one wants measures of lifelong learning that are linked to generally accepted content that seems to reflect the nation in general, these kinds of tests provide useful information.

Invalid Interpretations and Uses of Test Scores. Generally, the issue in the choice of a publisher's test is the match between the content of the test and what the state or district requires. For example, Arizona used the ITBS in the 1980s. A study by Noggle (1987) showed a low correspondence between the content of the ITBS and the state's content standards. This study motivated Arizona to abandon the ITBS and create a state test that was perfectly aligned with the state's content standards. This new test was also designed to enable school reform in the direction of focusing on abilities such as reading, writing, and mathematical problem solving. As was emphasized in Chapter 3, the content found in mandated state content standards or a school district curriculum should be the basis for teaching. If a mandated publisher's test is used, then the interpretation or use of test scores might be questioned. What are some of these invalid uses?

- Comparing states, school districts, and schools would be invalid because students come and go from these states, school districts, and schools and because the content is not closely aligned with teaching. It would be difficult to show that any state can be defined as having a uniform educational program that distinguishes it from any other state. The same argument applies to school districts and schools. Evidence is needed that precisely describes the uniqueness of any comparison unit before one can make valid evaluative judgments. This uniqueness should clarify to the public some reasons for why a school's or district's scores are higher than other comparable schools.
- Evaluating teachers or awarding merit pay would be invalid because no single test can capture the qualities of excellent teaching (Berk, 1988; Haertel, 1986). Even the definition of teaching is a considerable scientific enterprise.
- School closure would be an invalid interpretation because test scores are not good measures of school achievement specific to what was taught in a school during a specific period of time. Moreover, the attribution of cause to a school is inappropriate considering the many other factors identified in Chapter 1 that influence learning.
- The issue of the validity of passing or failing students on the basis of one of these tests is a matter of great importance. Thus, Chapter 6 is exclusively devoted to this type of high-stakes test score use.

These test publishers are very careful not to make false claims that their test scores can be validly used for these purposes. Although test publishers are interested in selling their products and services to the public, they typically stay within the framework of national testing standards (*Standards for Educational and Psychological Testing*, American Educational Research Association, American Psychological Association, & National Council on Measurement in Education, 1999).

Educators should always question whether each test score interpretation and use is valid. State and school districts like these publishers' standardized achievement tests mainly because they can make norm-referenced comparisons among students, classes, and schools, as was illustrated in Chapter 2. Although norm-referenced interpretations are always possible, the question must be asked: Are these norm-referenced interpretations valid?

Specific Subject Standardized Achievement Tests

Many test companies produce standardized achievement tests that have a narrower focus than the general, survey achievement tests discussed in the previous section. These specific tests serve a single school subject matter, such as reading, and may also serve a special population. These tests fill a need in the testing market for customers, usually school districts, concerned with deficiencies in specific knowledge, skills, or abilities of their students. The main purpose of these tests is diagnosis of specific problems in subjects such as reading or mathematics.

A good example of this kind of test is the Woodcock Diagnostic Reading Battery, which is published by Riverside Publishing (http://www.riverpub.com). This test is used to assess 10 aspects of reading achievement in various grade levels and into adulthood. The test has norms and diagnostic information that schools and teachers find useful in designing reading programs, spotting reading problems, and prescribing remedial instruction. It is a very popular test, due to its usefulness and years of development and validity evidence accumulated.

Another example is the Gates-MacGinitie Reading Tests™ (GMRT™) (fourth edition, 2000), also published by Riverside Publishing (http://www.riverpub.com). The stated purposes of this test are to (1) assess student and adult achievement in reading; (2) diagnose the reading needs of individuals and groups of students; (3) evaluate students for program placement; (4) plan appropriate instruction, intervention, and enrichment; and (5) report progress to teachers, parents, and students.

In the mathematics field, the Stanford Diagnostic Mathematics Test (fourth edition) is a good example of an achievement test that provides more in-depth analysis of student performance than that obtained from a comprehensive achievement test such as the SAT–9. The Stanford Diagnostic Mathematics Test has a wealth of validity evidence supporting its use as a diagnostic tool in the classroom. Refer to http://www.hbtpc.com/ for more detailed information.

KeyMath: A Diagnostic Inventory of Essential Mathematics is another good example in the field of mathematics. This test battery is an updated measure of understanding and application of mathematics concepts and skills for ages 5 to 22 that can be administered in less than one hour. Subscales include concepts, operations, and applications. The publisher offers four reports that provide users with different perspectives. More information is available from the publisher, American Guidance Service, on its webpage: agsnet.com/templates/productview.asp?Market=36&Category=285&Group =a26060.

Valid and Invalid Interpretations and Uses of Test Scores.   Valid use of these kinds of tests is in diagnosing learning difficulties in students in a specific ability to plan instruction to remediate this deficiency. A critical condition for validity here is that the content of the test matches the state content standards or school district curriculum.

Occasions might arise when an invalid use occurs. For instance, to use a reading test in English with a nonnative speaker who recently immigrated to the United States might misrepresent this student's achievement; the same could be said about a student assigned to a particular group for instruction who does not perform adequately due to boredom or frustration. Such a placement would argue for looking at the whole student rather than depending on a single test and test score for a placement decision.

With any proposed use, the publisher should be able to supply you with validity evidence supporting any proposed use. With that proposed use, a logical premise should exist that the test provides interpretations that you find useful.

Table 5.2 provides a sampling of specific achievement tests that can be used by schools interested in measuring a subject matter more comprehensively than can be found with the standardized, survey achievement tests like the ITBS, MAT–6, SAT–9, TerraNova-CAT, and TerraNova-CTBS.

State and School District Testing Programs

The state legislature initiates a state testing program to provide public accountability and to justify the use of state money to support specific programs and policies in each state. Because legislators are laypersons and usually not professional educators, these

TABLE 5.2   *Specific Subject Standardized Achievement Tests*

Name of Test	What It Measures	How to Use
Stanford Diagnostic Reading Test, Fourth Edition (SDRT 4)	Measures achievement in the reading process and pinpoints specific areas of difficulty for each student	Evaluates students for placement Determines reading strengths and weaknesses Provides special help for students who lack essential reading skills Identifies trends in reading achievement Provides information about instructional programs Measures changes over a specific period Determines where students need to improve
Orleans-Hanna Algebra Prognosis Test, Third Edition (grades 7–11)	Predicts success students will have in first-year algebra	Makes counseling or course placement decision regarding whether a student should take algebra Plans lessons Assists career awareness
Nelson-Denny Reading Test (high school, college, and adults)	Measures vocabulary development, comprehension, and reading rate	Assesses student achievement and progress in vocabulary, comprehension, and reading rate
KeyMath: A Diagnostic Inventory of Essential Mathematics	Measures concepts, operations, and applications	Assesses basic learning in mathematics for a wide range of mathematics achievement

legislators rely on professional advice to make policies and to allocate resources. Often, states have superintendents of education and a state board of education that may be elected, as in Kansas and Washington, or appointed. Initiatives for state testing programs usually come from the state legislature, the state board of education, or the state school superintendent. One would be hard pressed to find a state where the initiative for a state-mandated testing program came from a professional educators' association or from other educator organizations.

School districts have governing boards and operate very much like states. They range in size from very small to very large, and when resources are adequate, school districts will develop testing programs reflecting student achievement in key areas, such as reading, writing, and mathematics. Far too often, the easiest way to get school district assessment is to use a publisher's test, which provides a good substitute for a locally developed school district assessment program. The key issue in any such adoption is how well the content of the publisher's test aligns to the school district's curriculum. For the most part, this section will concentrate on state testing programs, acknowledging that school districts may have developed very fine testing programs without near the resources available to the state for a similar testing program.

State testing programs are very diverse and numerous. Mehrens (in press) reported that as far back as 1984, about 40 states were engaged in some serious form of state testing. All states have statewide testing policies (http://www.edweek.org/context/topics/issuespage.cfm?id=41), but states vary greatly in terms of the kinds of testing programs that serve each state. Many states (e.g., Michigan, Maryland, Ohio, Oregon, and Washington) develop their own testing programs, whereas other states (e.g., Hawaii and Tennessee) use a publisher's test, and some states (e.g., Arizona) use both kinds of tests.

Since there are so many of these kinds of testing programs in the United States, it may be helpful to review some key issues and unique features and then review what these testing programs have in common. It is not possible in this chapter to describe what all states are doing; however, Table 5.3 lists a few states and some of the unique features they contain.

Why Assess Students?   The main reason states initiate their own achievement testing programs is to assess each student's achievement over time, diagnose learning deficiencies, and give students, teachers, and parents feedback to evaluate and improve student learning. The focus in most states is the student, not a group of students. If the concern is about the achievement of groups of students, testing programs could use sampling techniques and state testing would be much smaller, less expensive, and less intrusive in the classroom.

Another reason for state and school district assessment is to improve instructional programs. By monitoring student achievement, educators can decide if students are progressing as they should. If they are not learning adequately, it might be attributed to the specific reading, writing, or mathematics programs in use or other factors. The test scores help educators think through the problem and its solution. Since the state is the larger unit of analysis, state testing provides norm-referenced information to make

TABLE 5.3   *State-Sponsored Testing Programs*

State/Web	Brief Description
Arizona ade.state.az.us	Arizona Academic Standards are assessed using the Arizona Instrument to Measure Standards. Tests are given in reading, writing, and mathematics in grades 3, 5, and 7. The high school test will be used for pass/fail decisions affecting graduation. The state also administers the Stanford–9.
Colorado cde.state.co.us	Colorado's K–12 Academic Standards is assessed via the Colorado Student Assessment Program, which measures reading, writing, mathematics, and science in grades 3, 4, 5, 7, and 8.
Florida firn.edu/doe	The Florida Statewide Assessment Program was started in 1971 and currently is designed to assess its Sunshine State Standards in reading (grades 4, 8, and 10) and in mathematics (grades 5, 8, and 10). Florida also gives the SAT–9.
Kansas ksbe.state.ks.us	Kansas Curricular Standards includes reading, writing, and mathematics, variously assessed in grades 4, 5, 6, 7, 8, 10, and 11. Science and social studies are scheduled to be assessed.
Michigan http:// www. meritaward.state. mi.us /	The Michigan Educational Assessment Program (MEAP) is based on the state's Model Core Curriculum Outcomes and the Content Standards. MEAP's purposes include comparing actual achievement to expected achievement and charting improvement over time. Michigan intends to target academic help where it's needed, mainly in poor communities. The state uses benchmark standards to chart progress of students and schools.
Minnesota cfl.state.mn.us	Minnesota Comprehensive Assessment measures the Basic and High Standards in reading and mathematics. Minnesota has a two-tier graduation standard. School districts have an option to use a publisher's nationally normed test. School districts can also develop their own tests, as long as the test measures state content standards.
Nebraska nde.state.us	School-Based, Teacher-Led Assessment and Reporting System uses Nebraska's content standards (Leading Educational Achievement Through Nebraska Standards). Reading/writing, mathematics, science, and social studies/history are covered. There is no state-mandated testing.
Ohio ode.state.oh.us	Standards for Ohio Schools drives Ohio's assessment program, which tests in grades 4, 6, and 9. Legislation has been passed making grade-level tests for promotion, with the caveat of providing remedial programs.
Oregon ode.state.or.us	Oregon has its Academic Content Standards and currently offers tests in reading, writing, mathematics, and science in grades 3, 5, and 7. The Certificate of Initial Mastery is a high school certification based on a high school test battery.
Washington k12.wa.us	Washington is undergoing educational reform. Its Assessment of Student Learning links to its state content standards, Essential Academic Learning Requirements. The state uses its home-grown assessment and the ITBS and ITED.

comparisons with other school districts within the state. Unfortunately, not all school districts have the same demographic context, so comparisons may not be valid.

Finally, the public demands to know how well students are learning and wants to know if its resources are sufficient to meet student needs. This need to know is fundamental to citizens in all states. Thus, it is unlikely that state-sponsored or school district achievement testing programs will disappear. In fact, it seems that state-sponsored testing programs are increasing as state officials see value in defining their own content standards and then using their own tests to measure these standards.

High Stakes. Chapter 6 is devoted to those achievement testing programs where the uses have significant consequences on students or their teachers. For the most part, these high-stakes testing programs are referring to high school graduation. About one-third of the states have or are moving toward some type of graduation testing. Chapter 8 reviews the potential or actual consequences of high-stakes testing programs.

Accountability. As discussed in various chapters in this book, accountability has two general connotations: (1) the public needs to know so that good decisions can be made about policies and resources assigned to education and (2) someone needs to be held responsible for student learning in each state. The first meaning of accountability seems to be the most widely shared and professionally acceptable. The second meaning may be growing in states that are looking to manipulate teachers into focusing on test results at the expense of a more comprehensive kind of learning experience. Chapter 8 discusses this second kind of accountability. The Texas Assessment of Academic Skills is a good example of an achievement testing program that may have disappointing results, according to a report by McNeil and Valenzuela (2000). Testing experts see this second form of accountability as having negative qualities (Linn, 2000). Accountability is explored more deeply in Chapters 6 and 8.

Value-Added. Test scores can be "contextualized" (i.e., provide a better idea about how students are doing) when more is known about the students' backgrounds. Chapter 1 provided a discussion of context, emphasizing social capital and intelligence as two factors that strongly influence learning and that reside outside of school. By taking into consideration external factors such as social capital and intelligence, people can get a better idea about how students, schools, and school districts are doing.

Tennessee was one of the first states to try a revolutionary method that may be spreading to other states and school districts: the value-added assessment. This method is based on the idea that teaching makes a big difference in student learning. The method assesses teacher effectiveness by examining gains of classes of students for a year based on year-to-year testing. Tennessee tests all its students annually in grades 3 through 8 with a customized version of McGraw-Hill's TerraNova test series. Called the Tennessee Comprehensive Assessment Program (TCAP), test scores are used to inform students, parents, and teachers about individual student achievement. The Tennessee Value-Added Assessment System (TVAAS) produces annual reports of aggregated student achievement gains attributed to each Tennessee teacher, school, and school district. The reports cover reading, language, mathematics, science, and social studies. Overall, Tennessee is very happy with this system (http://www.edexcellence.net/better/tchrs/16.htm#bm1), but there are many critics of this system as well (Peterson, 2000). The gist of the criticism follows:

- The system is usually put in place without consulting educators or parents.
- The system seems to emphasize basic knowledge and skills at the expense of fluid abilities such as reading, writing, and problem solving.
- The system ignores the problems of students at risk—namely, those with disabilities, those living in poverty, and those learning to speak English (discussed in Chapter 9).
- The system might augment cheating or other unethical methods to increase test scores (see Chapter 7).

Dallas (Texas) schools have been using a system like this since 1984 and the Milwaukee (Wisconsin) schools are currently considering a value-added system. The value-added trend seems to be growing nationally, as legislators and school boards are increasingly wanting to hold teachers responsible for student learning. (Chapter 8 argues that such emphasis ignores the context factors discussed in Chapter 1.)

School and School District Report Cards.   Another outcome of this increasing need for accountability is the school or district report card, which is like a student report card but generally refers to the state's, school district's, or school's academic achievement. Generally, there are two kinds of reports cards.

Menlo Park (an affluent community in the San Francisco area near Stanford University) uses a *profile report card* (http://www.mpcsd.k12.ca.us/sarc/sarc9900HV.html). It gives the most general information without any effort to pinpoint strengths or weaknesses in student learning.

The state of Kansas offers a good example of the other type of report card (http://www.ksbe.state.ks.us/). Unlike other states cited in this section, the state uses a publisher's test as its official state test. Kansas uses a webpage that has a state map of counties and school districts within counties. Thus, one can find any school district and school and obtain a complete report. A typical report will contain attendance, graduation, and dropout rates. The report card contains information about student achievement on all of Kansas's tests for different groups of students, such as English language learners. Although such reports may seem too detailed, even excessive, the report card provides the satisfactory detail about school achievement that even the most discriminating member of the public requires.

Report cards satisfy the need for one type of accountability. The most responsible report cards will disaggregate student data by different subgroups to help the public understand that some groups achieve more than others for various reasons. Students with disabilities, living in poverty, and learning to speak English are three distinct groups, though often overlapping, that usually have low achievement and require special instructional programs.

Performance Testing.   The tendency for modern education to embrace the teaching of fluid abilities has led to a substantial increase in performance testing in state-sponsored testing programs. Nearly all states are either planning or using performance testing. The most common form of performance testing is writing. Oregon is a good example (http:// www.ode.state.or.us/). Its writing model is one familiar to most educators. The writing modes are narrative, imaginary, expository, and persuasive. Six analytic traits are ideas and content, organization, voice, word choice, sentence fluency, and conventions, based on the six analytic traits model developed almost 50 years earlier at the Educational Testing Service. Students have a choice of writing prompts, as the objective is to increase the chances for each student to do his or her best.

Oregon has a very interesting mathematics performance assessment that addresses problem solving. The state's content standards include five strands: calculations/estimations, measurement, statistics/probability, algebraic relationships, and geometry. These five are very typical of many states' and school districts' content standards. However, their performance assessment involves mathematics performance problems that require the student to understand the problem, formulate a plan to solve the problem, solve the problem, and communicate the solution in writing or pictorially. Research on this type of assessment shows that girls, who typically are outscored by boys, are actually doing better than boys on these performance assessments, thus creating a higher status for young women in mathematics because of adding this performance component (Ryan & Demark, 2002).

Performance assessments are very attractive to those who want to see student learning focused on fluid abilities instead of knowledge and skills. However, teachers more easily teach the knowledge and skills, so tension exists between those who want quick results through multiple-choice teaching and testing of knowledge and skills and those who prefer more expensive performance testing that arguably offers measures of more important fluid abilities that may be the real objective of education. Despite the increasing accountability movement, we are likely to see more performance testing in state-sponsored testing.

Vermont Portfolio Assessment.   The *portfolio* has been defined generally as "a systematic and organized collection of student work used by the teacher and student to monitor growth of the student's knowledge, skills, and attitudes in a specific subject area" (http://www.sdcoe.k12.ca.us/notes/5/portfolio.html). For classroom teaching and testing, the portfolio is a highly regarded classroom evaluation tool (Haladyna, 1997).

One of the most unusual and controversial state-sponsored testing programs is the Vermont Portfolio Assessment, which was piloted in 1990–91. This project touched off a maelstrom of controversy and research. The Vermont project was designed by teachers and fully implemented in 1991–92. This assessment program required teachers to evaluate student classwork. The project was aimed at improving teaching rather than evaluating students. However, research on the Vermont experiment revealed many shortcomings of the portfolio assessment, including low rater and test score reliability. On the other hand, a Rand report concluded that many positive changes had occurred in teaching. Since the Vermont project was aimed at improving teaching, it appears to be working (http://www.ed.gov/pubs/IASA/newsletters/assess/pt4.html). An issue that states and school districts should address is the feasibility of portfolio assessment and the ultimate consequences or impact on students. Do the results justify the effort?

Valid Interpretations and Uses of Test Scores.   What is remarkable about state or school district testing programs is their diversity. Table 5.3 provides an unsystematic and probably unrepresentative set of state testing programs. Despite the diversity that seems to exist among these programs, some common themes exist as well:

- Most states want student achievement data to satisfy a basic need for accountability. The public needs to know how its children are doing in schools. Thus, the report card emerges as a method for reporting to the public.
- Another purpose of state testing is to provide information to teachers to help them evaluate and plan instruction or revise curriculum.
- Many states have decided to enter into high-stakes testing by making tests part of graduation requirements.

The validity argument for any of these test interpretations or uses needs to draw principally from the state's content standards and the alignment of that test to these standards. The test is usually secure. This security is important to ensure that teachers and others will not use previous tests and simply teach answers to test items, which most educators would not support as sound teaching. A state test can chart growth of students through grade levels and observe trends over time, which can be connected to special programs or changes in school district curriculum or instruction. Finally, even if states have their own tests, they often like to know how to link to national or international standards. There are ways to do this without extensively testing all students. So, state testing seems very desirable when the state thinks its citizens want a state-based set of content standards and tests are matched to that set of standards, so true accountability can be achieved.

State testing programs have great potential to positively affect student learning for several reasons. First, a state testing program reflects its own state content standards. If one truly intends such tests to help students learn, the tests can show the status of each student in each content area against standards and across time. Curricula, instruction, instructional programs, and teaching can be evaluated in the presence of reliable indicators of commonly agreed content standards. Like Vermont, states can improve the competence of teachers, thereby doing a great service to the public.

A major issue in most states desiring to have their own state-grown testing program is whether students will be compared or evaluated against national standards. The tendency is to want to have a state test for the obvious reason of matching the state's content standards, but also to give a nationally normed test, such as the SAT–9 or the ITBS, to learn how students are doing compared with students in other states. Interestingly, samples of students from grades 3 through 9 were given Oregon's content standards tests in reading and mathematics and the ITBS in reading and mathematics in 1992 and 1998. The results showed a very high correlation between the two tests (ranging from .74 to .85). These results do not take into account the fact that both tests have high, but not perfect, reliability, so the true relationship between the two tests is even higher than these coefficients show. This study, like other studies comparing a state with a nationally normed test, suggests that achievement tests measure a common underlying ability—in this case, reading and mathematics.

In summary, state-sponsored and school district-sponsored tests have the greatest potential to help students learn, because the tests are usually matched to the content standards that the state wants taught in the classroom. However, in states where a publisher's test is used, the alignment of test content to the state standards is a major issue and an important piece of validity evidence. Regardless of the test used, if state funding for schools is not equitable and students lack the equal opportunity to learn, no amount of testing will help. As a wise old Iowa farmer said, if you weigh the cow once and don't feed it and weigh the cow again, the cow still weighs the same. If school programs aren't nourished, then no one should expect dramatic results from the students.

National Assessment of Educational Progress (NAEP)

Mehrens (1998) reported from several national surveys that 57 percent of those polled representing the public favored national testing of students, whereas 69 percent of the teachers opposed national testing. The country currently has a single national testing program: the National Assessment of Educational Progress (NAEP). It is neither popular nor well known to the public, but it is arguably one of the best designed and administered achievement testing programs in the United States. The NAEP is a congressionally mandated project of the U.S. Department of Education's National Center for Education Statistics. Since 1969, the NAEP has assessed students' knowledge and skills in geography, reading, writing, mathematics, science, history, the arts, civics, and other academic subjects for students at ages 9, 13, and 17.

The purpose of the NAEP is to provide a fair and accurate measure of achievement in these subject-matter areas. No individual scores are reported, as the test is intended to give a national *snapshot* of the status of learning in these subject matters reflecting a generic, national curriculum. Indeed, the NAEP has developed impressive curriculum and assessment frameworks that include both content and cognitive behavior dimensions using panels of national experts.

The NAEP reports achievement data in a way that supports valid interpretations of trends. For instance, see "Statement" on the *NAEP 2000 Fourth Grade Reading Report Card* by Marilyn Whirry (http://nagb.org/) for an authoritative update on reading trends across the nation. The NAEP also includes information on special groups, including gender, race or ethnicity, and socioeconomic status. Annual reports are published about how the nation's students are doing in various subject matters. In addition, the NAEP makes its data available to researchers for studies of student learning. States are driven more by published reports of SAT–9s and ITBS-type test scores or passing rates on their graduation tests. If state-by-state comparisons are made by the NAEP, testing specialists have been quick to shoot down these spurious interpretations with compelling arguments about how such comparisons are invalid (Bracey, 1998). Indeed, if such analyses do not take into account out-of-school factors known to influence test scores, and if the NAEP tests' curriculum framework fails to match the state's frameworks, or if teachers are not using either curriculum frameworks, then what valid use are NAEP (or any other) test results?

The NAEP's national frameworks and other useful information about NAEP are available on its webpage: http://www.nagb.org/. Information available about student achievement based on NAEP tests at little cost is staggering in size and scope. Given the need for a national test to inform federal policymakers and decision makers, the NAEP is likely to continue. However, testing expert Michael Kean (1992) commented that national testing is unlikely to show the kind of results one wants until teaching essentially improves and links to national content standards.

International Testing and International Comparisons

According to the Third International Mathematics and Science Study's webpage (http://timss.bc.edu/TIMSS):

> The Third International Mathematics and Science Study (TIMSS) is the largest and most ambitious international study of student achievement ever conducted. In 1994–95, it was conducted at five grade levels in more than forty countries (the third, fourth, seventh, and eighth grades, and the final year of secondary school). Students were tested in mathematics and science and extensive information about the teaching and learning of mathematics and science was collected from students, teachers, and school principals. Together, TIMSS tested and gathered contextual data for more than half a million students and administered questionnaires to thousands of teachers and school principals. Also, TIMSS investigated the mathematics and science curricula of the participating countries through an analysis of curriculum guides, textbooks, and other curricular materials. The TIMSS results were released in 1996 and 1997 in a series of reports, providing valuable information to policy makers and practitioners in the participating countries about mathematics and science instruction and the achievement of their students. Technical reports and the complete international database also have been published.

Although the TIMMS has many laudable goals, considerable controversy surrounds it. Since the publication of TIMMS results, a lively debate has resulted in the media and among scholars about the validity of findings and interpretations. The United States does not rank as highly as other countries in the world, which has aroused national embarrassment.

Scholars, such as Berliner and Biddle (1995), have argued that not only are such international comparisons invalid but also the proof of U.S. education is in the success of its students. They further cite the excellence of American universities, which continue to draw students from around the world. They maintain that mathematics and science are not weaknesses in our educational system. Furthermore, they argue that Americans believe in a balanced lifestyle that includes a wider range of activities than in other countries and cultures. Thus, typical U.S. students are less likely to specialize or limit their activities to school and study in the early years of their education. Americans also value leisure time and other avocations. Thus, researchers and others argue that curricular variables exist that explain differences and the U.S. standing with other nations. The sampling of students for these tests is also called into question. By eliminating students of lower socioeconomic class from these test results, the United States would lead the world in all categories.

Stevenson (1987) described the Asian advantage in mathematics in terms of myths and reality. The decided advantage on TIMMS results would suggest that Asians are more intelligent than Americans. Asians get an earlier start in school and benefit from after-school classes. Asian mothers are more concerned about learning. Asian learning is mostly rote in nature, and therefore superficial. Finally, the psychological toll on Asian students is severe, manifesting itself in a high suicide rate. Ironically, U.S. mothers rate their children more positively than Asian mothers. Stevenson provided evidence and arguments of significant cultural and educational differences that account for performance discrepancies between Asian and U.S. children in mathematics, including the most telling factor: classroom time spent learning. Unlike Berliner and Biddle, Stevenson is concerned with the high regard the nation has for its students and the low regard it has for higher standards and expectations, early learning, and less emphasis in curriculum.

Another critic of TIMMS, Bracey (http://www.pdkintl.org/kappan/kbra9809.htm) points out many flaws in the TIMMS. One of these is that the sampling plan in each country is subject to quality controls that are not observed by most countries. Some countries see TIMMS as international competition and do not observe the rules. Bracey also argues that the countries differ in the age of students tested, differ in the types of educational systems existing in these countries, differ in enrollment rates, and fail to disaggregate the multileveled society of the United States (where most students do quite well in TIMMS, but students from neglected populations do quite poorly). Bracey dismisses TIMMS as a useful tool for evaluating U.S. education, and his essays will fill you in on the reasons for his discontent.

In a thoughtful essay, Latendre (1999) argues a middle ground. These international comparisons have serious limitations, but the findings do have some value. And Stevenson (1987) agrees that these TIMMS studies provide fresh insights into what might work and not work for improving student learning. Both authors encourage the thoughtful extension of discussion about the causes of student learning and differences in learning that seem to exist among cultures.

The TIMMS provides a wealth of information, curriculum frameworks, test results, actually released examinations, and a strong technical support mechanism that would seem to deflate criticism against it. International comparisons of student achievement will continue to be a topic of great concern to U.S. citizens. This testing program will survive, despite its critics.

Valid Interpretations and Uses of Test Scores.

Valid Interpretations and Uses of Test Scores.   As a basis for comparing the achievement of students from nations around the world, the TIMMS is one of the largest and most controversial testing programs in the world. The value of its data is considerable for generating arguments for and against U.S. education. Indeed, Phelps (2000) reported that the size of this assessment is increasing, now serving 45 countries in the world. Some countries rely on these assessments to monitor and diagnose their school systems and not for comparisons to other countries.

It seems fair to conclude that interpretations of comparative results should be done carefully. The United States has a unique diversity of people that creates disparities in achievement that makes the nation look like a third-world country when one looks at a certain group of students and the leader in the world when one looks at another group of students. Countries vary considerably on how and who they educate, the resources they put into education, and the emphasis and preparation they place on the TIMMS testing. As a research tool and as a means for studying world education, the TIMMS seems to have value. As a method for improving student learning in the United States, the TIMMS has not yet proven useful.

Evaluating Standardized Achievement Tests

So far, five categories of standardized achievement tests have been reviewed. Each section discussed some intended uses and identified possible misinterpretations and misuses, as determined from logical analysis and claims of publishers. As you consider interpreting or using any of these test scores, the following sections discuss strengths and weaknesses of all standardized achievement tests.

Strengths of Standardized Achievement Testing

Supporters of standardized achievement testing in the schools would compile a list like this one:

- The public demands accountability in its schools, and test information potentially gives fairly accurate descriptions of how individual students or groups of students are doing with respect to other students both nationally and internationally. These tests seem to satisfy the public's need for information about student learning.
- The content of most achievement tests generally reflects a normal school curriculum. Whether a state-developed test based on its content standards is used or a publisher's test based on a generic, hypothetical national curriculum is used, the content of these tests is very similar.
- Achievement tests are usually well designed, reflecting the kind of care and concern one wants with such tests. Poorly developed tests are often exposed by critics, and such testing programs are surely doomed to extinction.
- Achievement tests have norms that are useful for making comparisons, but not all comparisons can be made validly. (Chapter 3 provides a fuller discussion of this issue.)
- The scoring of tests and reporting of test scores is usually done responsibly by these companies or their agents.
- The cost of giving these tests and scoring and reporting multiple-choice test results is low compared with other options. If performance formats are used, the cost of scoring skyrockets.

Overall, it is easy to see why standardized achievement tests are so widely used. They provide useful information at a reasonable cost that the public wants.

Limitations of Standardized Achievement Tests

Critics of standardized achievement tests would compile a list like this:

- Although the public demands accountability, the kinds of accountability demanded with these types of tests is often inappropriate (e.g., teacher merit pay, test-driven reform, and demoralizing attacks on teachers whose students get low test scores).
- Test publishers believe their tests reflect a national or generic curriculum. School districts and many states feel that their curriculum is unique, so publishers' standardized achievement tests are a poor match to the curricula. Thus, a key issue is the content in scope and sequence offered by any test being considered by a state or school district.
- Norms are useful for making comparisons, but many members of the public and the media often make invalid comparisons, such as comparing and evaluating states or school districts. Such comparisons often reflect demographics rather than the quality of educational programs or teaching.
- The motivation to achieve high test scores on these tests leads educators to narrow the curriculum to fit the tests, to cheat, or to do other things that embarrass the teaching profession. (Chapters 7 and 8 discuss more fully some of these shameful activities and their consequences.)
- Critics argue that most of standardized achievement tests are limited to knowledge and skills and avoid the more expensive and less reliable complex mental abilities that are so highly valued, such as writing and mathematical problem solving.

Standardized achievement tests seem especially aimed at measuring mostly knowledge and skills that are found in most curricula throughout the United States. Most of these tests do not seem to be aimed at measuring types of higher-level thinking that reform-oriented educators would like. For instance, these published tests do not measure speaking, writing, and listening abilities or critical thinking, mathematical or scientific problem solving, or creative thinking. Some states have developed statewide assessments of abilities that run counter to the century-long trend of teaching and testing for low-level knowledge and skills. Those states with writing assessment and mathematics problem solving that involves performance and scoring guides (rubrics) reflect the newer orientation to testing. On the other hand, these traditional, knowledge-based standardized achievement tests can provide good insight into basic learning that all students need in the language arts, mathematics, social studies, and science. For this reason alone, such tests are not only valid for these interpretations and purposes but are also relatively inexpensive.

Dangers exist when laypeople—especially legislators, school board members, and the media—misinterpret or misuse achievement test scores. In other words, no evidence exists for certain interpretations or uses of test scores.

Summary

This chapter has reported on the usefulness of standardized achievement testing. As you can see, standardized achievement testing is very pervasive in U.S. education, mainly focused in delivery information about student achievement in the kindergarten through twelfth-grade range of students. Emphasis was placed on the appropriate and inappropriate roles of test scores resulting from administering these tests. Logical thinking about the use of standardized achievement test scores and supporting validity evidence go hand in hand in deciding whether a specific use is valid. This subjective judgment is made by noneducators—mainly legislators, other elected or appointed officials, and school board members. As educators, our professional role is to advise these policymakers to ensure that test scores are validly interpreted and used.

6

High-Stakes Testing for High School Graduation and Professional Certification and Licensing

High-stakes tests have very important consequences for test takers and perhaps significant consequences for the public and others involved in the development of the test taker. This chapter covers high-stakes tests for which educators make a pass/fail decision for each person taking a test. The intent of these high-stakes tests is to measure the knowledge, skills, and abilities specified as important in K–12 education or in a profession. Specifically, the term *high stakes* refers to situations such as the following:

- A high school student takes a certification or graduation test. Passing a state test based on content standards signifies that the student has met a standard and is qualified to receive a certificate of mastery or is eligible to graduate from high school, if other conditions are met as well.
- An elementary school student takes a grade-level, state-sponsored, or district-sponsored test reflecting the state's content standards or a well-stated school district curriculum. This test might be used for guidance in the student's education or for a pass/fail promotion decision.
- A teacher or a person in another profession passes a certification test that signifies high achievement in the profession, often leading to promotion, job opportunities, or pay increases.
- A teacher or a person in another profession passes a licensing test allowing that person to practice that profession in a state or some U.S. jurisdiction (e.g., Puerto Rico).

In all these instances, failing such a test has dire consequences. Those who fail have the opportunity to remediate the learning deficit and retake these tests until satisfactory learning has been observed.

This chapter has four sections: (1) elementary school monitoring and promotion and high school certification and graduation testing, (2) professional certification and certification testing, (3) professional licensure and licensing testing, and (4) teacher certification and licensure testing.

High-stakes tests have much in common: clear and precise definitions of what is measured by these tests, appropriate training or education preparing each candidate for the test, high concern for validity, fairly developed passing standards, and opportunities for remediation and retesting. If these conditions are not met, these testing programs are surely susceptible to legal challenges. Deficient testing programs are doomed to criticism and failure, as the public and law are becoming increasingly more sophisticated about testing and its issues.

Elementary School Monitoring and Promotion and High School Certification and Graduation Testing

According to Phelps (1998), surveys conducted over the past 25 years clearly reflect what teachers and the public expect for students. The public favors standardized achievement testing, higher stakes with these tests, and accountability. Phelps also reported that students are more likely to feel bored in school and unchallenged. Therefore, it is not surprising that many states have adopted or are considering adopting state testing programs for students that require higher test performance.

This section of the chapter looks at what several states and one city are doing and examines some issues affecting high school certification and graduation testing. First, however, it is important to consider the distinction between monitoring/certification and promotion/graduation because this distinction has entirely different high-stakes consequences.

A *monitoring* test score use is one in which elementary students are tested to see if they are on track for high school graduation. The state of Washington has such a test designed to measure its state-mandated content standards. Students in grades 3, 5, and 8 are classified into four categories: (1) not meeting standards, (2) approach standards, (3) exceeding standards, and (4) greatly exceeding standards. There are no consequences for falling into the first two categories, but surely a stigma will exist for any student, class, or school that consistently falls below standards. By measuring the achievement of students in their elementary school careers, parents and their children, teachers, school leaders, and others can monitor students toward successful completion of their K–12 education.

A *promotion* test can be used for making pass/fail decisions at a grade level. Chicago Public Schools use tests in this way. This practice is discussed more fully later in this chapter.

A *certification* test score use is one in which a high school student may show mastery of a subject matter by passing a test. Again, there is no dire consequence for failure, as the student is still eligible for high school graduation. Oregon has a certification test that will be featured in the next section of this chapter.

A *graduation* test score use is one in which the student has to pass the test or all parts of the test to be eligible for graduation. With either certification or graduation tests for high school students, remediation through self-study, special preparation courses, or classes is likely, and retests are permitted.

These kinds of test score uses are ongoing and increasing in scope in the United States and reflect the public's need for accountability. The public wants high standards for its students. This practice of holding students accountable has its critics and supporters. It may help to examine and evaluate state testing programs, one for certification and one for graduation. It may also help to examine and evaluate a public school testing program for elementary school students where pass/fail decisions are made.

The Oregon Experience: Certification Testing

Oregon has a high school certification test. Students take tests in reading, writing, mathematics, and science and must pass all tests to receive the CIM (Certificate of Initial Mastery). The state is also planning a CAM (Certificate of Advanced Mastery) that signifies higher attainment. Students who fail the CIM can still receive a high school diploma, but the CIM is seen as an added qualification for those seeking better employment or a college education.

Like many other states, the citizens of Oregon are interested in the education of their students. The State Board of Education prescribed content standards in English, mathematics, science, history, geography, civics, and economics to earn the CIM. The Oregon Department of Education has been responsible for developing tests to find out if students can meet or exceed passing standards set by panels of content expert educators in the state. Benchmark testing occurs in grades 3, 5, and 8 to evaluate if students are making satisfactory progress; the test in grade 10 is the test used to make pass/fail decisions regarding the CIM. Of course, failing students can restudy and take retests at other times throughout their secondary education. Oregon uses traditional knowledge-based multiple-choice tests and well-grounded performance tests in writing and mathematics, but has also introduced the idea of classroom-based work samples that will be included in the decision-making process. This system of education is ongoing, continuous, and evolutionary. Similar systems, such as those in California, have run aground with controversy and changes in political leadership. All such systems have a strong political base and the welfare and future of any educational reform is subject to changes in political leadership.

What distinguishes Oregon from other states that have graduation requirements is that certification is an optional rather than a mandatory requirement for any high school student who will be graduating. Local control by school districts is maintained, and the state has a basis for annually monitoring the status and growth of school districts. Thus, school districts can report to their constituency about how they are doing locally as well as compared to state standards and other school districts.

The purpose of the assessment system is to infuse into the classroom "best practices" regarding teaching and testing that correspond with the state's content standards. Thus, one of the more significant consequences of this system is how teachers are changing to prepare students for the content standards and how students are growing toward well-established goals of the state.

In subsequent years, more will be heard about the Oregon experience and its consequences on teachers and students. But for now, it is a more benign system than the harsher "if-you-fail-you-don't-graduate" attitude seen in many other states.

The Texas Experience: Graduation Testing

Graduation testing is enormously complex. According to an October 5, 1998, report in the *Arizona Republic,* 23 states require graduation tests. These tests are not without controversy. Proponents believe that "if we test it, teachers will teach it." They claim that the result of raising standards will be raising student performance and that students will be held accountable.

Opponents of graduation testing argue that three at-risk populations (students with disabilities, students living in poverty, and students with limited English proficiency) are hopelessly mired in low achievement. This kind of testing will not solve the learning problems of these three overlapping populations. Also, because school districts are usually not equally funded, students in low socioeconomic areas or students living in racial or ethnic enclaves seldom have the public resources dedicated to help these students. In addition, opponents believe that by focusing on a test, teachers will teach to the test and ignore other important learning.

One of the oldest and most mature high school graduation testing programs in the nation may be found in Texas. Perhaps more can be learned about graduation testing from studying what has happened there. Interested readers might consult a recent issue of *Applied Measurement in Education* (Volume 4, 2000), which is expressly dedicated to the Texas experience, the legal challenge it faced, and how Texas successfully defended itself from this legal challenge.

Texas has a growing immigrant population and faces considerable challenges in educating its 3.5 million students. A primary subgroup of these students is those with limited English proficiency (LEP), who traditionally score very low on achievement tests. Many of these students also live in poverty and a disproportionate number have disabilities that qualify them for special education.

Texas initiated statewide testing in 1980, like many other states. This test was designed to reflect what Texas educators thought were the essential objectives to be learned. They tested reading, writing, and mathematics in grades 3, 5, and 9. In 1983, this test was converted to a pass/fail test for high school students, beginning with grade 9. Ironically, students could still graduate with a high school diploma despite having failed this test.

The next generation of tests was started in 1984 and included more grade levels, and the fail decision on these tests was used to deny a high school diploma. School districts were held accountable for performance of students and required to provide remedial opportunities for failing students.

In 1990, the state went even further, initiating the *Texas Assessment of Academic Skills (TAAS)*. This program was more comprehensive with respect to content and focused on student performance in grades 3, 5, 7, and 9. The graduation test was offered at grade 11. This testing program has expanded to make it one of the nation's hallmark accountability systems with a variety of reports to parents and students at individual, school, and school district levels of analysis.

Sandra Stotsky (http://www.educationnews.org/analysis_of_the_texas_reading_te.htm) reported on a study of gains in the Texas assessment's reading scores for grades 4, 8, and 10. She examined the reading levels and difficulty of passages used for the test for more than four years. Her conclusion was:

> If the scores students achieved on the 1998 tests were higher than those achieved by their counterparts on the 1995 tests, the decline in the overall level of reading difficulty of the selections on these tests, as determined by the New Dale-Chall Readability Formula, suggests that there may have been no real improvement in their reading skills. There may have even been a decline. We simply don't know.

Researchers Clopton, Bishop, and Klein (http://mathematicallycorrect.com/lonestar.htm#link15) focused on mathematics achievement in Texas. These researchers concluded that the content of exit examinations in Texas is about equivalent of what one might ask of sixth-graders. They seem unimpressed with the Texas effort to reform education:

> The review of the examinations used in Texas is suggestive of a system wherein the power of statewide assessments has focused on raising achievement only to a minimal level. The low expectations evidenced by the exam items themselves, and the fact that instruction is geared toward these exams, is cause for concern. This concern is amplified by the indications that the system design may be insufficient to promote greater success in algebra and higher level mathematics courses.

Another study of TAAS was conducted by McNeil and Valenzuela (2000). Based on their own research and other studies, they drew several conclusions:

- There is a reduction in the scope of the school curriculum and a tendency to focus on low-level learning that pervades the state. Much of the school curriculum is neglected, replaced by an overemphasis on what is tested.
- Students with poor reading ability, especially LEP students, underperform on mathematics tests.
- A cumulative deficit is realized, and this continuous low-level teaching and learning results in students with limited ability in reading, writing, and mathematics.
- Students eventually become dropouts or "pushouts." The high-stakes test with its early warning system (testing in the elementary grades) tells students not to bother with school, because they are going to fail the graduation test. Thus, students leave school as early as possible, and this increases the state's performance as more and more low-achieving students leave school. (This result is corroborated by other studies, and is more fully discussed in Chapter 8.)

To add more fuel to this argument, a recent Rand Corporation report by Klein, Hamilton, McCaffrey, and Stecher (1996) reported that nationally normed measures of achievement from the National Assessment of Educational Progress (NAEP) were not well correlated with measures from the TAAS. These researchers concluded:

> The large discrepancies between TAAS and NAEP results raise serious questions about the validity of the TAAS scores. We do not know the sources of these differences. However, one plausible explanation, and one that is consistent with some of the survey and observation results cited earlier, is that many schools are devoting a great deal of class time to highly specific TAAS preparation. It is also plausible that the schools with relatively large percentages of minority and poor students may be doing this more than other schools. (http://www.rand.org/publications/IP/IP202/)

A frequent critic of high-stakes graduation testing, Alfie Cohn (2000) commented that the idea that high-stakes tests may be working should be weighed against logic and evidence. For instance, with Texas, the higher test scores in Texas may be sparked by smaller class sizes and court-ordered equalization of resources for rich and poor schools. Also, the higher achievement may come at the cost of forcing students out of school prematurely because of their poor learning history. Improvements in teacher training and teacher licensing or professional development may account for gains in a state or school district. As teachers and schools learn about a test such as the TAAS, teachers are wiser about what to teach and become good at drilling on skills that are sure to be on the test. Another factor is that these experiments with graduation testing are either starting or ongoing. A comprehensive database upon which to conduct a proper evaluation is lacking. Finally, it is important to realize that any standardized achievement test is simply an incomplete and partial measure of student learning, hardly sufficient for making graduation decisions. A broader more comprehensive set of data are needed before educators decide on a student's future with regard to high school graduation.

As you can see, this graduation testing program has sparked much controversy about high-stakes accountability testing. These findings raise serious questions about the limitations of reform and testing in Texas and in other states attempting to do the same thing. The Texas Education Agency homepage (http://www.tea.state.tx.us/student.assessment/) provides more information about this interesting and controversial high-stakes testing program.

The Virginia Experience

The purpose of Virginia's testing program is very much like that of most states: Set high, clear, and measurable academic standards on a statewide basis, then measure student progress in meeting those standards through regular testing. Ensure accountability by tying school accreditation to student achievement and high school graduation. The intent is not to put up barriers to student progress, but to ensure that the student has the knowledge and skills that he or she must have to be successful in the twenty-first century.

Katzman and Hodas (2000) described Virginia's increasingly familiar cycle of teaching and test reform. Then Governor George Allen led a reform for higher standards. The tests were dutifully developed and given to students. The passing score was arbitrarily set at 70 percent, resulting in a failure rate close to 50 percent in the state. The State Board of Education set a standard for schools that resulted in only 15 percent of the schools passing! As Governor Allen's term of office ended, the new governor and the State Board of Education relented to public pressure and adjusted standards. What is lacking in this story is that no support was given to low-performing schools to improve educational programs and teaching.

The report from the Virginia Department of Education, however, differs from this report by Katzman and Hodas. First, Virginia's tests are untimed, so no student is under arbitrary time pressure in taking the test. Second, all students have repeated opportunities to take the test if they need the test to graduate. Also, the high school tests are not barriers to promotion. Schools can use the tests as one factor in promotion/retention decisions in the elementary grades. In high school, the graduation tests will be phased in, beginning with the class of 2004. Problems with accreditation due to low test scores do not come into play until 2007. Thus, Virginia schools have an early warning about the status of its students, particularly since students are tested in grades 3, 5, and 8.

However, the state of Virginia does not directly address the problem of teaching students who traditionally do poorly on these tests. Although some schools are identified that seem to overcome the obstacle of having students at risk, Virginia has not yet identified the resources and strategies it will use to overcome the problems of these students. Yet the state makes clear that it intends to ensure accountability by tying school accreditation to student achievement as measured by its assessment. Currently, 98 percent of Virginia schools fail to meet these criteria. But the state is hopeful that reform will reduce this figure, and it provides evidence of that.

For the most part, Virginia's experience seems typical of most states undergoing this systemic reform effort with built-in high-stakes accountability. The state has experienced changes in leadership and has moved through cycles of evolution of high-stakes testing, but researchers do not yet have a complete evaluation of the consequences of this educational reform. Refer to the state's website for more information (http://www.pen.k12.va.us/).

The Chicago Experience: Using a Standardized Achievement Test to Fail and Then Remediate Elementary School Students

According to its webpage (http://www.cps.k12.il.us), the Chicago Public Schools includes 492 elementary schools, 93 secondary schools, and 16 charter schools serving 431,750 students, making it the third largest school district in the United States. About 84 percent of these students come from low-income families, and about 16 percent have limited English proficiency. With demographics like this, it is easy to see why Chicago has had a century-long problem of having a high percentage of its students achieve well below national levels on standardized achievement tests.

Beginning in 1997, Chicago city officials decided to use the ITBS (Iowa Test of Basic Skills) as a grade promotion test in grades 3, 6, and 8. According to the National Center for Fair and Open Testing (Fall 2000b), about one-third of U.S. eighth-grade students would fail by ITBS standards. Students not meeting standards in June were required to attend the Summer Bridge program, where they received intensive instruction in reading and math. In August, they were retested and if they met the criterion for their grade level, they were promoted. For those who did not pass, grades, attendance, and other factors were considered to determine if the student was promoted.

The National Research Council (NRC) of the National Academy of Sciences has questioned the use of tests for making pass/fail decisions. Research shows that grade retention is a poor remedy for a low-achieving student. The premise that having promotion tests (such as those in Chicago) will increase student effort and learning has not been proved true. The NRC supports early identification of students who are at risk for rigorous intervention and is not opposed to Chicago-style testing, but it believes that the tests should be used with other criteria to make the decision to promote a student.

According to the National Center for Fair and Open Testing (Winter 1999–2000), this experience has been a colossal failure. First, about 70 percent of the approximately 10,000 students who failed the first time they took the promotion test also failed the second time, despite the summer school and the extra year of learning. Second, the makers of the ITBS never claimed that the test was designed for this purpose and do not support this invalid test use. Third, sound pedagogy calls for alignment of curriculum, instruction, and tests. If the Chicago officials are educators, one might expect them to align a curriculum with the ITBS so that teachers could appropriately guide instruction to match the curriculum and the test. Since this is not the case, it is invalid to use such a test for such a purpose. Test results were also used to place schools and school leaders on probation, which is another invalid use of the ITBS scores. Interestingly, the article reports that small increases in percentages (3 percent at grade 3, 7 percent at grade 6, and 12 percent at grade 8) met the cutoff criteria the next year. However, there is ample evidence that such small gains might be caused by any of a variety of test-polluting practices (discussed in Chapter 7), one of which is teaching to the test and another is simply cheating on the test. In a related article on the Chicago experiment in the same issue, familiar signs of unethical practices surfaced: Summer school sessions focused on extensive test preparation, cleaning of stray marks on the answer sheet, an invitation to correct wrong answers, and circulating copies of the ITBS to help teachers prepare for the test. Chapter 7 discusses more fully these problems, which seem to occur at epidemic proportions in this nation's schools.

The webpage of the Chicago Public Schools reports a three-year success with this program, claiming that test scores are climbing and that accountability is working (http://www.cps.k12.il.us/AboutCPS/):

> "We're absolutely thrilled with these results which show improvement in every school, region and neighborhood at every level across the board," said CPS' CEO Paul Vallas. "They show three consecutive years of improvement among elementary schools in reading and math and two consecutive years of improvement among high schools in reading and math." Vallas said schools with the highest concentration of low income families reported some of the highest gains.

Evaluation of the Chicago experiment is continuing and future research reports should reveal the breadth and depth of this effort to improve schooling in a system where failure in the past has been historic and extensive.

The General Equivalency Degree (GED) Alternative

High school dropouts are known to be one of the at-risk populations. Dropouts have fewer employment opportunities and fewer chances to earn a living wage when compared to high school graduates. The GED testing program allows any person at least 16 years old who is beyond compulsory high school attendance to earn a GED, which is considered the equivalent of a high school diploma. This diploma is recognized as a key to employment opportunities, advancement, further education, and financial rewards. So for those not graduating from high schools, the GED provides a very valuable alternative. This testing program is administered in all 50 states. Most people prepare for the GED tests through review classes, studying, or practice. Courses are offered throughout various state and county agencies. Many students already have the knowledge and skills they need to pass the GED.

In order to receive the GED, a student must pass five tests: writing skills, social studies, science, interpreting literature and arts, and mathematics. The 7½-hour tests are not easy. An estimated 70 percent earn passing scores. Successfully passing these tests shows that the student has acquired a level of learning that is comparable to that of high school graduates. A national standard was set for the minimum score needed by a student to pass the GED. People who pass the GED tests have stronger reading skills, on average, than graduating high school seniors. About 14 percent of students earning a high school diploma each year do so via the GED route. More than 95 percent of employers nationwide employ GED graduates on the same basis as high school graduates in terms of hiring, salary, and opportunity for advancement. Since 1942, more than twelve million adults have earned the GED. Thus, the value of using test scores for awarding the GED seems well established based on the good that this testing program has achieved.

As high-stakes certification and graduation testing increase, more students will be pushed out of high schools. The GED program will probably expand to accommodate the higher number of high school dropouts seeking this alternate route to a high school diploma.

Advanced Placement (AP)

From the Advanced Placement (AP) webpage (http://www.collegeboard.org/ap/stateinit/), AP gives students an opportunity to take college-level courses and tests while still in high school. There are 33 courses in 19 subject areas offered in 13,000 secondary schools. More than 1.2 million tests are given to 750,000 students in the United States.

Students elect AP courses for many reasons. Usually, it is an honor for teachers as well as students to participate in this program. Also, many universities give credit for completed AP courses. Faculty at colleges and universities report that AP students are better prepared for college, and this information motivates students to get more AP classes and credit by passing the test.

The District of Columbia and 26 states provide support to the AP program by encouraging participation. These states' support includes encouraging or mandating AP courses in high schools, helping teachers attend AP workshops and seminars, subsidizing examination fees, and establishing statewide AP policies for universities in the state. Because of the leadership shown by legislators and educators in these states, the growth in their students' participation in AP has been truly remarkable. The federal government has provided $15,000,000 in grants to states for the payment of tests for low-income students. Overall, the AP program is one of the most successful education programs in the country. Its growth is assured by the broad base of support in education and by government.

Bias in High-Stakes Student Testing

One of the main arguments against high school graduation testing comes from the fact that children who live in poverty typically score low on all cognitive tests, thus raising the specter that such tests are biased against these students. In Chapter 1, this population was characterized as having low intelligence and achievement as well as a collection of social problems that are associated with low intelligence and low achievement. Unfortunately, certain social, racial, and ethnic groups are disproportionately represented among the 15 percent of Americans who fall into this category. The issue is determining whether tests are biased or whether the tests simply reveal the effects of living in a subculture of the United States that provides little impetus or opportunity for learning and success in American life.

Most test publishers are highly cognizant of bias in testing and have developed simple and sophisticated methods for studying test bias (Cole & Moss, 1989). It is the ethical duty of these test publishers to routinely conduct item sensitivity reviews to determine if test items are inappropriate for social, ethnic, racial, or gender categories. Offensive items are removed. Items are written to reflect a balanced representation of social, ethnic, racial, and gender representations and roles (Haladyna, 1999). Statistical studies of test item bias are routinely recommended in national testing standards (American Educational Research Association, American Psychological Association, & National Council on Measurement in Education, 1999).

The study of test bias is a large and active area of research in testing. Thus, test sponsors and developers will continue to study bias and try to achieve fairness in testing. The fact that a large segment of U.S. society performs poorly on tests is not evidence that test scores are biased. In fact, quite the opposite is true. If students achieve poorly, then such tests should clearly reveal this sad fact so that appropriate action can take place. Thus, these tests are simply doing what they were designed to do: measure the knowledge, skills, and abilities of students.

Legal Challenges to High School Graduation Testing

As pointed out in Chapter 1 and discussed further in Chapter 3, the validity of test score decisions have been legally challenged. The public has a right to challenge inappropriate test use, and the nation has a history of such challenges for high school testing. Two landmark court cases were *Debra P.* vs. *Turlington* and *The GI Forum* vs. *The Texas Education Agency.*

With the *Debra P.* case, the plaintiff argued racial discrimination against a high-stakes test and won. In Florida in 1979, after the test had been administered three times, approximately 2 percent of the white seniors had not passed, compared to approximately 20 percent of the African American seniors. The foundation for the suit was systemic segregation and lack of opportunity to learn for many students. This case established two major requirements for high-stakes graduation tests. The first is *adequate notice,* which requires that students be told what a graduation test will cover several years before the test is implemented. The second is *curricular validity,* which means that the schools are teaching what is being tested (http://www.ncrel.org/sdrs/areas/issues/methods/ assment/as8lk11.htm).

With the *GI Forum* case, at issue was the passing rates of students identified as African Americans and Hispanic, whose average performance was lower than the passing rates of other types of students. The case was resolved in favor of the state of Texas. The major considerations in that ruling were as follows:

- *Professional standards:* In the opinion of testing experts, Texas followed professional testing standards (American Educational Research Association, American Psychological Association, & National Council on Measurement in Education, 1999; Mehrens, 2000).
- *Validity:* Compelling evidence of validity was presented that the TAAS measured knowledge, skills, and writing ability, which were the objectives of the state's curriculum.
- *Reliability:* As one important aspect of validity evidence, reliability was found to be satisfactory.
- *Content standards:* Clear content standards reflected the public's desire for a state curriculum.
- *Opportunity to learn:* Unlike the *Debra P.* vs. *Turlington* case in Florida, it was shown that the state of Texas had historically encouraged school districts to monitor student performance and provide remedial instruction to low-performing students.
- *Retesting:* Opportunities were available for retesting after remediation.
- *Passing standards:* The passing scores for all tests were determined in ways that met professional testing standards.
- *Adverse impact:* When differences between groups of minority and majority students are larger than expected, adverse impact is noted.
- *Technical issues:* A variety of technical issues were argued by both sides in this case. These issues involved use of a single score for pass/fail decisions and retesting, passing parts of the entire test versus a single pass/fail score, differential item functioning, and other statistical studies.

Through expert testimony and careful examination of validity evidence related to professional testing standards (American Educational Research Association, American Psychological Association, & National Council on Measurement in Education, 1999), the conclusion was drawn that the TAAS met professional standards (Mehrens, 2000). Thus, this court case sends a message to all states and school districts that high-stakes graduation and promotion testing can work if proper attention is paid to professional test standards.

Summary

Elementary and high school accountability testing seems well established and here to stay. Monitoring and promotion testing in the elementary school seem less established and may not survive because of potential negative consequences to these students. Until the nation solves the problem of how to educate students with disabilities, students living in poverty, and students with limited English proficiency, such testing does not seem to help them. One important and valuable point is that such testing identifies the learning deficiencies that the country needs to address. The failing of these students, however, may not seem to be in their best interests. In time, the consequences of this social policy of accountability for students, teachers, and school districts will be studied and evaluated to determine if this kind of testing is really doing the good that was intended.

Professional Certification and Certification Testing

This part of the chapter examines a type of achievement testing that profoundly affects many adults in the United States. Professional certification is a large field that is also growing worldwide. The public wants to be assured that practicing professionals have met high standards. Professions take great pride in their high standards, and the certification boards that regulate these standards appear to be growing in number and size.

What Is Professional Certification?

Professional certification is simply a recognition that a person has trained for a profession, practices in that profession, and has completed requirements for a certificate that acknowledge high achievement in some specific area of that profession. The certifying board creates the requirements and monitors each candidate's progress toward certification. For example, physicians may seek certification in one of 23 medical specialties (e.g., cardiology, ophthalmology, internal medicine, otolaryngology) or in a subspecialty (e.g., cosmetic surgery, hair restoration, facial plastic and reconstructive surgery, sports medicine).

In many instances, an internship or fellowship experience that develops a professional person's ability in the specialty or subspecialty is required. After this experience, a certification test is used to decide who receives or does not receive the certificate. This certificate is sometimes a condition for employment and often has important implications in the professional development of the certified professional.

A master's degree or doctorate is a type of certification. Students attend school, earn credits, have experiences, and complete a performance test or project called a thesis or dissertation. Earning the certificate (degree) enables these students to seek higher levels of employment in business, industry, education, and other settings. In some professions, the master's degree or doctorate is a requirement for employment. For example, most college professors must have earned an appropriate doctorate in a field of study for employment at a college or university.

Another kind of certification comes from nonprofit organizations whose charter it is to educate persons in a field. For example, the American Compensation Association provides educational training to thousands of people who work in human resources departments in businesses and other institutions (http://www.acaonline.org). Earning credits helps these people advance their careers by providing them with job knowledge as well as skills and abilities that they can apply.

Another highly successful educational program comes from the Association of Investment Management and Research (AIMR), which enrolls more than 80,000 students worldwide (http://www.aimr.org/). The AIMR offers a three-year home-study course. Students passing three rigorous annual examinations earn the certificate for Chartered Financial Analyst (CFA) and have entry into positions in finance. The stakes for earning the CFA are extremely high, as the career options are very attractive.

Another growing field is certification via the Internet for those wanting to increase their technology skills. Companies such as Cisco Corporation have large training centers and certify their employees through the Internet (http://www.cisco.com/). Cisco's fast-growing testing program, which is one of the largest in the world, has three levels of certification: associate, professional, and expert.

As you can see, certification is an active and growing aspect of American standardized testing, one that has implications for millions of people who are entering into the nation's complex work force at the highest levels of specialization and complexity.

Generally speaking, certification is a good enterprise because it affords all people the opportunity to advance in their chosen profession without the stigma of failure. Although some individuals fail in their quest for certification, the consequence is not loss of opportunity to work in one's chosen profession. Instead, the consequence is usually the loss of opportunity to advance as quickly as compared to if the certification had been earned.

Licensure and Licensing Testing

Unlike certification, professional licensure and licensing testing has a legal basis that is found in all 50 states and U.S. jurisdictions (e.g., Puerto Rico). As with certification, the public wants to be assured that licensed professionals have met high standards, and the licensing boards assume the grave responsibility of regulating licensing in their state.

What Is Licensure?

Licensure is a complex system of government regulation with the purpose of providing public protection. A license is a formal permission to practice a profession in a state. For professional people, licensure is a more serious type of professional advancement than certification, because a person cannot legally practice a profession in a state or other jurisdiction until all requirements are met, including passing a test or battery of tests and meeting other qualifications. All 50 states in the United States and some U.S. jurisdictions require licenses for professional practice in such professions as architecture, accounting, dentistry, dietetics, law, medicine, nursing, and pharmacy, to mention a few. The requirements for a license vary by professions, but states pass laws about the requirements for each licensee. Many professions have national examinations. The test results are accepted by member states that agree to use the test information in helping decide who will be licensed to practice. In some professions, licensing is done by regional testing organizations, such as in dentistry. In professions such as teaching, licensing can be done by emerging national or regional examinations or each state can develop its own examination.

How extensive is licensing? According to Schmitt (1995), licensing has grown enormously in the last 50 years. In 1952, 80 occupations were licensed in the United States. Another study showed that in 1968, states licensed between 25 and 57 occupations, with the median being 37. In 1986, another report showed 800 professions licensed, and a later report listed over 1,000 professions, although only 60 were regulated in most states. Because licensing meets a public need, state legislators will continue to require licensure for more and more professions and occupations, as long as they perceive a threat to the public from unlicensed people.

Characteristics of a Licensing Process

Testing programs vary by profession, but generally a licensed professional has received accredited training in a professional school, often at a university that sponsors the program. Usually the licensed professional has to complete an internship, where practical skills are acquired and the professional ability is polished. Then a licensing examination is given that is most often multiple choice, knowledge based, with some problem solving. However, the licensing examination can include essay, oral, or performance formats. For instance, candidates for dental licensing in all states must bring patients to the testing center for actual supervised treatment. The skill at which they treat the patient determines their success on the examination.

Competency is usually an ability representing the professional that consists of knowledge and skills, an emotional component, and the capacity to use knowledge and skills in some complex way that shows the ability reflecting that profession. Licensing tests are intended to measure competency, including both what is learned in the professional school and what is found outside of school (Messick, 1989). Thus, competency is developed from classroom instruction, practical experiences in the profession, and overall contact with the world. Those with the greatest breadth and depth of formal education and real-life experience tend to do best in these tests.

Requirements of a Licensing Examination Board

Professional licensing boards consist of dedicated organizations of professionals who form a nonprofit board for the purpose of recognizing members of those professions who meet certain standards, which always include training, experience, and testing.

Board members are highly respected within their profession and volunteer to serve on the board. They contribute their time and expertise to advance their profession.

Whether the board serves as a licensing authority or a certification authority, two responsibilities they assume are legal and ethical. Both responsibilities are considered in designing and administering a licensing testing program, and these requirements apply equally to certification licensing. The requirements come from the *Standards for Educational and Psychological Testing* (American Educational Research Association, American Psychological Association, & National Council on Measurement in Education, 1999) and the *Code of Fair Testing Practices* (Joint Committee on Fair Testing Practices, 1998). Both documents provide sensible advice in the form of concepts and recommended principles and procedures. These principles and procedures as well as other ethical concerns for testing are discussed in Chapter 10.

Legal Issues in Licensing

Because licensing tests are so life altering, it is not surprising to find that legal issues abound. One of the most prevalent is that some social, ethnic, racial, and gender groups typically do poorly on these licensing tests in contrast to European American men, thus raising the specter of bias in testing. The most notable court case was the Golden Rule Insurance Company's lawsuit against the Educational Testing Service, who developed the Insurance Agent Licensing Examination for the state of Illinois. In 1984, the court ruled in favor of the plaintiff and thus "the golden rule" was created. Simply stated, this rule forces test developers to choose test items that reduce the difference between a high-scoring majority and a low-scoring minority. Thus, the content of these licensing tests remains the same, but any test item that widens the gap between these two groups is avoided. This simple remedy increased the number of minority candidates passing the test, but since that court ruling, the gap between higher-scoring majority candidates and lower-scoring minority candidates continues to be too wide.

Legal and testing expert Bill Mehrens (1995) commented that if a licensing test is developed following professional standards, it is likely to withstand legal attacks. In other words, the courts are inclined to permit states to license occupations and professions as long as the procedures it uses for test development reasonably following professional testing standards (American Educational Research Association, American Psychological Association, & National Council on Measurement in Education, 1999).

Teacher Certification
and Licensure Testing

With all states requiring teacher licensing and with nearly three million teachers in the United States, teacher licensing is a huge testing enterprise. Most other professions typically have a national examination, but teacher licensing testing programs are still fragmented. Many states offer their own testing programs, but a few national tests are emerging.

As with any other profession and many occupations, licensing is a legal entitlement. State legislatures pass laws mandating that certain requirements be met before someone can be licensed to practice in the state. For teachers, these requirements normally include certifications or college degrees reflecting adequate teacher education preparation; often internships and/or clinical experience, such as student teaching; and other requirements, including paying the fee for the licensing test. Most of these testing programs are nonprofit and funded by candidate fees. These examinations can be written, oral, or performance based. Currently, teacher testing seems to be aimed at several types of achievement. The state of Arizona is a good example of a typical state teacher licensing testing program.

The Content of Teacher Licensing Tests

The public's need for accountability in education is well documented to have started in the mid-1800s (Haladyna, Haas, & Allison, 1998). One of the first attempts at teacher testing was the oral examination where teachers stood on a stage and were grilled on their knowledge by citizens of the community. In some ways, the current methods do not differ that much, except the grilling is more systematic and standardized.

At the heart of any teacher licensing test (or any other professional licensing test) is that the content should be based on a systematic study of the knowledge, skills, and abilities needed in professional practice. The traditional study that is done is known by various names, including *job analysis, practice analysis, role delineation,* and *task analysis.* The study is usually a survey of practicing professionals who are asked to rate the importance of some knowledge or skills. These results are translated into a table that reflects the balance that topics receive in the test.

If the job analysis is not done or is not done correctly, there are legal precedents that demonstrate that inadequate content foundations for tests will be rejected by the courts. The National Center for Fair and Open Testing (www.fairtest.org) provides several good articles it has published on teacher testing. One of these articles describes when Alabama and Georgia courts struck down teacher licensing tests that discriminated between races. Both states had to recall their examination results and pay heavy penalties to teachers losing certification through test results. It is important in situations such as these that the teacher licensing test be conceived on knowledge and skills thought to be important to teaching. Scores on this test should be moderately to highly correlated with other criterion measures of teacher effectiveness.

Teaching Ability or Teaching Skills. Teaching ability or teacher skills are best measured via a performance test or a teacher-made portfolio that displays teaching ability or teacher skills (Kelley & Haladyna, 2001). For example, the Scottsdale (Arizona) School District in their Career Ladder teacher evaluations uses a teacher-made portfolio to document each participating teacher's accomplishment over a year's time. This is a standardized portfolio. States have adopted teaching content standards that have clearly established the need for teaching performance tests measuring teaching ability and skills, but progress on actual implementation is very limited. One of the main issues with measuring teaching ability is that a performance test has to be designed that is cost effective and that leads to reliable and unbiased test scores. Since performance test results have to be professionally judged, reliability and bias are persistent problems.

Professional Knowledge. Professional knowledge includes facts, concepts, principles, and procedures that surveys of teachers have shown are important in the profession of teaching. Most professional licensing and certification boards conduct surveys of practicing professionals who are asked to rate the criticality of knowledge and skills important for teaching or to rate the importance of each. The boards then develop multiple-choice tests that adequately and defensibly sample this knowledge.

Content Knowledge. Content knowledge is a category that the public would strongly support. The typical content knowledge expected from teachers includes reading, writing, and mathematics. Thus, the tests are nothing more than the kinds of tests seen with the SAT-9 or the ACT Assessment. State legislators and the public usually think that teachers should easily pass such tests, and when teachers do not, the public seems outraged that such persons are teaching in the nation's schools. Thus, testing for content knowledge is likely to continue.

Is Teacher Licensing Important or Necessary?

The teaching profession is one of the most honored and respected among all professions, according to a national survey conducted by Peter Harris Research for Recruiting New Teachings, Inc., a nonprofit organization aimed at improving teacher recruitment (*Arizona Republic,* November 25, 1998). When respondents were asked which of eight professions gave the most benefit to society, education won by a 3–1 ratio over the other professions, including medicine. The respondents to this survey also believe that good teaching makes a difference in student learning, and more than 80 percent of those polled wanted higher standards for the licensing of teachers. With this popular public support for higher standards, it is easy to see why teacher licensing is important. In another poll printed in the *Arizona Republic* (November 25, 1998), Barrett reported that 75 percent of parents surveyed thought that fully qualified teachers were hired in their school districts but 25 percent felt there was a problem of poor quality teaching. About 80 percent were in favor of strengthening teaching licensing requirements and an equal number felt that raising salaries was appropriate. More than half of those surveyed felt that teacher quality was crucial to student learning. The greatest influence seems to come from the combination of forces that exist outside of school.

In 31 states, bonus pay is offered for teachers who meet standards for certification in a national teacher certification test. Many states offer certification if teachers meet educational and experience requirements that allow them to earn high pay or have access to more responsible positions within the state and school districts. As in many other professions, added education and experience may result in access to high-paying jobs.

Teacher Licensing Testing Programs

This section examines several teaching licensing testing programs with the idea that one of these is likely to emerge over time as the national licensing test.

National Board for Professional Teaching Standards. The 1983 report by the President's Commission on Excellence in Education published a scathing attack on public education in *A Nation at Risk*. This report triggered a number of responses, one of which was an initiative to develop a National Board of Professional Teaching Standards (NBPTS) in 1987. Two years later, this board issued a policy about what teachers should know and be able to do.

The NBPTS is a nonprofit, nonpartisan, independent organization governed by 63 members, 52 of whom are teachers. Its mission is to create teaching standards and to design and operate a national teacher certification testing program. By doing this, the board believes student learning will be increased. The NBPTS has five core propositions they follow:

1. Teachers are committed to student learning.
2. Teachers know the subjects they teach and how to teach these subjects.
3. Teachers are responsible for managing and monitoring student learning.
4. Teachers think systematically about teaching and learn from their experience.
5. Teachers are members of learning communities.

The examination includes a submitted portfolio, videotapes of teaching, lesson plans, and samples of student work. Applicants must have at least three years of teaching experience. As of November 1999, the NBPTS reported that almost 4,804 teachers in 48 states had been certified, contrasted with 282 teachers in 1995 (http://www. whitehouse.gov/WH/New/html/edprogress_report.html). The certificate is good for 10 years. Clearly, this teacher certification program is national in scope and gaining momentum.

The $2,000 administration fee is necessary because trained examiners must evaluate the complex materials submitted by the teacher. At least 35 states offer some subsidies for this test, providing fee support and/or pay increases when the standards are met. The federal government also provides substantial subsidies for this nonprofit testing program, believing that this will increase the number of high-quality teachers in the profession.

While validity evidence accumulates for this testing program, caution must be exercised regarding the part of the testing program that involves performance, videotapes, and portfolios, due to their limitations as measuring instruments. For instance, videotapes are subject to the threat of dishonesty in the portrayal of teaching. Sampling would be another issue in these tests. Does the material selected for evaluation represent typical or best work? Validity evidence would have to substantiate that such evaluation is both reliable and free from serious bias in professional judgment by the scorers of these tests. The NBPTS's webpage provides more information on this promising new teacher certification testing program (www.nbpts.org).

The Praxis Series.   The Educational Testing Service (ETS) in Princeton, New Jersey, a highly respected, nonprofit testing organization, has undertaken a long-term development effort in teacher testing that includes the Pre Professional Skills Test (PPST) and the National Teacher Examination (NTE). Their efforts have evolved into the Praxis Series, which is a coordinated set of tests and services that states can use in their teacher certification or licensing (http://www.teachingandlearning.org/licnsure/praxis/). The Praxis Series is even useful to colleges and universities that are screening candidates for teacher education. The Praxis Series consists of three parts: Praxis I: Academic Skills Assessments, Praxis II: Subject Assessments, and Praxis III: Classroom Performance Assessments.

Praxis I: Academic Skills Assessments.   This initial assessment is intended for admission to teacher education or for the early stages of teacher education. The assessment includes reading, writing, and mathematics, similar to what is seen on many state assessments of students, in standardized achievement tests such as the ITBS or the SAT-9 (featured in Chapter 5), and in state graduation tests (discussed later in this chapter). The Praxis I has two formats. The first is the PPST, a paper-and-pencil three-hour examination that is mostly multiple-choice format but has one essay item. Despite the use of the word *skill* in the title of this test, the PPST does not measure skills but measures knowledge and, in some instances, knowledge of skills. The content of the PPST might be interpreted as reflecting what students learn in the elementary and secondary schools. Thus, policymakers and the public are likely to accept the PPST as a worthwhile entrance requirement or exit requirement in teacher education, based on the reasoning that any teacher should have this basic knowledge before entering into teaching. Hicken (1992) presented a study showing a low correlation between the PPST and measures of teacher competence. He argued that the PPST was measuring something that was not important to successful teaching and thus prevented many candidates for teacher education from entering into the teaching profession.

The second test in the Praxis I is a computer-based test (PI-CTT) also measuring reading, writing, and mathematics. The intent of using this type of test is to see if students have the basic knowledge skills necessary to enter into teacher education or teaching.

Praxis II: Subject Assessments.   This battery of tests is far more complex and intended to be directly related to subject matter the teacher will teach. The Core Battery Tests include general knowledge, communication skills, and professional knowledge about teaching. Praxis II also includes Subject Assessments/Specialty Area Tests and Multiple Subjects Assessments for Teachers, which was developed jointly with the state of California for its teaching licensing requirements. A fourth part of this series is the Principles of Learning and Teaching Tests, where case studies are used to measure knowledge of teaching principles and procedures for different grade levels.

Praxis III: Classroom Performance Assessments.   The most important and comprehensive of the Praxis series are the Praxis III assessments (Dwyer, 1994). Teachers must perform in the classroom and be evaluated by trained examiners, usually during the first year of teaching. As noted earlier, these exams are the most complex, expensive, and difficult to administer and score. Reliability and rater bias are potential problems.

The Praxis Series represents the single-largest testing program for teacher certification and licensure in the nation and is perhaps the heir apparent for the national teacher licensing program that this country lacks. Given its current scope of service to more than 30 states, it may eventually be accepted universally in the United States.

Locally Developed Teacher Licensing Testing Programs.   States such as Arizona prefer to develop their own testing programs based on their own content standards. Such testing programs do not derive the benefit of a collaborative effort (like the NBPTS and the Praxis Series) and depend strongly on the resources available in the state where the test is being developed. Most follow the same procedures: legislative mandate, content standards, test development, test administration, standard setting, test scoring, and score reporting. Most of these programs also focus on the three major types of achievement: abilities, professional knowledge, and content knowledge.

Such tests are local to the state's needs and desire for independence from higher authorities. The limitation of such a belief is that the cost of developing a high-quality testing program is so expensive that compromises have to be made. Thus, such programs are unlikely to compare with better-funded national or regional testing programs that reflect more jurisdictions.

Where Is Teacher Licensing Going?

Virtually all professions feature a national licensing examination. If they do not, then they are evolving toward such an eventuality. Teaching seems to be moving slowly toward national licensing based on universal content standards that include knowledge about teaching, content knowledge, and teaching skills and ability.

The National Board of Professional Teaching Standards seems to offer a viable, high-quality teacher certification test that some day may be accepted by states as a licensing test. This test's detrimental cost is mostly due to the need to use portfolios and videotapes of teaching performance.

The Praxis series is also an impressive challenger for a national test. The commitment for research and development from the ETS is considerable. Many other professional certification and licensing examinations cost considerably less than these two contenders for a national teaching licensing examination. But most of these testing programs do not yet have these performance criteria as part of the test. They certify performance through internships or clinical experiences. In teaching, the licensing process includes student teaching at the teacher training institution.

State-based tests are doomed to extinction, as the long-term trend seems to be toward a national examination. Further, the implied rationale for state tests is weak (i.e., teachers in any state have a distinctively different set of knowledge, skills, and abilities than those needed in other states). As in medicine, law, and pharmacy, national standards make sense. The same national standard of high-quality care and concern with public safety is desirable in all states. National programs have more financial and human resources and can produce a better examination with more validity evidence backing up its use for licensing. Consider the accomplishments of the NBPTS or the

Praxis Series, for example. Finally, since Americans are mobile, the general public would like teachers who are licensed in one state to have easy access to teaching positions in other states, particularly in states where there are teacher surpluses and shortages. With a national examination, the United States would have reciprocity that enables teachers to move seamlessly from one state to another.

The Future of High-Stakes Testing

With licensing and certification in the professions and especially in teaching, high-stakes professional testing is only getting stronger. The public is comforted by testing programs that screen some of the largest professions—namely, teachers, police, nurses, and social workers, but also certified public accountants, dentists, architects, lawyers, and even golf professionals. Those who hold licenses and certificates in these professions are the greatest supporters of licensing and certification, offering their volunteer time and support for testing programs that license and certify. Indeed, this sector of high-stakes testing is growing stronger and stronger.

The National Center for Fair and Open Testing (www.fairtest.org) (Fall 2000b, 2000d, 2000f; Winter 2000–2001a) reported that a national revolt is brewing against high-stakes testing for elementary and secondary school students. (This backlash is discussed more fully in Chapter 8.) A combination of poorly designed tests and politically inspired standards may have led to test uses that will simply have dire consequences on students and society in general. Opposition may cause legislatures to reduce the scope of these high-stakes testing programs or to delay implementation. Yet, the communities of parents, businesses, and other leaders want these high-stakes tests, as polls often attest. So the great experiment in high-stakes testing in schools will probably continue, but not without protest and constant public scrutiny. The media always play an important role in this overview of state testing programs.

Summary

High-stakes tests certification, licensing, and graduation tests affect the lives of those wanting to graduate from high school and practice in a profession. From the public's view, high school graduation test requirements are important to ensure that U.S. students meet certain requirements before reaching adulthood and entering the world of work. Certification and licensing in occupations and professions are part of the process of human development through which many of us have to pass. Although anxiety provoking and costly in terms of time and money, certification, licensing, and graduation testing are necessary for the betterment of society. But a crucial issue that needs to be addressed within any certification, licensing, or graduation testing program is validity. Is it valid to make a life-altering decision based on the performance of a single test or a battery of tests? A related concern are the costs and consequences of such testing. Does the good the test brings outweigh the bad? For instance, with high school graduation testing, what are the consequences to society of students who fail these tests? Chapter 8 addresses the issue of consequences of high-stakes testing on U.S. society.

Issues in Standardized Achievement Testing

Part III raises many issues that we educators and the public should understand, discuss, and resolve.

Chapter 7 deals with the topic of test score pollution, which is a constant source of error in interpreting test scores. Test score pollution can lessen the validity of any test score interpretation or use. The goal of the chapter is to increase your awareness about this topic.

Chapter 8 discusses the pervasive consequences of interpreting and using test scores in a high-stakes environment affecting students, teachers, and the public. The issue is how to weigh the good and bad consequences of each high-stakes test score interpretation and use.

Chapter 9 raises the subject of testing and reporting scores of students who are typically the lowest-achieving (and lowest-scoring) students. Three student populations are discussed: (1) those needing special education, (2) those from poverty, and (3) those with limited English proficiency. Race and ethnicity are excluded from this discussion, and a rationale is presented for this decision.

Chapter 10 focuses on prescriptions and principles that all educators should follow in interpreting and using standardized achievement test scores.

The Epilogue provides a brief closing message about the value of standardized achievement testing.

7

The Pollution of Test Score Interpretations and Uses

This chapter examines a threat to valid interpretations and uses of test scores: test score pollution. Many studies and essays have fueled a growing awareness of this problem. Some sources of pollution are intentional and downright unethical, whereas other sources of pollution are unintentional. Educators must guard against pollution creeping into test scores and be cautious in interpreting and using test scores when pollution is potentially present. This is especially important when the use of a test score has high stakes.

What Is Test Score Pollution?

All test scores contain random error, which can be positive or negative and small or large. One never really knows the direction of random error or its size, but the reliability coefficient provides an estimate of the proportion of variation in test scores that one might attribute to this random error. For instance, a set of test scores with a reliability coefficient of .90 shows that about 10 percent of the variation of test scores is random error, and a reliability coefficient of .60 show that about 40 percent of the variation of test scores is random error. Random error is uncorrelated with a student's true score, so random error can be annoying when trying to interpret or use a test score, especially when making important pass/fail decisions.

As contrasted with random error, which is assessed via the reliability coefficient, test score pollution is a systematic error. Test scores can be systematically increased or decreased due to a factor unrelated to what the test is supposed to measure. Messick (1989) used the term *construct-irrelevant variance* to describe this idea of systematic error. Since the objective of any intelligence or achievement test is to measure a true score, test score pollution makes the quest for the true score more difficult. Table 7.1 captures the array of test score polluting influences that are discussed in this chapter.

TABLE 7.1   *Categories of Sources of Test Score Pollution Discussed in This Chapter*

Source	Aspects
Instructional environment	Two conditions should be met before interpreting test scores: curriculum alignment or match to the test and students having equal opportunity to learn the material to be tested.
Test preparation	Students can be prepared for tests in two contrasting ways: one is recommended by testing specialists and the other is objectionable.
Test administration	Three conditions may increase test scores artificially: exclusion of low-scoring students, altering the administration of the test, and not providing enough time for students.
Cheating	A series of actions, activities, or practices range from questionable to outright cheating.
Test anxiety Test motivation	Several factors may have variable unwanted influences on test scores: motivation, test anxiety, and fatigue.
Students with disabilities Students with limited English proficiency Students living in poverty	Student achievement can be underestimated without appropriate accommodations or modifications to remove the influence of the disability on test performance. Students living in poverty lack fundamental needs (food, shelter, rest). Students learning to speak English are at a distinct advantage. To what extent are test scores valid indicators of their learning or learning potential?
Scoring tests	In the process of scoring tests, many documented activities may affect the accuracy of scoring: rater bias, answer verification, scoring foul-ups, and test norm errors.
Contextualized reporting	When reporting test scores to the public, misinterpretation can occur when the context for test performance is not provided and scores are lumped together without regard for factors that may have caused these scores.

In the late 1980s, physician John Cannell raised some serious questions about standardized test scores in the United States. In his 1989 book, *How Public Educators Cheat on Standardized Achievement Tests*, he found that 48 of 50 states performed above average on these tests. A high percentage of students were above average, when average should actually be the 50th percentile (half of the test takers above this point and half below). Cannell blamed test publishers and educators alike. Publishers tend to produce only one or two forms of any test. Thus, unscrupulous educators tend to teach to the test or, worse, cheat.

The main purpose of this chapter is to raise your consciousness about test score pollution as a threat to valid test score interpretation and use. We teachers need to examine our classrooms, schools, and school districts to see if test score pollution is present.

If present, we need to take steps to remove or reduce these sources of pollution. Also, we need to examine the causes of test score pollution, which may be test-based accountability. While inappropriate strategies for assessing accountability is a more systemic problem in U.S. education and politics, as has been noted in several places in this book, its influence on educators is considerable and mostly negative.

As an introduction and overview to test score pollution, Table 7.1 lists 10 sources of test score pollution that comprise this chapter. These sources will be discussed in detail throughout this chapter.

Two Factors Contributing to Test Score Pollution

Two related factors seem to be contributing to test score pollution. The first is test-based accountability, and the second is the quest for higher test scores that follows from test-based accountability.

Test-Based Accountability

The public wants to know how the schools are doing. This need has translated into national testing that broadly surveys achievement over time and across the grades. State and school district testing programs attempt to satisfy this need for accountability by administering tests each year at most grade levels. But the issue is: Who is accountable for student learning? In many settings, teachers are held responsible, as if they are the only factor that influences student learning. For instance, Arizona teachers were offered a $1,200 bonus if their students exhibited higher test scores on a state-mandated SAT-9, which, curiously, is not directly linked to the state's own highly regarded content standards. Holding teachers accountable is illogical from many standpoints, as Chapters 1 and 3 have shown. Many factors contribute to student achievement that reside outside the school. And most school systems are seldom adequately funded to provide what teachers need to make up for the deficits found outside of school. Finally, teachers have little voice in policies and resources affecting student learning.

The need for accountability continues to focus on teachers as the responsible party for student learning and a single test as the criterion measure of student learning. This narrow view of student learning has done considerable harm to the educative process, according to many critics of this practice (Haladyna, Nolen, & Haas, 1991; Paris, Lawton, Turner, & Roth, 1991b; Smith, 1991b). Darling-Hammond (1991) commented:

> Making schools genuinely accountable for student learning will require involving teachers in the development of methods and modes of assessment that measure what students know and are able to do. In this way assessment can be tied to instruction, improvement of practice, and the creation of greater knowledge and shared standards across the educational enterprise as a whole. (p. 220)

Indeed, a more enlightened approach to accountability would view education in a larger context—one that involves legislators and school boards as the policy formulators and resource allocators, but vitally involves the parents, other members of the public, and educators in this collaborative process. The outcomes of education, as described in Chapter 1, become part of this enlightened view, and the external and internal causes become part of the working model that makes accountability something that will motivate everyone to seek and obtain a better education for all students.

The Fallacy Behind the Quest for High Test Scores

According to Sherman Dorn (1998), statistical accountability is part of the political culture. The public demands numbers showing how schools are doing. Policymakers resort to using a single test as a convenient and simple indicator of the success of schools and its teachers. So, the public conveniently turns to available and inexpensive standardized achievement tests as that indicator. Given that most standardized achievement tests reflect a small sample of student learning from a broadly defined school curriculum, is it right to use such a test as a criterion to make a judgment about school success?

Haertel and Calfee (1983) disagree with the notion that high scores on a survey achievement test are a good criterion. Not only is a test score a small sample of student learning, but learning is supposed to generalize beyond the test to problems one faces in life. Under pressure to produce high test scores, we teachers end up teaching to the content found on a test. By doing so, we narrow the scope of learning to simply content on these tests and not to the total domain of learning that a test is supposed to sample. This "narrowing of the curriculum" reduces teachers to technicians, drilling a few facts into students' heads over a long period of time. The mastery of a few facts on the test will lead to a false, inflated interpretation of test scores—that a student (or a group of students) knows much more than is true. This widely practiced deception is attributable to the need to produce high test scores. Legislators and school board members seem to fuel this need. The media make this need known to the public. And so, we educators will do virtually anything to get high test scores—even cheat.

Another aspect of the problem is that most standardized achievement tests fall short of measuring the kinds of outcomes that modern, reform-oriented educators and the public expect. In the technical jargon of testing, Messick (1989) called this *construct underrepresentation*. The construct that is intended to be measured is not completely measured. Rather, the tendency is to test the simple aspects of student learning and forgo the more complex aspects of learning. So instead of tests that focus on problem solving and critical thinking in lifelike and realistic settings, most standardized achievement tests measure isolated bits of knowledge and skills that, on the surface, are necessary for all learners, but this knowledge and these skills are seldom applied in complex ways that are normal for society's citizens. Thus, focusing on getting high test scores inherently turns the public away from the kind of learning outcomes that they really want in their children—namely, to solve problems and to think critically and creatively.

The result of this quest for high test scores is a reduction of student learning. Students are taught only what teachers believe will be on the test. Many educators argue that this is one way of corrupting the value of education. Professional educators do not equate effective learning with teaching the content that is tested. Today's students need to develop reading, writing, speaking, and listening abilities that they can apply to critical thinking, creative thinking, and mathematical and scientific problem solving. They also must learn a variety of social abilities that may fall into this emerging category of emotional intelligence. As Chapter 1 suggested, the outcomes of schooling are more complex than any publisher's test battery can measure. Overreliance on a test as a criterion of student learning is a costly mistake.

The categories of test score pollution featured in Table 7.1 will now be discussed.

Instructional Environment as a Source of Test Score Pollution

Three related issues arise in the category of instructional environment that contribute to test score pollution. The first is the curriculum that drives both teaching and testing. The second is the match or mismatch of teaching in the classroom to the desired content and the content of the test. The third is the students' opportunity to learn the content that will be tested. The educational experiences of the students should be linked to content standards, but test-based accountability perverts this ideal.

Curriculum and Standardized Achievement Testing

Given a state or school district, there are three conditions that presents us with a problem.

State Content Standards and a Matched Test.   Many states have decided to adopt content standards and build testing programs that are aligned with their tests (Arizona, Florida, Michigan, Ohio, Oregon, Texas, and Washington, to name a few). These examples provide a strong case for systemic reform in which teachers are virtually mandated to teach to an implicit state curriculum knowing full well that the state-mandated achievement test will be matched to this curriculum. In fact, in many states, teachers, parents, and other school leaders have a strong voice and role to play in developing these tests, so there is a shared responsibility.

State Content Standards and a Mismatched Test.   Some states take a simple shortcut by using a nationally normed standardized test such as the SAT-9 or the ITBS. Having state content standards is a positive step, but by using a mismatched test, teachers, parents, and other school leaders are confused as to what to stress in curriculum and in teaching: the state's content standards or the content of the adopted standardized achievement test. Should the state standards be universally adopted and followed, or should teachers follow the implicit curriculum linked to the state's mandated test? This situation occurred in 1987 in Arizona, where the ITBS was the state-mandated test, but only about 25 percent of the items were clearly linked to state content standards (Noggle, 1987).

No State Content Standards and a Mandated National Test.   In the middle of the last century, standardized achievement test scores had more benign uses. State content standards did not exist, and a nationally mandated publisher's test let school districts and their personnel know how their students matched up to a norming sample. If scores were low in mathematics reasoning, for example, curriculum and instruction were more strongly emphasized in that area in the next year. Many school districts operated in this way for a long time, until the age of accountability resulted in content standards and high-stakes testing where states, school districts, schools, classrooms, and teachers were exposed in the media and pitted in competition with one another. The onset of this age of competitive accountability seems to be a major cause of test score pollution. Some school districts or schools simply decided that the curriculum represented by the state's mandated test was the one to use. By doing this, the test matches the curriculum perfectly. Of course, not all school districts do this. At the year's end, schools that have aligned their curriculum with the test are compared to schools that are not aligned. Thus, some schools may look better than other schools simply because they chose to realign to match the mandated test, while other schools chose to stick to their own curriculum. As you can see, the practice of curriculum alignment to match the mandated test is very debatable. Does it pollute test score interpretations? I think so.

Curriculum is a perpetual battleground of educators' and the public's values, hopes, and dreams. Most school districts and states spend millions of dollars and instruct personnel on the development of curriculum to represent the educators' and the public's ideas about what students should learn. The sad story about high-stakes standardized achievement testing is the frequent, recurring practice of pitching the school district or state curriculum at a time before the standardized achievement test is given so that students can concentrate on the content that is likely to be tested soon.

Instruction and Standardized Achievement Testing

Three dubious possibilities arise when examining the classroom and what the teacher does.

Teaching to the Content of the State-Mandated Publisher's Test.   As teachers, we can accept the test as a measure of student learning and teach only the content that we know will be tested. By making this choice, we know that by concentrating on 40 to 70 items on the test, we need only teach 40 to 70 facts, concepts, principles, and procedures for that school year. Then our students will score high and the public will be satisfied with our teaching. Few educators would subscribe to this approach to test preparation, yet in the Nolen, Haladyna, and Haas (1992) survey, 65.9 percent of elementary school teachers reported that they focused on knowledge and skills that were going to be tested, 57.9 percent used sample questions, 11.5 percent used actual items from last year's test, and 10 percent reported teaching items from the current test (a practice that is blatant cheating). A survey by Herman and Golan (1993) also provided good information on the extensiveness of some of these practices. In a more recent study by Walt Haney of Boston University, 12 percent of the teachers and 12 percent of the principals he surveyed reported giving tests in nonstandard ways (National Center for Fair and Open Testing, Summer 2000c). These practices included giving more time and changing answers. As Mehrens and Kaminski (1989), among many others, have argued, such practices run the risk of increasing the public's perception of student learning without materially affecting actual student learning. This kind of teaching is a major type of test score pollution.

Teaching to the Content That the Test Represents.   This activity is very much like the former, except that the teaching focuses on a real or hypothetical curriculum that the test represents. Thus, the teacher (or sponsoring school or school district) is saying that the standardized achievement test reflects a national curriculum that he or she will use. The teacher trusts the test company to build a curriculum that he or she can use, and the test nicely matches that curriculum. This approach to test preparation is not necessarily a bad one. Indeed, test publishers invest heavily in making sure that their test content is current with what national advisory committees, consisting of teachers and curriculum specialists, want students to learn.

Teaching to the State Content Standards.   Most educators would support this practice. If the state's content standards are developed by representatives from the teaching community, and if national standards are employed, such as those from the National Council of Teachers of Mathematics, then this kind of test preparation is consistent with best practices in teaching. Noted testing authority Jim Popham (2000b) recently captured the ideas expressed here as a game that we teachers play for the public that has to do with test scores and the public's acceptance of test scores as an indicator of how successful we are. Table 7.2 shows six cases that exist in schools that reflect the gamut of teacher actions. Please note that Popham does not support any of the case scenarios except the first, where both teachers and students win. The only reasonable approach to teaching is to follow the school district curricu-

TABLE 7.2   *Popham's Score-Boosting Game: Six Possible Scenarios for Teachers*

Case	Teacher Action	Score Impact	Game Results
1	Teacher teaches content domain of knowledge and skills. The test is a sample of this domain.	Scores go up.	Teacher wins. Students win.
2	Teacher does not teach the domain.	Scores don't go up.	Teacher loses. Students lose.
3	Teacher teaches the items on the test and ignores the domain, and teacher gets caught.	Scores go up.	Teacher loses. Students lose.
4	Teacher teaches the item on the test and ignores the domain, and teacher does NOT get caught.	Scores go up.	Teacher wins. Students lose.
5	Teacher relaxes test administration, and teacher gets caught.	Scores go up.	Teacher loses. Students lose.
6	Teacher relaxes test administration, and teacher does NOT get caught.	Scores go up.	Teacher wins. Students lose.

Source: Adapted from Popham (April 2000).

lum, case 1. Case 2 is gross incompetence. Cases 3 through 6 are examples of unethical test preparation or test administration.

Opportunity to Learn (OTL)

At the heart of the problem of test score pollution is a simple concept of teaching that should strike fear into any state's attorney general who addresses legal challenges to some state-mandated high stakes pass/fail test. This concept, *opportunity to learn (OTL)*, simply reflects the situation wherein if a high-stakes, state-mandated test is indeed built on a set of content standards, before a pass/fail decision is made for any student, students should have received adequate instruction. The standard for OTL, however, goes farther than a student simply receiving instruction. According to the Goals 2000: Educate America Act, the OTL standard calls for adequate resources, practices, and conditions necessary for learning at each level of education, including classrooms, schools, school districts, and states. Herman, Klein, and Abedi (2001) claim that researchers focus on curriculum, strategies, and resources when considering the extent of opportunity to learn. National OTL standards provide a means for motivating states to provide adequate educational opportunities.

In any state or school district where accountability is desired, the cornerstone of that system should be the opportunity to learn. One remedy that many responsible jurisdictions take is to hold back on the date when high-stakes testing programs go into effect. Interestingly, student portfolios can be used as major pieces of OTL evidence if they are collected in the classroom and relate to a state's content standards (Haladyna, 1997; Porter, 1995). The OTL becomes a friend to American education, providing a high standard for legislators and school boards to meet in an atmosphere of accountability and high-stakes testing.

Without documented opportunity to learn, high-stakes decisions would seem to be invalid. If students lacked appropriate instruction, holding students and their teachers responsible seems blatantly unfair. The courts are said to be highly cognizant of OTL. If it cannot be documented, a state or a school district will have a hard time defending its use of test scores for pass/fail decisions. Herman, Klein, and Abedi (2001) show that OTL can be assessed inexpensively by using surveys, so OTL studies are feasible.

Unethical Test Preparation as a Source of Test Score Pollution

Most testing specialists recommend test preparation as a worthwhile activity that is intended to prepare all students to perform at their highest possible level without interference from any factors that may limit this performance, such as test anxiety (Haladyna, Nolen, & Haas, 1991; Mehrens & Kaminski, 1989; Miyasaka, 2000; Mehrens, Popham, & Ryan, 1998; Smith, 1991b). Several potential sources of test score pollution fall into this category of unethical test preparation.

Item Formats

This category of potential test score pollution addresses how some educators use actual tests to practice for a forthcoming test. As you might expect, the practices range on a continuum from downright unethical to ethical.

Current Test Form Exposure.   This year's test is handed out and students practice directly on the test. This practice, which is blatantly unethical and clearly violates professional standards, should never be tolerated.

Using a Previous Test Form as Practice.   School leaders and teachers may obtain last year's test and use it as a basis for instruction or test preparation for this year. Since the content and item formats will be similar, such preparation will give these students an unfair advantage over students who did not practice with last year's form, because not all other students receive this advantage.

   Imagine this scenario: A nearby school district takes the SAT-9 each year. Some teachers actually develop a "Stan Fordnine Test" that looks very much like last year's SAT-9. This test appears to have been designed by teachers who want their high school students to practice with item formats and test content that is likely to be tested in next year's SAT-9 test. Although the test is not linked to the state's content standards, getting high scores is valued in that school district to the extent that teachers spend their valuable time developing this test and use valuable classroom time preparing students for the SAT-9. The items on such a test may likely be clones of actual items used in the SAT-9. To what extent would you as a member of the public or the profession of education be inclined to accept this practice as ethical? Beneficial to students? Or healthy to education in general? This practice is deceptive to the public and should not be tolerated.

Same-Format Preparation.   If certain test item formats are used in the standardized achievement test, teachers or school leaders might decide to develop learning activities designed to familiarize students with these formats. This kind of test preparation is highly recommended. Lack of familiarity with test item formats might cause some students to be confused and perform poorly, below their potential, especially students in early grades. The problem with same-format preparation is that those who receive it may outperform those who do not receive it. Unless the same-format preparation is uniform throughout the school district or state, this practice is a potential source of test score pollution. Nonetheless, same-format preparation is an ethical practice.

Test-Taking Strategies (Testwiseness)

The ability to take tests and maximize performance is known among testing specialists as *testwiseness*. So, one could conclude that all students should be equally testwise. Anything less would penalize students, not because they have learned less but because they do not have the strategies to do their best on these tests. Chapter 10 promotes teacher use of these strategies because they are nonpolluting. However, if some students get extensive training in testwiseness and others do not, does that fact pollute some test scores? As you can see, teaching test-taking strategies is a good thing, but by *not* teaching these strategies, your students' test scores may be polluted.

Timing of Test Preparation and Speededness

As reported earlier in this chapter, surveys of teachers reveal that many teachers cram students for the standardized achievement test, starting several days to several months before the test is given. If this preparation is aimed solely at the content on the test, one should call into question the timing of this activity. Is it intended to improve student learning or simply artificially boost test scores? This is called *cramming* for the test. Short-term memory is used to cram facts into the head and to forget everything after the test. Timing for test preparation is the issue. Generally, testing specialists recommend that test preparation be year-round and include content that is related to the state's or school district's content standards.

Research on Test Preparation Effectiveness

Research reports provide mixed findings about the effectiveness of various test preparation strategies. A prudent conclusion here is that more and better research is needed before one can fully understand how effective various types of test preparation are.

   Samson (1985) did one of the earliest research syntheses on test preparation. From the 24 studies he examined, Samson reported that the effect of test preparation would raise student scores from the 50th percentile to the 63rd percentile. He also reported that longer test preparation courses did better than shorter test preparation courses. A later analysis by Bangert-Drowns, Kulik, and Kulik (1983) on achievement tests and by Kulik, Bangert-Drowns, and Kulik (1984) for intelligence tests also corroborate these findings. Scholes and McCoy (1998, 1999) reported two studies of test preparation by students taking the ACT Assessment. They reviewed the research on test preparation and reported that, with their samples, test preparation had a very small effect on student performance on this college admissions test. Deaton, Halpin, and Alford (1987) supported this conclusion that test preparation may have only a small, negligible effect on test scores. However, Scholes and McCoy also found that some types of test preparation were slightly more effective than others. But in evaluating this research, one needs to know the content of test preparation, the age or developmental level of the students being trained, the kind of test used (ability or achievement), and the extensiveness of the training. As researchers pay more attention to these factors, more definitive answers to the question of effectiveness of test preparation training will become available.

   A good point made by Smith (1991b) is that even if the effect of ethical test preparation is small, this effect can translate into a grade-equivalent score of one month on a publisher's test, which affects the validity of interpreting a test score. Factoring into the evaluation of the effectiveness of test preparation, the amount of time spent on test preparation, and the types of test preparation, including the arguably unethical types, how much harm or good is accomplished? If this test preparation time were spent on instructional activities that were correlated with a state's or school district's content standards, might this time be better spent? Further, when one school or school district provides this helpful instruction and other schools or school districts do not, the differences, even if they are small, are not due to teaching or learning but to how much helpful instruction on test-taking was provided. Nonetheless, the trend in the larger number of research studies is that test preparation can be effective in improving test scores; therefore, test preparation becomes a source of test score pollution that should be treated. The remedy is clear: Test-taking skills should be uniformly taught to all students in all grade levels so that it cannot be a source of test score pollution in the future.

Test Administration as a Source of Test Score Pollution

Sources of potential test score pollution in the area of test administration are excluding students, extending the time limit, and monitoring answer sheets.

Exclusion

In Austin, Texas, a scandal unfolded in a newspaper article by Kurtz (1999) exposing the fraudulent tampering of dropout lists in Austin's school district to increase the scores of schools in danger of being labeled "low performing." The deputy superintendent was indicted for tampering with governmental records. In Hartford, Connecticut, a curious reporter revealed a ruse to make it appear that Hartford students were increasing in achievement over a five-year period. Each year, an increasing percentage of low-scoring students were excluded from taking the test. Over five years, scores increased as did the percentage of excluded students. A local Phoenix, Arizona, high school expelled 30 to 40 troubled students each year just before state tests were given. The removal of these students increased the average performance in the school. The recipient school that admitted these students, of course, experienced the reverse effect—lower scores each year.

These vignettes reveal a systematic pattern to mislead the public about the effectiveness of schools and school districts by excluding certain students the schools know will score low on these tests. If you, as a school leader or teacher, really need to produce high test score results, the simplest, most direct strategy is simply to eliminate the source of low test scores by dismissing the students most likely to score low or to destroy or remove the test results of these students so that the official record shows what you want: higher scores. Of course, this is blatant misrepresentation of what students are learning, but the excuse offered in these circumstances is that the test is not intended to measure what is taught anyway, so exclusion gives the public what they want. As you can see, there is a twisted nature to the quest for high test scores that drives many teachers to do things that do not make them proud as educators.

Time Limits

One of the dilemmas in test design is the setting of time limits for students. In most published standardized achievement tests, time limits are imposed for practical reasons.

Since not all students will finish at the same time, some realistic limit has to be set so that the majority of students who have finished the test can be dismissed in a timely way. Most testing programs allow for enough time for all or most to finish the test.

There are valid reasons why students do not finish the test. Some students, called *plodders,* are slow and methodical. In the quest for efficiency, a time limit overlooks plodders, and their scores are lower than they would be if they were given more time. Some students learning to read, write, speak, and listen in English will perform slowly on these tests. They run out of time because they are translating in a language that is unfamiliar to them. Thus, the use of a time limit will usually result in lower scores than if these students were allowed more time. Also, students with high to moderate test anxiety tend to perform poorly under time conditions, according to Plass and Hill (1986). Their previous research and other research on test anxiety show that this condition has a very debilitating effect on student performance. Research also shows that the tendency for test anxiety is especially strong for boys.

Since national norms are based on timed tests, students gain an unfair advantage if they are given extra time. Keep in mind that a standardized test assumes that all students take the test *under the same conditions.* Extending the time limit for some students makes the test less standardized and lets test score pollution creep in.

One way to atone for slow test taking is to teach students time-management strategies. These strategies are discussed in Chapter 10 as essential testwiseness learning for students. Another effective strategy is to use untimed tests and give all students sufficient time to complete the test. There is some controversy about the effectiveness of this strategy, but if the time limit is extended, students will take the extra time to ensure that all test items have answers, even if random guessing is used. Students will also be careful to make erasures complete. (The optical scanning machine will mark a poorly erased answer wrong because the machine scans two answers for an item, which will result in an error.) Extra time seems like a simple way to give students opportunities to mark each item and check for erasure errors.

Answer Sheets

With high-speed optical scanning of test results, students must not only know content and be familiar with item formats but they must also know how to mark their answers on the answer sheet. Although this act may seem mundane and trivial, one research study by Cashen and Ramseyer (1969) actually showed a test score pollution based on whether a separate answer sheet was used or if students marked answers in the test booklet. This effect dissipated with older students. If a testing program uses answer sheets, it might introduce a source of test score pollution for their younger students, who may perform lower than they would have if they had marked in their test booklet.

Cheating as a Source of Test Score Pollution

This topic is obviously unpleasant, but it is worth mentioning that educators and students have cheated on tests (Cannell, 1989; Cizek, 1999; Mehrens & Kaminski, 1989;

Nolen, Haladyna, & Haas, 1992; Qualls, 2001). Cheating has two sides: one dealing with test givers who are interested in getting good results, and the other dealing with test takers who see the value in cheating and fail to see the liabilities. Readers who are interested in a very comprehensive treatment of this subject or who have any doubts that cheating is a problem in testing should consult Cizek (1999), which is the most extensive treatment of this subject available. Following are only a few well-documented sources of cheating, presented here to give you an idea of the extensiveness and variety of cheating as a source of test score pollution.

Student Cheating

In the November 22, 1999, issue of *U.S. News and World Report* (pp. 55–65), writers Carolyn Kleiner and Mary Lord reported that almost everyone is cheating on tests. Polled college students reported that 84 percent cheat on tests. Of course, the kind of cheating they discussed is more pervasive than cheating on standardized achievement test. But their point is that cheating is so ingrained into U.S. culture that the lines between cheating and honest school behavior are often blurred.

How do students cheat? Cizek (1999) lists 10 different methods of cheating, including asking for copies of test questions for a forthcoming test, copying answers from another student's paper, letting another student copy one's answers, asking another student for answers to questions on a forthcoming test, previewing a test from an illegal test file, delaying the submission of work with a false excuse, double marking a multiple-choice item, claiming to have handed in a paper, taking a test for another student, and getting an advanced copy of an examination. He missed one. An *Arizona Republic* article (October 30, 1996, p. A2) reported an incident of coded answers appearing on a pencil during a testing session for the Graduate Management Admissions Test.

Not surprisingly, technology is employed in cheating. Micro recorders and photographic equipment can be used to copy secure examinations, such as those used in licensing and certification tests. As technology improves, the effectiveness of cheating will also improve; thus, this problem may only worsen when standardized tests are used in high-stakes settings.

Since cheaters earn higher scores than they deserve, they contribute a form of systematic error that reflects one of the many sources of test score pollution. As cheating increases in a specific setting, test scores may increase, leading the public to think that students are learning more, when the opposite may be true!

Educator Cheating

As the incentives for teachers increase if their students score high on mandated tests, the temptation to cheat increases (Qualls, 2001). This is particularly disturbing if the teacher knows that the test is not well connected to the state or school district curriculum. Thus, it may seem understandable to some that certain teachers will resort to cheating because it is the only way they can see to satisfy the test-score hungry public, legislators, school board members, and media.

The main idea behind cheating is that the score a student, class, or school receives is higher than what it would be if some activity (i.e., cheating) did not occur. Following is an examination of practices that could arguably be called *cheating*. Most of these practices are subtle and devious. None of them is connected to good teaching and higher student learning.

How widespread is educator cheating? A recent review by Qualls (2001) suggests that high-stakes test score use has increased the incidence of educator cheating nationally. Zwick (2000) reported a cheating scandal in Sacramento, California, where teachers illegally photocopied the SAT-9 so they could teach to its content. One unique example of teacher cheating was on a teacher licensing test. At least 52 candidates in five southern states were nabbed after paying up to $1,000 for extra time and assistance from test administrators of the PRAXIS teacher licensing examination (National Center for Fair and Open Testing, Fall 2000f). This section discusses some of the methods used to cheat and the consequences of cheating. Two of the largest educator cheating scandals occurred in New York and Louisiana.

A total of 47 principals, teachers, and staff members from 32 elementary and middle schools were involved in cheating on highly competitive standardized tests in New York City (http://www.nytimes.com/library/national/regional/120899ny-cheat-edu.html). According to investigators, teachers and principals at some schools let students mark their answers on scrap or notebook paper, then told them which answers to correct when they filled in the bubbles in the official test booklets. At other schools, teachers directed students to erase incorrect answers or changed the answers themselves. Note that an increase of several points in a test for a class average would increase national ranking significantly, so the amount of cheating need not be blatant or large. Just one or two answers will suffice, especially if the class is close to the national average. Review Figure 2.1 in Chapter 2.

Charges of widespread cheating from 1995 through 1999 were made against 32 New York City elementary and middle schools, involving 43 teachers, 2 principals, and 2 paraprofessionals. One student's scores jumped from the 12th percentile to the 81st percentile after she was given answers. The next year, the girl's score fell to the 19th percentile.

Investigative reporter Jeff Meitrodt of the *New Orleans Time-Picayune* uncovered a pattern of scores on the California Achievement Test (CAT) administered in local parish schools that spiked erratically (http://www.nolalive.com/speced/toogood/main.html). One school went from the 24th percentile to the 67th percentile. The investigation uncovered a principal who invalidated the scores of 10 of 289 students. These students were destined to get very low scores. The parish policy is to test all students, which is a national standard as well. Meitrodt's investigation uncovered a systemic pattern in the New Orleans schools of tampering with the tests. Some schools with high gains used test preparation materials condemned by the test publisher because the exercises too closely resembled the CAT. Teachers at several schools were permitted to copy tests and teach answers to students. Some principals let students work in small groups when taking the test, making it easier for teachers to coach the students. More and more students are being classified as having a disability, which entitles them to special treatment, such as having their answers recorded by their teachers. Although this is highly recommended for students who are truly disabled, liberal application of this rule may inflate scores.

Reading Answers to Students.   This type of cheating is risky because, if exposed, it can jeopardize a teacher's career. In a published report in the *Arizona Daily Star* (April 28, 1996), an Arizona elementary school principal reported that some teachers read sections of the test to students and gave special inflections when reading the right answer. Other teachers posted mathematics formulas on classroom walls to help students during the test. In Texas, a principal and three teachers were fired after a nine-month investigation turned up evidence that they gave oral prompting to test questions on the Texas test.

Erasures.   This type of cheating is more subtle and occurs after hours. The teacher simply makes systematic or random corrections in student answer sheets, erasing several wrong answers and replacing them with right answers. An erasure of a student's wrong answer to a right answer in a random manner cannot be detected but may substantially affect the standard score and ranking of a class relative to other classes. This form of cheating is devious and relatively easy to do. Few school districts, state testing agencies, or testing companies have the resources to investigate this possibility. In the most obvious instances, where wholesale erasures are done, answer sheets can be examined for excessive erasure and investigations might uncover cheating, but this is a remote and unlikely possibility (Qualls, 2001).

Sanitizing Answer Sheets.   Another test score pollution that comes from erasures should not be considered cheating but does increase test scores. Parents or volunteers are asked to clean up answer sheets by making sure stray marks are erased and that erased answers are completely erased. This is done because teachers and other educators know that if an erasure is done poorly, the scanning machine will mark the item wrong simply because the machine reads the answer to an item as double-marked, which is an automatic disqualification for the item. Thus, vigilant parents and volunteers do a great service to their school or school district by cleaning up answer sheets. Although what they are doing is laudatory, not all schools and school districts do that. So when a state or school district report is issued, the public does not know who had their answer sheets sanitized.

Using Test Preparation Services.   As high test score stakes increase, companies are beginning to provide test preparation services that are sold to schools or concerned parents. The *Wall Street Journal* (November 2, 1989) reported that this practice amounts to sophisticated crib sheets. As these companies try to clone items likely to be found on the test, they find themselves more and more successful at boosting test scores. But is the increase real learning or artificial? The same issue arises when one group of students uses the test preparation service and another group does not: Is the difference attributed to test preparation due to the service? Does the service provide real learning experiences or in some way artificially contrives to boost test scores?

Consequences of Cheating.   One of the problems with teacher and other educator cheating is that there is little collective experience in dealing with cheating teachers and less diligence in challenging teachers and other educators. In 1989, Gloria Guzman was accused of cheating on Arizona's mandated test (http://www.azstarnet.com/public/packages/iowatest/121-4945.htm). Guzman was recognized by peers and parents as an excellent teacher. Her second-grade class test scores jumped 62 percentile points above other comparable second-graders in the school. The following year, these same students' test scores declined, matching their low-scoring classmates who were with another teacher. Despite the suspicion and evidence mounting against her, the State Board of Education never took decisive action. In South Carolina, a teacher was dismissed for giving students crib sheets containing answers to the test (*Wall Street Journal*, November 2, 1989). South Carolina has specific laws governing such behavior. In some states, this kind of wrongdoing can result in dismissal, probation, shame, embarrassment, or no action. Thus, certain teachers may take such a risk, knowing full well that in most states, the consequences are more likely to be positive than negative.

Causes of Cheating.   What drives the desire to cheat on these tests? Test-based accountability and high-stakes test score use seem to be the primary motivations for these cheating scandals. School leaders and teachers are expected to produce test score gains that reflect good instructional programs and good teaching. Some cheaters want to improve their reputations and further their careers. In New York, five district superintendents were removed because of low student test scores. School principals are judged, in part, on test scores. Some schools base merit pay on test score performance. Instead of attacking the root cause of this cheating problem, some jurisdictions (e.g., New York) ratchet up vigilance in administering standardized tests. But as long as these test scores are used invalidly, there will be educators who will cheat to assuage the public's demand for high test scores in a test-based accountability environment.

Test Anxiety and Motivation as Sources of Test Score Pollution

Two significant emotional characteristics that constitute major sources of test score pollution are test anxiety and motivation. Both are well documented in the research literature as contributing to invalidity.

Test Anxiety

Test anxiety is a major debilitating condition for many people. One estimate of the extensiveness of test anxiety is about 25 percent of the student-age population, but others have estimated the extent of test anxiety to range between 33 and 50 percent (Hill, 1984). Anxiety is complexly related to expectations for learning, test scores, and other factors (Hill, 1984; Hill & Wigfield, 1984). Students with especially high and low anxiety tend to perform poorly on these standardized achievement tests. Hill and Horton

(1986) reported that correlations between anxiety and test performance were fairly high in the second grade and increased in later grades. Thus, with older students, anxiety seems to be more debilitating. Anxiety is prevalent in all socioeconomic levels and with students from a diversity of cultural backgrounds and ability levels. Since postsecondary testing is growing in the United States, the extent of anxiety must be considerable. In other words, test anxiety strikes everywhere.

Fortunately, test anxiety is treatable. To reduce test anxiety, target those students for continued attention to their performance problem. Provide a positive learning environment, instill confidence in learning, provide multiple opportunities to take tests, and make tests instructive if performance is low. Also, students who are well prepared for a test tend to have lower anxiety going in. Thus, test preparation (as described in Chapter 10) is highly recommended. Poor testing practices, high-stakes tests, and poor teaching only exacerbate anxiety. Optimal testing conditions should be present—for example, adequate opportunity to learn, adequate test preparation, and motivational approaches that are positive as opposed to debilitating. Finally, teachers need adequate preservice and in-service training to create awareness and remedies to reduce test anxiety.

In summary, disappointing student performance might not necessarily reflect low achievement but be caused by test anxiety. This certainly gives reason to exercise caution in interpreting any standardized achievement test score that seems greatly different from a student's classroom performance.

Excessive Motivational Practices

We educators have a great influence on the mental states of students when they take a standardized achievement test; one of our responsibilities is to serve as motivator, encouraging students to do their best on the test. Paris, Lawton, Turner, and Roth (1991) reported that young students are typically motivated to perform well, but as they grow older, they realize that the test has no bearing on their lives. Consequently, the performance of older students may not be their best. Student teachers have reported that incentives—such as pizza parties, dances, field trips, and the like—serve as great motivators for students to do well. The *Arizona Daily Star* (April 26, 2000) reported that some schools held pep rallies before the big test and that high-scoring students are honored. Such events are highly correlated with excessive test preparation activities, which also constitute a potential source of test score pollution.

Sometimes students are threatened: no pizza party, no graduation ceremony, no school prom or dance. Sometimes they hear that teachers will lose their jobs unless students perform well. The use of heavy-handed motivational techniques may seem justified to some, but mental health experts, teachers, and parents seem to be rightfully dubious about such tactics to boost test scores.

Although one might naively support such motivating practices, keep in mind that not everyone motivates students this way. If motivation makes a difference in performance, then the differences on the achievement test are not the result of achievement but in the motivation that the students received. In these circumstances, comparisons among classes and schools reflect nothing more than how much motivation schools or teachers generated in students to take the test. If motivation is important in test performance, then motivation should be consistent from state to state, across school districts, schools, and classrooms.

Students with Disabilities, with Limited English Proficiency, and Living in Poverty as Sources of Test Score Pollution

In Chapter 9, three commingled student populations are discussed that have serious performance problems on standardized testing. One might also argue that these three populations, on average, perform more poorly on such tests than other students because the learning levels of these three groups of students are usually commensurately low. But as educators and responsible citizens, we should also examine the premise that many of these students underperform due to existing disabling conditions. Federal legislation recognizes some of these problems and provides guidelines for us. This section examines the premise that students so classified are likely to be victims of test score pollution.

Students with Disabilities

Students with disabilities must often take mandated tests that may have very high stakes. These students typically have an individual education plan (IEP). The 1997 amendments to the Individuals with Disabilities Education Act (IDEA) mandates that children with disabilities must be included in state and district assessments with appropriate accommodations where necessary (IDEA, section 612 (a)(17)(A)). Unfortunately, this legislation does not specify what these accommodations are or how they should be provided.

The fact that student performance can be underestimated in a test due to a disability is the justification for this legislation. Thus, students with disabilities comprise a population of students where test score pollution is an imminent threat.

The key to eliminating this source of test score pollution is *accommodation.* Hollenbeck (in press) and Phillips (in press) view this problem along a continuum, where accommodation is at one end and modification is at the opposite end. Accommodation is the action taken to eliminate test score pollution by making changes in the testing situation. Modification creates a unique situation where the test scores from the test modification cannot be considered equivalent to the test scores from a standardized administration. Chapter 10 will further discuss how testing accommodations are an important element in interpreting and using test scores.

Students with Limited English Proficiency (LEP)

As a nation built from waves of immigrants, the United States has the continual challenge of educating students in English whose natural language is some other language. Most of the recent students are from Central or South America and speak Spanish, but an increasing number of students come from Africa, Europe, Eastern Asia, and the Middle East. The problem of educating non-English speakers has been present since the birth of this nation and continues today.

Students with limited English proficiency (LEP) score below average on achievement tests. Since the most fundamental purpose of achievement testing is to help students learn, blending the scores of LEP students with the rest of the population obscures the fact that these students are not achieving as well as those with English language proficiency. Coupled with the fact that many LEP students tend to live in poverty and some may also have disabilities, we have students with compounded disabilities that strongly influence their success in school. Consequently, evaluation of student learning is weakened by blending scores of students from this population. As with students with disabilities and students living in poverty, disaggregating these scores lets the policymakers, public, and educators gather better information about these populations of special learners. Moreover, with disaggregated scores, there is a distinct profile of LEP students that helps educators pinpoint their learning problem and seek resources and treatment that have a more successful track record than regular education.

Students Living in Poverty

The Elementary and Secondary Education Act of 1965 recognized the need for providing equal opportunities for education for all students. This act was amended in 1994 (http://www.ed.gov/legislation/ESEA/toc.html). In this amendment, the Congress of the United States recognized two needs:

> (1) although the achievement gap between disadvantaged children and other children has been reduced by half over the past two decades, a sizable gap remains, and many segments of our society lack the opportunity to become well educated;
>
> (2) the most urgent need for educational improvement is in schools with high concentrations of children from low-income families and achieving the National Education Goals will not be possible. (http://www.ed.gov/legislation/ESEA/sec1001.html)

The official designation for these students is Title I. New Title I provisions for states link its services with each state's content standards. Each state is expected to implement some type of assessment reform that addresses the problems of Title I students and fair testing using content standards. Testing student achievement is crucial, and closing the gap between students living in poverty and other students is a national priority.

In Chapter 1, a model for school learning provided a perspective of student learning, showing the types of outcomes desired in education and the internal and external factors influencing learning. Poverty is one of those influences existing outside of school that has a debilitating effect on student learning. Students living in poverty seldom achieve very highly and seldom do well in school. These students often lack opportunities that the rest of the student population takes for granted, such as adequate shelter, food, and rest.

Reporting student test scores without reference to Title I seriously misinforms policymakers about the status of children living in poverty and their educational problems. Planning educational programs and providing resources for Title I students is a legal responsibility of state and school boards.

Scoring Errors as a Source of Test Score Pollution

Modern standardized achievement testing benefits from automation and technology, as might be expected. Machine-scannable answer sheets and computer programs provide a variety of testing services, but there is always a chance that a test score will be corrupted by the scoring process. Even test companies experience scoring foul-ups that contaminate scoring and the uses to which test scores are applied.

Key Verification and Alternate Right Answers

The most obvious thing about any standardized achievement test sponsored by a test publisher, a state, or a school district is the scoring key that contains a list of right answers. A simple error in identifying the right answers can cause many students to lose a single point. A single point may seem trivial, but students who are at the borderline for a pass/fail decision will fail as a result of a key error. But is this possible?

Content experts typically provide a keyed response for each item; however, if the committees are not composed of experts or the review process was faulty in some way, test items might be miskeyed or deserve a double key (have two right answers). If the sponsor of the test is sloppy in the detail of formulating the key, key errors occur. Such errors are invisible to the public, and there is little or no safeguard in place to catch such errors.

Scoring Foul-Ups

Growing evidence exists that in many states and jurisdictions, scoring problems have arisen (National Center for Fair and Open Testing, Summer 2000a). In the summer of 1999, the Educational Testing Service (ETS), one of the world's leading test companies, reported a serious error on its May examination of the Scholastic Assessment Test I. An omission by the optical scanning machine that records students' marks on the answer sheets resulted in scores that were 50 to 100 points lower than deserved. In California, a missing Federal Express package of student answer sheets resulted in 650 students retaking the test. In Florida, 14,000 test documents were lost from a total of 1.4 million. Since schools are ranked, the lost documents can affect rankings. In New York City, a scoring foul-up resulted in a large number of students being assigned low scores, causing them to enroll in summer school to make up for their low learning. In Minnesota, 8,000 students were wrongly informed that they failed the state's graduation test and had to attend summer school (National Center for Fair and Open Testing, Summer

2000a). A smaller error in that state involved sending letters to selected African American students who actually met state standards, inviting them to enroll in a remedial program for students who did not meet the state standards (National Center for Fair and Open Testing (Winter 2000–2001b).

Another aspect of this problem is delay in scoring. Test scores from the Florida test were delayed due a shortage of graders of essays. Michigan had delays in their scoring for two consecutive years. And the Arizona mathematics test had one item incorrectly scored, resulting in costly delays and loss of credibility. A scaling error occurred in Tennessee, creating a need for rescaling and a delay in reporting results. South Carolina experienced a scoring delay. Mississippi students had to wait five months for test results.

What has been learned from these experiences is that with massive testing, scoring errors and delays occur that disrupt the process and give critics ammunition to attack the testing process. If students are to be served by such testing, then teachers, parents, and students need to receive test scores that can be validly used to guide instruction. Scoring errors and long delays undermine the value of the use of such tests.

Rater Bias

A growing number of tests require that student performance be judged by professionally trained judges who use descriptive rating scales. Writing assessments are the most common type of performance test. A review of research by Haladyna and Ryan (2001) shows that judges differ in their degree of severity. Some judges are consistently harsh; others are consistently lenient. This research also shows that unlucky assignment of harsh judges to a borderline student may result in a failing grade; conversely, the lucky assignment of easy judges to the same borderline student may result in a passing grade when the opposite is true.

State- or district-sponsored testing programs using this performance format should be alert to the possibility that a rater is a source of test score pollution. If this test is used in a high-stakes setting, then the individual student is at risk of being misclassified due to rater error instead of performance.

Other forms of rater bias exist that are seldom mentioned in these assessments. For instance, research has shown that some raters rate in paradoxical ways, called *idiosyncratic* rating. Some raters commit the *error of central tendency*, tending to rate in the middle of the scale. For a high-stakes test in which a higher passing standard is used, central tendency ratings would tend to fail more students than is fair. The *halo error* ignores the value of different traits and gives each student about the same score, regardless of the trait being analyzed. This practice produces spuriously high reliability, lulling the test sponsor into thinking that the test scores are more reliable than they actually are.

An emerging science of rater analysis is increasingly sophisticated and sensitive to such problems, but there is little documented evidence of attention to this serious problem. Legal challenges in the future might focus on whether rater bias is addressed in scoring performance test results.

Testing Norms

Testing companies usually collect data from representative samples of students around the nation. From these test results, norms are built that show typical performance levels by grade. The National Center for Fair and Open Testing (Fall 1998a, p. 6) reported that the SAT-9 showed a peculiar drop from grade 8 student scores to grade 9 student scores. Speculations were offered about this curious phenomenon in reading without a corresponding drop in mathematics and other subjects tested. But reports like these cause one to question the basis of interpreting scores relative to a norming group when the norming group might not be representative of the nation. In other words, test companies may do their best but cannot provide assurance or evidence that their norming sample resembles the national population. In Chapter 5, the NAEP was the only test that demonstrated a representative national sampling plan, so that interpretation could be made from test results to the nation at large.

Scoring the Test

As you can see, scoring an achievement test is not a simple matter. With an increase in performance testing, scoring is more complicated than ever. With the testing industry booming, qualified workers are in short supply. Educators and the public need to be legitimately concerned about test scoring. The smallest error can have grave consequences on a large number of students, but even if an error results in the failing of just one student, there should still be a concern.

Contextualized Reporting

Invalid interpretations results when the public, including elected personnel and the media, view achievement data out of context. For example, any state summary of student achievement will show that students with disabilities, living in poverty, and with LEP score lower than any other groups of students. Chapter 1 offered explanatory evidence for low scores. This evidence comes from nonschool factors. Other evidence presented elsewhere in this book suggests that these students receive a lower quality of education, which further contributes to their problem of learning. Yet, test scores can be routinely aggregated at a larger level of analysis to show how a school or school district is failing. These "failing schools" usually have high rates of students with disabilities, with limited English proficiency, and living in poverty. Thus, the problem is not so much with the school or the teacher, but with existing social conditions and lack of resources provided to these three groups of students. Chapters 9 and 10 offer more discussion and arguments for contextualized reporting and the value of disaggregating data to pinpoint learning problems of students from these three categories. The important point in this chapter is that test score interpretations are misguided by ignoring the causal factors behind test scores for students who live in poverty, who have disabilities, and who are limited in English proficiency.

What Can Teachers Do about Test Score Pollution?

As discussed and documented throughout this chapter, the threat of test score pollution is real. Whether you teach or are a school leader, legislator, school board member, parent, or concerned citizen, we all need to express our concern at national, state, and school district levels about these undesirable influences. So, what can we do specifically?

- The most effective test preparation strategy is good teaching, which involves using your state content standards and/or your school district curriculum, which should be aligned with your state content standards. Provide all students with adequate opportunities to learn and relearn the content that will be tested.
- Plan and conduct ethical test preparation for all students taking the test. Ensure that the curriculum for test preparation is extensive and publicly defensible. (Chapter 10 contains a section devoted to ethical test preparation.)
- Refrain from aligning your school or school district curriculum to an externally mandated, misaligned test such as the SAT-9 or the ITBS. The district curriculum or state content standards should be your guide for teaching content. To align with a mandated test essentially links you to a test that is *not* strongly connected to content that your state or school district expects you to teach. However, as Smith (1991b) has shown, when a state or school district unfairly mandates such a test and misuses it, you are put in a difficult position ethically and professionally. There is not much you can do in this situation, short of resigning in protest or caving in and complying with this mandate to teach to the test.
- Administer the test in the recommended way.
- Don't cheat. Cheating not only has negative effects on students but it may also lead to being expelled from the teaching profession.
- Avoid excessive motivational practices that create an unfair comparison between those so motivated and those who have typical motivation.
- Consider the effects of anxiety in testing. If a student performs below expectation, look for indicators of test anxiety and take the appropriate action. Test anxiety should be treated as a disability, employing programs for curbing it or invalidating a test score. Test scores of test-anxious students should be interpreted cautiously.
- Consider the problems of students with disabilities; students who are learning to read, write, speak, and listen in the English language; and students who live in poverty and probably lack the multitude of opportunities to learn and perform as students who live above the poverty level. Take appropriate measures to accommodate or modify assessments and provide the students with suitable and meaningful instruction.
- Ensure that adequate quality controls are instituted in scoring test data that protect students from rater severity and scoring errors.

Summary

This chapter has established that test score pollution is a threat to valid test score interpretations and uses. Some types of test score pollution are intentional and others are accidental. Regardless of the type, state and school district policies must be vigilant against these threats, and caution must be exhibited in interpreting and using test scores when pollution is possible or present. However, a larger problem exists that may be the cause of pollution. A narrow view of accountability is that a test is the best criterion for measuring student learning and that the teacher or the school is responsible for that score. Thus, teachers are motivated to produce what the public wants: higher test scores. An enlightened type of accountability would have everyone play a role in improving education with shared responsibility. A variety of indicators should be used to measure student achievement. Contextual factors surrounding the student both in and out of school should be considered. Teachers play an important role in accountability, but responsibility for student learning should be shared.

8

Consequences of Standardized Achievement Testing

This chapter examines the consequences of standardized achievement tests on students, teachers, parents, and the public. Does testing really help students learn? Do testing results really provide information to satisfy accountability? What are the benefits of standardized achievement testing? What are the deficits?

Many essays and research studies have contributed to a growing realization that standardized achievement testing does not necessarily support wise policy and practice. In fact, many of the low-stakes uses of standardized test results that were observed in the 1950s and 1960s gave way to test uses that had more significant implications for students, parents, and society. Testing specialists have lamented that new test uses were not valid or justified, and were downright harmful to the students that the tests were supposed to be helping. Research on consequences of standardized achievement testing is a new field of study. This chapter will report some of the emerging trends and issues.

The chapter begins with a discussion of the role of politics in standardized achievement testing. High-stakes testing and accountability are then examined, two major reform efforts that are intertwined. This is followed by a discussion of the consequences of current high-stakes standardized achievement testing on students, schools, teachers and other educators, and the public, including students' parents.

Politics and Standardized Achievement Testing

It should come as no surprise that politics plays a very influential role in standardized achievement testing. Federal and state legislators and school board members are elected officials who create educational policies and allocate resources in their jurisdictions. Each of these groups of elected officials sponsors achievement testing programs. For example, note the Chicago Public Schools experiment with promotion testing that was discussed in Chapter 6, or the NAEP that the U.S. government has sponsored for many years. Most states have an achievement testing program that includes a home-grown test of the state's standards or a publisher's test such as the SAT-9, ITBS, MAT-7, or TerraNova-CAT or TerraNova-CTBS.

In discussing the influence of politicians in education, House (1991) portrays the country's two-party system as reflecting differing values regarding education. The conservative side of this two-party system views education for the masses as a poor investment, with the underclass seldom achieving and seldom contributing in positive ways to the national good. Thus, resources allocated to this group should be minimal. The liberal side views education as a means for achieving equity in society. Those with perseverance and ambition can earn higher status and lead more productive lives by working hard and getting a good education. Thus, more resources need to be allocated to those who have the highest risk for failure, the underclass. The main difference between these two extreme poles seems to be how the general public deals with those students who are least likely to achieve in society. (These students, which are the focus of Chapter 9, include students with disabilities, students living in poverty, and students with limited English proficiency.)

A prevailing sentiment often expressed at local, state, and national levels comes in the form of a condemnation of public education. House (1991, p. 23) writes, "The failure of the educational enterprise, especially education of the poor, was a major cause of the national failures, domestic and educational." The argument continues to be made that education has not succeeded with the underclass. As Chapter 1 discussed, education is not the sole cause of low achievement; rather, the causes come from *two* sources: out of school and inside of school. Yes, education often fails to meet the challenge of adequately educating this at-risk population. But the responsibility for educating these students must be shared by society. Social policies need to improve conditions for this underclass. Within any school district, state, or the nation as a whole, politics continues to play a crucial role in shaping policies regarding educating students. Knowing the political climate within any governing authority helps one better understand the legal mandate and level of resources given to education.

Politics is a very active and important player in education. Reforms such as cultural literacy, accountability via testing, promotion and graduation testing based on content standards, minimal competency teaching and testing, and performance testing may come and go. But the problem of dealing with this hardened, unchanged underclass remains. Elected officials will likely continue to seek remedies, but historically educators are not players in this game. Nonetheless, we educators can play an important role in shaping educational principles and procedures that drive education, and educators can keep the public informed about education and standardized achievement testing. Consequences of achievement testing is an emerging field of study—one that will enlighten the public about the value of standardized achievement testing.

Consequences of High-Stakes Testing and Test-Based Accountability

In previous chapters, high-stakes testing and accountability have been characterized in different contexts. In this chapter, the context is the consequences of high-stakes testing and test-based accountability.

High-Stakes Test Score Use

As noted earlier in this book, *high-stakes testing* implies that the test taker faces significant consequences when approaching a testing situation. Chapter 6 introduced us to three high-stakes uses, each involving pass/fail decisions based on test scores. Test scores may be used to promote students, as is done in the Chicago Public Schools. Increasingly, test scores are being used to make pass/fail decisions for high school graduation or certification. And there are many instances of pass/fail decisions being made on the basis of test scores for professional certification and licensing. The financial and emotional consequences of failure is certainly significant in all three instances, but few studies have evaluated these consequences. Table 8.1 presents an overview of some high-stakes test score uses.

The use of test scores also increases the risk of legal challenges to test score decisions (Mehrens, 1995; Phillips, in press). As the stakes go up, the tendency for attacks on the testing program also increase. Indeed, the American Educational Research Association (2000) issued a position statement about high-stakes testing that warns about the dangers inherent in such testing and offers some principles to guide educators in high-stakes testing programs. Chapter 10 presents and discusses these principles. Test sponsors must be very careful about the validity of making pass/fail decisions. If the testing program fails to meet certain criteria for validity, these programs are liable to legal challenge.

High-stakes testing will probably always be present in American life, particularly in professional certification and licensure. But the role of high-stakes testing for pass/fail decisions for elementary school promotion or secondary school graduation is still very debatable in terms of its benefits. The idea regarding bonus or merit pay for good test score performance from students has many flaws, yet remains popular with policymakers. The use of test scores for personnel decisions also seems flawed.

Accountability

As discussed in previous chapters, accountability has two meanings:

- The passing of information to policymakers to help them set policy and assign resources

TABLE 8.1 *Some Typical High-Stakes Test Score Uses*

Making pass/fail decisions	Students are tested for promotion, certification, or graduation. Those entering or in a profession are tested for certification or licensure.
Merit pay or pay bonuses	Teachers and other educators are offered financial incentives for increased student performance, as defined by standardized achievement test scores.
Personnel decisions	School superintendents and other school leaders and teachers may have their future employment linked to achievement test scores.

- Holding someone (teachers) responsible for student learning on the basis of test scores

The first meaning is what legislators and school board members do as policymakers: consume information and make wise decisions. Testing in this first meaning of accountability provides information to policymakers to create the optimal conditions for student learning. The second meaning of accountability seems to imply that if there is a test result, people want to hold someone responsible for that test result. As Chapter 1 made clear, teachers do not have control over many factors that influence student learning or the resources needed to support special programs for students at risk. Teachers' influence is limited to about 900 hours of contact with students each year, usually working with limited resources. Holding teachers accountable transfers responsibility from policymakers to teachers who are powerless to affect policy and have to work with the limited resources given to them.

Another crucial issue with students is what will become of students who fail to meet the high standards issued in challenge to these students. Senator Paul Wellstone stated, "Why do we then honor and declare 'accountable' policy makers and politicians who use tests on children in a way that the test manufacturers have said is effectively unsafe?" (National Center for Fair and Open Testing, Spring 2000c, p. 9). Senator Wellstone was referring to the many test-polluting practices described in Chapter 7 but also was addressing the effects of this high-stakes testing atmosphere on student learning and the prevailing attitude toward school and education. He raises an important issue: What harm are we educators doing to our students with high-stakes testing?

Another issue is that with either meaning of accountability, a state-mandated test is simply too blunt an instrument to delicately and sensitively measure student learning to provide teachers with the information they need to help students learn. Because such tests are broad surveys of knowledge and skills, the tests are not substantial enough with respect to sampling to be that useful. More precisely aimed diagnostic tests are needed to help students learn.

Recently, highly respected testing specialist Robert Linn (2000), after having worked for more than 40 years in the field of achievement testing, concluded that accountability has probably done more harm than good. Teachers might agree with Linn's conclusion. High school mathematics teacher Nancy Watson (1998) argued that publishing test scores can do considerable damage to the reputations of teachers and other educators. Although Watson supports high-stakes uses of test scores and accountability, she believes that educators could do a better job of implementing these testing programs.

William Mehrens, another highly respected testing specialist, is more cautious (Mehrens, in press). He has argued that if one looks at opinion, then it might be argued that accountability and high-stakes testing have gone too far, but if one examines evidence, the drawn conclusion might be more tentative. Mehrens contended that more studies are needed before one can be certain about the positive or negative consequences of achievement testing. He stated that rhetoric about the evils of high-stakes testing might overshadow actual evidence. Mehrens has reviewed research on consequences and has difficulty finding conclusive evidence about consequences of high-stakes testing at this time. However, he and others have acknowledged that this is a new field of study with many challenges and problems ahead. More research on consequences is expected, particularly as a public backlash to high-stakes accountability testing occurs.

Despite the limited evidence available about consequences, Mehrens does draw some tentative conclusions based on evidence he cites:

- Combining logical argument with sketchy evidence, high-stakes state testing may lead to teacher burnout, decrease morale, and increase cheating. Chapter 7 provides evidence of increased cheating, and evidence reported in this chapter supports the notion of more teacher burnout and lower morale.
- The use of a single standard for all students and assuming that all students can achieve beyond this single standard defies logic and what experts know about learning and testing. Setting a single standard based on this false premise only sets everyone up for a major disappointment when one-third of the nation's students still fail to achieve.
- In any high-stakes situation, such as graduation testing, test scores will increase, but the issue is whether the increase is legitimate or some form of test score pollution. Mehrens has repeatedly made the important point that any increase in test scores should correspond with increases in student learning. Test score polluting practices create what testing specialists call *construct-irrelevant variance,* which is commonly referred to as *bias.*

The next sections are devoted to a discussion of the effects of testing from various perspectives. First will be a look at the effects on students, followed by a discussion about the effects on classrooms and the school curricula, teachers, and the public, which includes parents and the elected officials who make these testing policies and allocate funds for education.

Effects of Standardized Achievement Testing on Students

This section evaluates the effects of standardized achievement testing on students drawing from a variety of sources. One of the best sources is a review of research and essays by Paris, Lawton, Turner, and Roth (1991). They argued that when one considers standardized achievement testing from a psychological perspective, one can better understand the effects of achievement testing on students. This psychological perspective complements the political and testing perspectives, which, although necessary, cannot provide the entire story about standardized achievement testing.

How Do Students View These Tests?

According to Paris and colleagues (1991) and others who study children, younger students have positive views of themselves and their abilities. As they become older and take tests, receive grades, and make comparisons, many students become less confident. They tend to attribute their success or failure to bad luck and other factors beyond their control. As a result, these older students show less interest. Tests victimize these students. The low-achieving students become disillusioned and less motivated, resulting in less effort to learn and a greater inclination to make bad decisions about schooling. Successful students feel the opposite. Tests empower them, giving them greater motivation and confidence in their ability to learn.

Younger students tend to think that standized achievement tests are useful, and their effort reflects this serious interest in testing. Older students often fail to see the value of testing. These older students report receiving test-taking training (testwiseness) but they are less inclined to use these strategies in the classroom. They report more frequently a tendency to mark randomly and to show inattention to the test in other ways. A related point made by teacher Marc Richmond (1998) is that many children fail to take the test seriously. As a result, familiar response patterns are seen on answer sheets: random marking, silly pattern marking, or unfinished marking where many items are unanswered. Students also tend to be less motivated to perform on these tests as they get older. The earlier feeling about the usefulness of tests leads to a better understanding that the test is part of public policy that affects state legislators, school boards, schools, and their representatives. The value of test scores to these students is unclear. As a result, there are many reports concerning a lack of effort. This is particularly true with tests given at the high school level, unless, of course, the test is a high school requirement for certification or graduation. The fact that test scores become a basis for social comparisons sets up a system within schools for "winners" and "losers." Those who typically score low will usually attempt to invalidate the process by admitting they did not try or the test is invalid as a measure of their social worth.

As Chapter 7 reported, test anxiety is a large problem. High-stakes testing exacerbates test anxiety—especially if students think the teacher will be punished for low test scores, as might be the case. Imagine the young child who is told by a parent, playmate, or another person, "If scores are low, your teacher may not be here next year or may not get her pay increase." Moreover, test anxiety is correlated with low achievement and anxiety worsens as children get older. Low performance on these tests tends to increase this anxiety. So the interaction of anxiety and test performance work together to worsen an already bad situation for low-scoring students.

As you learned in Chapter 6, Texas has one of the most rigorous standardized achievement testing programs, the Texas Assessment of Academic Skills (TAAS). The program has been ongoing since reforms in the 1980s. Overall test performance jumped from 55 percent in 1994 to 74 percent in 1998. Students with certain racial or ethnic origins who previously scored low improved from 32 percent passing to 56 percent passing for one group, and from 41 percent to 62 percent passing for another group. The important question to answer is: Is the gain in Texas due to enriched curriculum and more intensive and extensive teaching or better test preparation and unethical practices (as discussed in Chapter 7)?

A study by McNeil and Valenzuela (2000) tells a different story. In one Texas district having a population of low-income Spanish speakers, virtually the entire budget was dedicated to test preparation, so the students could be drilled on the low-level mathematics that the TAAS was sure to measure. Teachers reported that although TAAS scores increased, students were deprived of high-quality teaching and their ability to read and handle assignments, and their quality of work declined. Reports such as this are troubling. On the other hand, Texas has committed to smaller class sizes and special programs for students with limited English proficiency (*Education Week*, April 29, 1998). Two of the consequences of high-stakes testing, then, are resources and programs that make a decided difference.

Testing Very Young Children

Reputable national educational organizations recommend against testing children in grade 2 and below (Haladyna, Haas, & Allison, 1998; Kohn, 2000). The National Center for Fair and Open Testing (Fall 1998a) cited a *Washington Post* story about first-graders in Virginia taking a standardized achievement test and crying, feeling sick, collaborating on answers, or simply quitting the test. This recent report is consistent with other reports (e.g., Nolen, Haladyna, & Haas, 1992) with a more diverse sample of teachers from all grade levels. Highly respected testing expert Jim Popham (2000a) also documented the problems with testing young children. In a study reported by Kohn (2000), young children reported that they could orally answer questions that frustrated them during the standardized test session. Thus, they underperformed on the test. These students easily become frustrated and feel stress during such tests.

Other Negative Side Effects

The National Center for Fair and Open Testing, a nonprofit organization that monitors standardized achievement testing, argues that the heavy reliance on multiple-choice formats limits teaching and learning to knowledge, at the expense of skills and abilities, such as critical thinking, creative thinking, and problem solving. Traditional achievement tests rely on testing knowledge in "bits and pieces." Learning is viewed as simply the aggregating of this knowledge. This traditional learning theory seems outdated. Modern learning theory is, of course, concerned with knowledge but also with the integration of knowledge and skills in ways that lead to solving problems and to thinking critically and creatively. Thus, traditional achievement tests have an approach to testing that is not compatible with cognitive learning theory.

Teachers and other educators are at a crossroad, according to one widely respected testing expert, Lorrie Shepard (1991). She found in her survey that educators either had embodied the traditional theory or were embracing this newer theory of learning. Mary Lee Smith's excellent studies (1991a, 1991b) support this trend in Arizona, where reform has thrust teachers into the modern age of student learning with mixed results. Some teachers were "there," teaching students to develop abilities, while others stayed with the traditional way of teaching.

Weighing the Evidence about Consequences on Students

Each policymaker needs to examine the evidence of the effects of testing on students, asking if the good outweighs the bad. In particular, the three populations featured in

Chapter 9—disabilities, poverty, and limited English proficient—should be considered. Students from these three groups have the most to lose in high-stakes testing. When weighing the evidence for and against high-stakes standardized achievement testing, the focus should be on what happens to the students. Early indications are not good, but more evidence is needed.

Effects of Standardized Achievement Testing on Classrooms and Schools

In the 1970s, objective-based instruction and criterion-referenced testing were instituted as major school reforms. This approach made a rigid connection between teachers' student learning objectives and tests designed to measure these objectives. Quite a bit of research focused on matching these sets of objectives, instruction, and tests so that all children could have equal opportunities to learn. However, several researchers questioned the legitimacy of standardized achievement testing (Freeman & Porter, 1989; Leinhardt & Seewald, 1981). Mehrens (in press) summarized the body of evidence about this period and concluded that teachers seldom used standardized achievement test results, so the content had little or no influence on what teachers taught. Indeed, this current educational reform may be undergoing the same phenomenon. Teachers must make changes in instruction if reform is to work. New content standards and strong initiatives to teach abilities such as critical thinking and problem solving may not change teaching styles and content emphasis.

As noted in the previous chapter, one way to increase test scores on the standardized achievement tests is to eliminate or reduce time spent on areas not tested and to concentrate teaching efforts on topics that are sure to be tested. Educators have long argued that good teaching involves specifying worthwhile learning outcomes clearly to students, providing appropriate instruction, and testing accordingly.

The use of the standardized achievement test for some high-stakes purpose, such as teacher merit pay or student promotion, may force teachers to narrow their focus. Indeed, a series of studies conducted in the 1980s revealed much of the then current thinking about the role of textbooks and standardized tests in teaching (Freeman & Porter, 1989; Freeman, Belli, Porter, Floden, Schmidt, & Schwille, 1983; Freeman, Kuhs, Porter, Floden, Schmidt, & Schwille, 1983). These studies cited an instance where five students in a case study spent an entire semester studying 23 fourth-grade objectives, because the teacher knew that the students would be extensively tested on these 23 objectives. Thus, these students did not receive as much instruction in other areas untested by this test. The researchers concluded that it matters which test and which textbook the teacher used.

In a pretrial report on the Texas Assessment of Academic Skills, Linda McNeil of Rice University (National Center for Fair and Open Testing, Summer 2000b) reported that teachers reduced time spent on untested subjects to emphasize topics tested on the TAAS. Indeed, teacher Terri Goyins (1998) described her innovative mathematics teaching and how she abandoned it to prepare for the state-mandated testing program that focused on mathematics calculations, because that is all that would be tested. So, not only are the topics taught reduced, but the nature of the content is reduced to factual recall and easy-to-learn material that is most likely to be tested and produce improved test scores. Sure-fire remedies are used instead of costly and time-consuming teaching and testing that develops abilities such as reading, writing, and mathematical and scientific problem solving.

A study by Walt Haney of Boston College corroborated McNeil's findings (National Center for Fair and Open Testing, Summer 2000b). In his survey, 82 percent of teachers he surveyed said they were gearing teaching to the state-mandated test and 88 percent reported spending more time on types of items that were likely to be on the test. Thus, school district curriculum or state standards are being abandoned unless the test is well designed and reflects the school district curriculum or state standard. This finding is well documented in many other studies (Allington & McGill-Franzen, 1992; Koretz, Linn, Dunbar, & Shepard, 1991; Smith, 1991b). Smith reported that about 100 hours were spent in test preparation at one school in her study. Since the school year has about 900 hours of student time, a 100-hour commitment to test preparation significantly detracts from classroom instruction—a very powerful factor causally related to school learning.

The evidence seems to be mounting in favor of a conclusion that test-based accountability and high-stakes testing influence the school curriculum, narrowing it to fit what the test measures. If the public wants this, then the trend is a good one, but most educators seem to think that this trend is not beneficial to the education of their students.

Effects of Standardized Achievement Testing on Teachers

The basic purpose of high-stakes testing is to increase the achievement of students across the nation. But the attempt to do this is usually sponsored by states, with school districts also sponsoring specific initiatives. The main idea of this educational reform is to get school districts, schools, and teachers to evaluate what they are teaching and how they are teaching, to make changes to better student learning. They need to bring local curricula in alignment with national standards. While this kind of educational reform may be laudatory, most teachers see educational reform that is test driven as undesirable for their students and for themselves.

Edelman (1981) reported on teacher perspectives about mandated testing in a time where high-stakes testing was just beginning. Her survey of 104 third-grade California teachers, who were undergoing one of California's frequent test reform efforts, reveals that most teachers (92 percent) believed there was too much testing. Most teachers did not think the tests measured student learning accurately. These teachers mainly concluded that the benefits did not outweigh the costs.

Since that report, there has been an increase in high-stakes achievement testing and an outpouring of research on the effects of testing on teachers. Some of the best research has been done in Arizona by Mary Lee Smith and colleagues (Smith, 1991a, 1991b). This research involved extensive visits and interviews with teachers. The findings of these studies were confirmed by surveys conducted by Nolen, Haladyna, and Haas (1992). Following are eight documented outcomes of accountability and high-stakes testing.

Publishing Student Achievement Scores

Little good comes when test scores are published. Teachers have very little control over the students they receive, the resources provided to them, and school organization and leadership. Yet, when scores are published, it is the teacher who comes under scrutiny. The reaction from teachers, accordingly, is: "Their (teachers') statements on questionnaires, in interviews, and during conversations, in meetings and (in teachers') lounges reveal the anxiety, shame, loss of esteem, and alienation they experience from publication of test scores" (Smith, 1991b, p. 8). Test scores are reduced to the solitary indicator of success, and family and home conditions and intelligence of students are not considered. Thus, invalid interpretations are made by the public about the success of teachers in low-scoring areas. Teachers feel that the test is poorly connected to what they teach, so they must either change their teaching to reflect the content of the test or follow their own ideals and teach what the school district curriculum and their conscience dictates.

The National Center for Fair and Open Testing (Fall, 1998b) reported on a crisis with teachers in North Carolina when student scores were published. This state has made testing an important factor for high school graduation and grade promotion. A report from an organization in North Carolina stated that teacher morale is diminishing, that teachers elect to leave low-scoring schools that are located in the poorest areas of the state, that teaching is reduced to rote memorization and test-taking skills, and that there is extensive placement of students into remedial and special education classes, when the trend in special education is for inclusion in the regular classroom. This evidence shows that the push for student and teacher accountability hurts the schools and the students who need the most help.

Invalidity of Test Score Interpretation and Test Score Use as Justification to Compromise Ideals

Teachers believe that misaligned tests are invalid measures of what they teach, and the dissonance that sets in with them contributes to their low morale. How can teachers teach to a test that offers less than valuable information? This attitude sets up considerable dissatisfaction with teaching as a profession. One of the most alarming aspects of this perceived invalidity of the uses of these tests is that a few teachers will actually cheat on the test, because they know that the results have no bearing on their students. They cheat to placate school leaders, school board members, the media, and the public, but the psychological cost to them—although difficult to assess—is probably not very good. Very little is known about this effect on teachers, but as high-stakes testing continues, the nation may see more of this attitude that "we give the public what they want."

Another side to this issue is the increasing practice by legislatures to provide incentive bonuses based on test score performance. For instance, in Michigan, Governor John Engler was reported in the *Grand Rapids (Michigan) Press* (Sunday, April 2,

2000) as initiating an $8.5 million program that has backfired in many ways. First, students are reported razzing their teachers about how they hold the fate of teachers' pays in their hands. Second, teachers are more reluctant to collaborate or share teaching ideas because the awards are competitive. And third, large groups of teachers have protested, saying that they will contribute their bonuses to charity.

Schools in Denver and Pennsylvania have adopted similar plans. These programs are linked to a faith that the sole indicator of learning is a test and the teacher is the sole influence on student performance. While this social experiment is underway, there is no research to argue effectively for or against it. Nevertheless, one thing is certain: Test pollution is bound to occur if the past is a good predictor of the future. Cheating is a major type of test score pollution. Based on earlier studies, one might expect that some unscrupulous teachers will "earn" their bonuses by cheating.

Emotional Impact on Children

As the previous section shows, testing has a known effect on students. Most students hate this experience. Moreover, teachers see that their students' efforts are being wasted on testing that has no value to the students or the teacher. The emotional distress on students rubs off on their teachers. According to Smith (1991b), teachers feel anxiety and guilt for putting their students through this experience.

Time Lost for Instruction

The amount of time effectively spent in teaching is directly related to the amount of learning. If the time for teaching and learning is significantly reduced because of week-long standardized testing, this time is lost time for student learning. Another aspect of this problem is that reports such as those by Nolen, Haladyna, and Haas (1992) and Herman and Golan (1993) show that considerable amounts of time may be spent preparing for the annual test instead of teaching the school district curriculum. As mathematics teacher Judy Bodenhausen stated,

> Tests take time from teaching. I will lose a whole week so that I can help administer California's standardized test—one that is not correlated with the new curriculum standards. . . . I must face media criticism when some students do poorly on this inappropriate test, although most low achievers are transients who have been in our district only a short time. (1998, p. 9)

Katzman and Hodas (2000) reported from an interview with a teacher in the high-stakes setting that she spends 50 percent of her time with students in test preparation for two months before the test. Such is the frenzy generated by high-stakes testing.

There is one argument that counters with if teachers do spend two months preparing for a mandated test, students must be learning something. Isn't that good? The key to the validity of this argument is the extent to which the mandated test matches the state content standards or the school district curriculum.

Is lost time important? Is the learning relevant to the annual test more important? In a survey reported by Herman and Golan (1993), most teachers believe the former.

They also think that the test results are not very useful. Thus, the time spent preparing for tests, taking the test, and discussing results with students and parents is not time well spent (McGuinn, 1999). Since many states and school districts have content standards or well-established curricula, the time spent preparing and taking standardized achievement tests robs students of more relevant learning opportunities.

Narrowing the Curriculum

This topic has been treated several times in this book and is relevant here. Teachers will reduce the content that they teach if there is a mandated test used for test-based accountability and other high-stakes uses. As one teacher revealed, "OK, if languages arts and mathematics are all that will be tested, my daily schedule will be language arts in the morning and mathematics in the afternoon. We will skip everything else, because nothing else counts." This facetious conclusion reveals the dilemma that good teachers face. The mandated test dictates what they must teach, and any variance from this mandate weakens the students' chances for performing on this test and succeeding, as judged by the students' performance. Most of these good teachers would argue that the lessons they had prepared for expanding student abilities will be scrapped in favor of the drills and practice that will affect test performance.

Some teachers take the opposite position: "My contract doesn't say increase test scores; it says to teach." So they teach what they think is correct and ignore the pressure to narrow the curriculum to increase student performance. But the pressure of accountability will force these teachers to strongly consider their alternatives: Teach to the test or else.

The Exclusive Use of Multiple-Choice Tests

Multiple-choice testing is not bad in and of itself. In fact, this item format is very good for measuring knowledge as well as limited forms of problem solving and even critical thinking (Haladyna, 1999). But if teaching is dominated by learning knowledge at the expense of cognitive skills and fluid abilities (discussed in Chapter 1), then students are receiving only one part of an education. The heavy emphasis on knowledge in standardized achievement testing contributes to this narrow, limited scope of student learning. Good teachers teach fundamental knowledge and test with multiple-choice questions, but they also use a variety of other assessments to measure skills and abilities.

Teachers' Increased Feelings of Numbing Helplessness

An ever-growing perception among teachers reported from many sources is that teachers are powerless to effect change in schools, particularly with students from populations that are typically low performing (e.g., students living in poverty). The ideas of high-stakes testing and test-based accountability do not emanate from teachers—they have virtually nothing to say about these practices. Smith (1991b) reported that teachers feel helpless with respect to the publication of their students' scores, causing them emotional distress and the incessant badgering in the media as if they were the only ones who influenced these scores.

Teacher Morale

Undoubtedly, test-based accountability and other high-stakes test uses have taken their toll in teacher morale and stress (Mehrens, in press). This conclusion is compounded by recent reports that about one-half of the country's current teachers will be retired before the end of this decade. The teacher shortage is current and will be ongoing, especially if teachers are driven out of their profession by inappropriate educational policies. The added stress of test-driven teaching and holding teachers responsible for student performance will continue to erode the supply of dedicated professionals. Teacher Jane Ellen Glasser of Norview High School in Norfolk, Virginia, has observed:

> The media make headlines of my gloom: "American Education in Crisis." Test scores read like obituaries. Politicians get busy. Mandates fall like bricks from detonated school buildings. School systems get busy. There are new standards, new curricula, new textbooks, new strategies. Teachers get busy. We are so busy throwing out the old and moving in the new.... I am overwhelmed. The problem is bigger than my classroom, bigger than public education. The tenement of failures in school is a product of our culture. (1999, pp. 16, 17)

A report in the *Christian Science Monitor* (May 24, 1990, p. 1) exposed cheating in Rochester, New York. Some teachers were reduced to tears regarding the fierce competition over high scores. Answer sheets were distributed to teachers. Some teachers said they would do whatever it took to get high scores. Cheating was also detected in 40 elementary schools in California. In a study by Haas, Haladyna, and Nolen (1990) about 9 percent of teachers confessed that they cheat and how they cheat. These unprofessional behaviors are demoralizing both to those who do not cheat as well as those who do.

In a report from the National Center for Fair and Open Testing (Fall 1998c, p. 3) a survey of North Carolina teachers showed that 52 percent of the teachers were beginning to develop negative attitudes toward low-scoring students. Some teachers would consider leaving their jobs if their schools were "exposed" as low performing. North Carolina has threatened to give teachers a competency test if their schools are highlighted as low performing. Indeed, salaries tend to be lower in such school districts, so there is a pronounced tendency for teachers to abandon schools where achievement is low and public scrutiny is high.

Never has the profession of teaching looked so bleak. Teaching in an environment where some public policies seem blatantly wrong, allocations of resources for teaching seem minimal, and social problems that are known to contribute to low achievement are at an all-time high (Hixson, 2000).

The Public and Backlash to Test-Based Accountability

Surveys of the public generally show that education is important, that schools are doing a pretty good job, and that high standards are good. The public also believes in standardized achievement testing and trusts the results of these tests. Thus, newspaper reports of schools and school districts do much to reflect the condition of education. However, although standardized achievement test scores may reflect student learning over a life-time, the lack of match between what teachers teach during a school year and what that annual test measures does not serve education very well. The public mainly likes the idea of holding students and schools accountable for achievement through high-stakes testing, but a public backlash seems to be growing in most states where such testing exists. When the idea for a high-stakes testing program begins, legislative support and policymakers seem to reflect the public's mood for educational reform and accountabil-ity. But as the program gets implemented, the public begins to notice the consequences of high-stakes testing.

Parents in Chicago (www.pureparents.org) won a victory over the Chicago Public Schools following a complaint to the Office of Civil Rights of the U.S. Department of Education. As discussed in Chapter 6, the old policy was to use the Iowa Test of Basic Skills scores for pass/fail promotion criteria. The new policy is to allow other criteria to influence the decision. These criteria include grades, attendance, and teacher recom-mendations. An appeal for student review must come from parents. What is important about this decision is that about one-third of all students test below Chicago's standard nationally. Thus, this decision might support further protest in other jurisdictions for pass/fail decisions based on a single test.

According to the *U.S. News and World Report* (April 3, 2000), 33 sites and hun-dreds of teachers and parents in Ohio protested the use of a fourth-grade test for promo-tion decisions. A survey of current and prospective lawmakers in Ohio indicated that changes in the Ohio test were forthcoming as a consequence of this public dissatisfac-tion. In Louisiana, parents filed a protest with the Office of Civil Rights, like Chicago parents did earlier. The argument in Louisiana was that the state's test has adverse impact on minority and poverty students. Challenges are also being made in Massachu-setts, where a survey of teachers found that most were opposed to high-stakes testing (National Center for Fair and Open Testing, Winter 2000–2001a). In New Jersey, the state's school administrators have called for a five-year moratorium on the state's test-ing program after widespread dissatisfaction (National Center for Fair and Open Test-ing, Fall 2000e). One response has been the state's readjustment of passing standards after an alarming number of students failed—a familiar story repeated in other states. In Virginia, a parent-led campaign is railing against the state's Standards of Learning tests. A survey of 800 parents showed a lack of confidence and credibility in this test.

Upper-class parents are seeing enriching activities—such as field trips, special projects, and other benefits of an affluent school district—disappear as the focus turns to getting higher test scores. The National Center for Fair and Open Testing (Winter 2000–2001b) reported public protests against high-stakes testing and predictable gov-ernmental reactions in Alabama, Alaska, Arizona, California, Delaware, Maryland, Massachusetts, Ohio, and Wyoming. Thus, the backlash movement seems to be real and gaining momentum.

A Chronology of Backlash in One State

Arizona provides a good example of the public's backlash against test-based account-ability. Its educational reform test, AIMS (Arizona's Instrument to Measure Standards), was constructed to measure student achievement in grades 3, 5, 8, and 10, in reading, writing, and mathematics based on the state's adopted content standards. The tenth-grade test was a high school graduation requirement, with five tries permitted for students to show mastery. Table 8.2 provides a chronicle of events culminating in a small backlash.

Despite Arizona's medial standing on nationally normed SAT-9 tests, most students failed to meet the state's high standard. Many of these students had taken and scored above average on college admissions tests. Hasty development of the testing program, coupled with results showing that 80 percent of the state's minority population was failing this test, has caused statewide alarm (*Arizona Republic*, November 29, 2000, p. B-1). The public is growing increasingly angry about the test. Criticism from the business community, educators, parents, students, and others is broad in scope but consistent:

- Passing standards are much too high. Most adults would have trouble meeting them.
- Results are not available in time for teachers to find them useful.

TABLE 8.2 *Developmental History of High-Stakes Testing*

Date	Event
May 1995	Elected education superintendent announces plan for high-stakes high school graduation test.
October 1995	Content standards drafted with the help of teacher committees.
August 1996	State board approves standards.
September 1998	Some 76,000 students take pilot test (and don't do very well).
November 1998	Graduation test implementation delayed from 2001 to 2002.
May 2000	Tests are given statewide, including grades 3, 5, and 8.
July 2000	Mathematics test deemed too hard by state board; graduation test delayed to 2004.
September 2000	Results: 80% fail mathematics; 70% fail writing. What are we going to do?
November 2000	Disproportionate number of minority students will fail this test. Outcries from advocacy groups.
Spring 2001	Mathematics test changed; harder content removed and passing level lowered. Date for implementation delayed again.
Fall 2001	Superintendent resigns. New superintendent initiates changes that include educators. Date for implementation delayed.
2002	Elections and a new wave of reform???

- The content standards are not yet fully implemented in the classroom.
- Emphasis on reading, writing, and mathematics detracts from students whose interests and career paths may be toward the arts, science, computer science, technologies, and other fields.
- Teachers will focus lessons only on content that is sure to be on the test.
- The schedule for implementation is much too fast. No one is ready.
- The program does nothing for students from neglected populations (students with disabilities, students living in poverty, and students with limited English proficiency). These students are most likely to leave school early and this program only accelerates their exit from formal education.
- Money is spent on testing that does not help students learn.
- This is a politicians' test conceived to advance politicians' agendas.

Although the validity of each criticism has to be weighed against the evidence, the outcry from the public is significant and increasing, showing a shifting of opinion when they become aware of the consequences on the students. The high projected fail rates seem unrealistic when one looks at other indicators of student achievement, such as grades and test scores on nationally normed tests. Experiences in states such as Arizona provide painful lessons on educational reform by mandating testing. The consequences of any such reform effort should be mainly positive but the evidence that appears to be developing in various states seems mostly negative.

Reactions to Backlash

About 27 states currently link tests to promotion or graduation. However, it is likely to see these states backing away from the use of test scores as the public becomes angrier with tests containing content for which students have not yet received appropriate teaching, unequal funding of schools, high standards that even most adults could not meet, and testing and scoring foul-ups and errors that reduce the public's confidence in such testing.

Surveys continue to show that people like high-stakes testing (National Center for Fair and Open Testing, Fall 2000a), but how far to go with high-stakes pass/fail decisions is another issue. A key issue in this argument is what to do with the students who fail in this high-stakes setting. Another related issue is how high-stakes testing programs are implemented. A growing tendency that is supported by professional educational organizations (see Chapter 10) is to use supplemental criteria for making pass/fail decisions, as done in the Chicago Public Schools.

If the public was better educated about standardized achievement testing and realized that the quest for accountability using one test has caused teachers to abandon what they thought was good teaching and focus their teaching only on what counts on the test, the public might act more aggressively with policymakers about accountability and high-stakes testing.

Is There a Positive Message Here?

Despite the gloomy message throughout this chapter about the consequences of test-based accountability and high-stakes achievement testing, it might be encouraging to close on a positive note. Florida teacher Lee Bailey (1998), a veteran teacher who has seen it all, writes that prior attempts in Florida to start and successfully use high-stakes testing failed, but the most recent version, the Florida Comprehensive Assessment Test (FCAT), was linked to professional standards and produced benchmarks for performance. The test used a variety of item formats, including a performance component. The FCAT generated discussion among teachers. There are no consequences to students, as yet, but the demand that schools and districts must make systemic changes in low scores persists. The testing program will cause teachers to work together and articulate teaching better to bring students into line with the state's content standards.

Summary

Recent interest in the consequences of testing on various constituencies has helped explain that all education policies and actions will have some effect: good or bad. Unfortunately, the current state of achievement testing in the United States seems to be more negative than positive. This is not to say that many tests discussed in this book are inherently bad, but that the way people interpret and use tests may not be in the best interests of the citizens being served. More time is needed to sort out the consequences, good and bad. But clearly, accountability and high-stakes testing will likely endure, and test developers, legislators, policymakers, school boards, principals and other administrators, teachers, and the public will continue to learn more about the consequences of their actions.

9

Standardized Achievement Testing of Students at Risk

This chapter focuses on the interpretation and uses of three groups of students who are at risk of not achieving satisfactorily in school. These students include those with disabilities, those who live in poverty and are classified as Title I, and those with limited English proficiency (LEP).

First, the chapter deals with the problems of these students and shows how education typically falls short of helping these students learn. Next, you will learn about how the achievement of these students may be underestimated and what can be done about that. Finally, the chapter examines the rationale for the ideal role of standardized achievement testing in dealing with low-achieving students.

The reporting of achievement test scores of these students in responsible ways is crucial to creating awareness for legislators and policymakers about the urgent needs of these three groups of students.

What Is Known about Students at Risk?

According to Lomax, West, Harmon, Viator, and Madaus (1995), an original reason for mandated standardized achievement testing was to identify the disparities in education for students at risk and to close the gap. As a nation, we should be identifying those students most in need of remedial education and provide them the necessary instruction to help them succeed in school. This is especially urgent, since these students are most likely to fail high-stakes tests. Denial of high school diplomas for students at risk will have very negative consequences for them in their postschool lives.

Unfortunately, such standardized achievement testing exposes a significant problem in education without helping the nation close the gap between students at risk and the rest of the students. Lomax and colleagues (1995) believe that students at risk suffer more from standardized achievement testing than other students. Indeed, other researchers have hypothesized that students from these at-risk populations may have language, social, and cultural differences that contribute to their malaise. Lomax and associates found that teachers in their study who taught students at risk spent more time on test preparation, motivation, test-specific materials, and practice tests. In other words, these students did not receive a high-quality education. A study reported by Herman and Golan (1993) of elementary school teachers showed that students living in poverty are most likely to receive inappropriate test preparation, which many teachers equate to poor teaching. Another report (CRESST, 2000) repeated this chronic finding about students from at-risk populations. These researchers also reported that students not considered to be at risk tended to perform more poorly than expected when joined with students who are at risk. Thus, a context effect seems to exist, fueling the idea that attending a school with a mixture of students at risk and students not at risk puts the latter group at risk as well.

Several important studies and essays have voiced a common theme of the large test score gap that exists between these three at-risk groups of students and everyone else (Bemiller, 1993; Good & Brophy, 1987; Goodlad, 1984; McGill-Franzen & Allington, 1993; Oakes, 1992). Without any reservation, the difference between at-risk groups and other students is large. These students need better educational programs to make up the differences that exist between them and other students.

An important point made by Bemiller (1993) is that students from at-risk populations are less likely to be identified and placed in high-ability groups where instruction is regarded as most progressive or of highest quality. Thus, not only are these low-achieving students not doing well in school but also their opportunities seem to limited. Bemiller also reviewed and cited research about the common misconception that "all children can learn." He stated, "When we confront teachers and school systems with expectations that all children should be performing at or above age-normed 'grade levels,' we ensure 'failure' for a significant proportion of children or teachers" (1993, p. 9).

Children from at-risk populations are so disadvantaged that they are unable to perform the complex tasks that modern achievement testing requires. The consequences of asking these children to do what they cannot do is abject failure. The cycle of not learning lessons presented in class compounds in future lessons, resulting in a virtual halt in learning. Toward the goal of helping these children, any educational intervention should require mastery of basic knowledge and skills in a sequential fashion before students move on to the complex tasks required in state content standards, usually in writing and mathematics. Thus, an implication of this instruction for students at risk is a nongraded environment where mastery is the preferred method of teaching.

Who Are These Students at Risk?

At-risk students often fall into more than one of the three categories of disabled, poor, and limited English proficient. However, making distinctions among the three populations is useful because each population has a significant profile of educational disadvantage with a rich history of what might work and not work. Each of these three populations has very low standardized achievement scores (National Center for Educational Statistics, 2000). Any report from the school, school district, state, or nation will show this to be true. In many instances, these scores truly reflect low achievement, and in some special circumstances, the low scores reflect a bias that is working against reporting the true status of these populations.

The U.S. government uses four factors to identify children at risk: (1) mother with less than a high school education, (2) living with a family using food stamps or receiving cash welfare payments, (3) living in a single-parent household, and (4) having parents whose primary language is not English (National Center for Educational Statistics, 2000). Added to this list should be students with disabilities, because they have the same low achievement that these other students do, and students living in cultural isolation, such as a Native American reservation or a racial or ethnic enclave (barrio, ghetto, 'hood).

What about Race and Ethnicity?

There is a marked and indisputable disparity between students classified as "white" and three other racial/ethnic groups—Native Americans, African Americans, and Hispanics/Latinos—on virtually all cognitive tests administered in the United States in the English language for as far back in history as tests have been given. The cause of this gap has been widely discussed (Herrnstein & Murray, 1994; Jensen, 1969, 1980) and widely debated by sociologists, educators, psychologists, and others. The issue is complex. The nation should never sidestep the responsibility to close any gaps among groups of students by providing equitable opportunities to learn. Educational intervention is required to improve learning of low-performing students, regardless of their race or ethnicity. Table 9.1 uses college admission test data to illustrate the size of the differences among various groups of students.

The differences between all groups listed in Table 9.1 and Caucasian American/White are quite large, given that the standard deviation of the ACT assessment is 4.0 and the standard deviation of the SAT1 is 100. What Table 9.1 does not tell you is the family income level of these students. Another report using NAEP data gives a similar profile (http://www.whitehouse.gov/WH/New/html/edprogress_report.html). Students

TABLE 9.1   *ACT Assessment and SAT1 Scores*

Group	ACT	SATV-SATM
Low family income	19.1	459–469
American Indian/Alaskan Native	19.0	482–481
Mexican American/Hispanic/Latino	18.6	453–460
Caucasian American/White	21.8	528–530
African American	17.0	434–426

Source: Adapted from National Center for Fair and Open Testing (Fall 2000b).

living in poverty cut across all racial and ethnic groups and are more distinctly defined as students at risk.

Race and ethnicity are social constructions. True race and true ethnicity are hard to establish scientifically. Moreover, terms such as *people of color* are so misleading that they defy clear definition. The few racial and ethnic classifications that tend to be used (African American, Hispanic/Latino, Native American) do not conveniently fit all people. Racial and ethnic identities are becoming more blurred as students are increasingly unsure about in which group they belong. Stereotyping and racial profiling are unfortunate and unfair characterizations of groups of people who vary considerably in all human characteristics. Despite the gap between racial/ethnic groups of students shown in Table 9.1, there are incredibly gifted people from all racial and ethnic categories.

The emphasis in this chapter is placed on students who clearly fall into categories that place them at risk regarding receiving a good elementary and secondary education. Students with mental, physical, and emotional disabilities are an at-risk group that performs well below national averages, and these students come from all racial, gender, and ethnic categories. There is little doubt that students living in poverty, regardless of race or ethnicity, are very likely to have low achievement records and lack many opportunities that other children have. There is little doubt that students with LEP face the same plight that students face who live in poverty. These LEP students may be mostly Hispanic, but their national origins also include Africa, South America, Europe, and eastern Asia. Moreover, many LEP students also live in poverty, thus compounding their problem. In all cases, these three groups of students are classified equally, without regard for race or ethnicity. Attention directed to the three groups discussed in this chapter are more inclusive than social agendas that focus on a single ethnic or racial group at the expense of all other students who are at risk of not receiving an adequate education.

The Unique Problem of Teaching and Testing Native American and Native Alaskan Students

Given the previous discussion about inclusiveness in dealing with students at risk, the Americas have a native population that is uniquely different from all other populations. Their achievement records in public schools in the United States is persistently and troublingly low. Toward the goal of providing equal opportunity to this native population of students, many important testing issues arise that need attention.

There are about two million Native American students in the United States, mostly living in Alaska, Arizona, and California in 550 recognized tribes speaking about 250 native languages. Thus, the problems reported here are similar to those of LEP students, one of the featured groups of at-risk students in this chapter. However, the problems encountered by Native Americans are more profound than those witnessed with LEP students. Many of these Native American students live in poverty.

One easily recognizable distinction is that Native American students either live on a reservation or are integrated into U.S. society. The price of isolation from a mainstream culture or a world culture is well documented by Thomas Sowell (1994). Societies that live in isolation from other societies tend not to develop at the same rate as culturally diverse societies. The problem with education and testing is: By whose culture does one impose curricula and measures of student learning? In Native American societies, elders assume the responsibility of educating youth and providing standards. In mainstream America, the responsibility for educating and providing standards is more diffuse.

A very thoughtful analysis about this problem of educating and testing Native Americans comes from Estrin and Nelson-Barber (1995). The summary presented here does not do justice to the complexity of this problem. Today, Native Americans are mostly taught at public schools, but federally supported reservation schools have existed for quite a long time. These schools are almost nonexistent now, but nonetheless, reservation schools do exist that consist mostly of Native Americans. Modern curricula and mandated achievement tests are very foreign to most Native Americans. Social studies education generally links students to their cultures, but typical U.S. curricula seldom contain such linkages to Native American culture.

Estrin and Nelson-Barber (1995) argued that a sociocultural perspective to the problem is needed, and this perspective will include cognitive learning theory, an understanding of Native American cultures, and effective and appropriate instruction. They argued that Native American culture is devalued in modern U.S. curricula and instruction, and, of course, tests. Standardized achievement testing seems patently wrong to teachers of Native American students (Haas, Haladyna, & Nolen, 1990). Score reports do not do justice to these students or provide meaningful information to help teachers teach these students more effectively. When using current U.S. standards as a benchmark for this population, the attention given to these students in public education deservedly should be on what kind of education is provided for any and each of these at-risk student populations. Higher-quality educational programs are needed to bring about higher achievement for Native American students.

Practically speaking, what can we teachers do with Native American students who require not only appropriate instruction but also testing accommodations and modifications? Making the transition from one set of cognitive tools in a native society to the larger inclusive modern American society requires changes in instruction and testing. Estrin and Nelson-Barber (1995) have argued for adaptive testing that allows students more opportunities to express their answers orally or in writing, as opposed to multiple-choice test formats. These students certainly seem well suited for significant testing accommodations and modifications both on standardized achievement tests and classroom assessments.

Low scores often earned by Native American students might be interpreted as the degree to which they have made the transition to this other culture instead of a prediction of their academic potential. Estrin and Nelson-Barber (1995) have offered the following specific advice for testing this special population, with the proviso that appropriate instructional changes have been made. (Their excellent recommendations may apply equally to any and all students.)

- Link assessments to instruction. Avoid tests that are not geared to instruction. (In other words, do not use standardized achievement tests unless they are curriculum relevant.)

- Embed assessment in instruction.
- Tailor the content of assessment to the student's cultural experiences.
- Use open-ended test formats so students can orally answer.
- Allow for sufficient time to respond.
- Allow for reflection and deliberation.
- Give students choices of assessments.
- Allow for cooperative assessments.
- Minimize the influence of language in the assessment, as many students lack language proficiency. Another strategy is to simplify language in tests or read the items aloud.
- Prepare students for the standardized test experience by telling them the purpose of the test and the meaning of the scores.
- Validate the value of the student's culture in learning and testing.
- Document the context for the assessment. In some circumstances, you may want to invalidate test scores.

Students with Disabilities

Approximately 11 percent of all elementary and secondary school students have disabilities that include a multitude of conditions, including autism, mental retardation, specific learning disabilities, emotional disturbances, traumatic brain injury, speech or language impairment (e.g., stuttering), visual impairment, deafness and other hearing impairments, orthopedic impairments, developmental delay, deaf-blindness, other health impairments (e.g., allergy, asthma, diabetes, epilepsy, heart conditions, hemophilia, leukemia, rheumatic fever, sickle cell anemia), and multiple disabilities (Salvia & Ysseldyke, 2001).

Perhaps the most common student disability is attention deficit disorder, or ADD. According to a report from the National Institutes of Health (1998), about 3 to 5 percent of children have ADD. They are characterized by low attention and concentration, distractability, hyperactivity, and impulsivity. Although there is still more to be learned about the profound effects this disorder has on children, it can be diagnosed and treated.

Regardless of the disorder, students with disabilities are at risk in many ways: (1) diagnosis of a disability may be incorrect or not made (e.g., diagnosing ADD is mainly behavioral and usually flawed, but recent research points to better diagnosis using electrocenphalography [Sterman, 2000]); (2) a disability often impairs learning and therefore students with disabilities are at risk of not achieving adequately; (3) a disability often prevents students from obtaining equitable and effective education; and (4) when tested, these students' scores typically are underestimates of their true achievement.

Federal laws now provide a legal basis for teaching and testing these students—for example, the *Americans with Disabilities Act (ADA),* passed in 1990; the *Improving America's Schools Act (IASA),* passed in 1994; and the *Individuals with Disabilities in Education Act (IDEA)* passed in 1997. The sum of these three acts forces the issue about students with disabilities.

Emerging from this legislation is a general principle governing the testing of students with disabilities: All students are entitled to equal opportunities to learn. Inclusion is an important principle in modern education. Many states and the federal government expect students with disabilities to be adequately instructed and appropriately tested. However, most testing programs and the federal government recognize that about 1 to 2 percent of the population is so profoundly disabled that standardized achievement testing is not warranted, so exemptions are granted and alternative assessments are required.

In some circumstances, school officials have resorted to shameful practices, such as excluding students with disabilities because they tend to score lower than average on standardized achievement tests. By excluding these students, school district or school averages will be higher, suggesting to the public that the district or school is more successful. This is one of many sources of test score pollution discussed in Chapter 7.

By law, every student with a disability has an individual education plan (IEP) and a team that makes and implements this plan and monitors student progress. The team may request that accommodations or modifications be made in the test or they may request an exemption. However, IASA and IDEA require that some form of assessment be used to document exempted students' educational progress. The following sections describe the test choices you have.

Accommodation

Accommodations are allowable changes of the test format or administration conditions where the resulting test scores are interpreted as if no accommodation were present. In other words, the accommodation eliminates the influence of a disability without altering what is being measured. The finding of equivalency is established empirically, through research. Figure 9.1 shows typical types of accommodations.

Out-of-Level Testing

A major type of testing accommodation is to administer a test at a grade level well below that of the student. This action is consistent with the idea that each student should take a test at a level where the student actually functions. Many students with disabilities perform well below grade level. Thus, the administration of a test below grade level provides a more accurate description of achievement than a grade-level test. This accommodation can be justified and is consistent with IDEA guidelines.

Modification

A test modification is any change to the test format or administration conditions that has not been empirically proven to be equivalent to the unmodified format or administration conditions. Another test modification is when the interpretation is different. The goal within any assessment system is to eliminate modifications for students and provide accommodations, or, even better, to eliminate the need for accommodations. But with some students, modifications are necessary. For example, a student with a severe read-

FIGURE 9.1   *Types of Accommodations Typically Offered to Students with Disabilities*

- *Modifying Timing*   Extend the time limit. Follow a flexible administration schedule. Give the test in several shorter sessions. Give the test over several days. Allow frequent breaks.

- *Personal Assistance*   Use sign language. Repeat directions. Have student demonstrate understanding of directions. Use both oral and written directions. Allow student to answer orally. Cue the student to remain on task. Read or have computer read aloud the test items. Check to see that the student is marking correctly. Provide physical assistance. Clarify the items. Simplify the language in the directions. Provide cues when to start and stop.

- *Presentation Changes*   Use braille or large-print versions of the test. Use sign language. Use enlarged answer sheets. Provide written steps for directions. Highlight key words or phrases in directions. Mask portions of the test to direct the student's attention. Administer individually.

- *Environmental Changes*   Allow the use of a study carrel. Test in a separate room. Increase or decrease opportunity for movement. Reduce stimuli in the testing area. Use preferential seating. Secure papers to the work area with tape or magnets. Provide special lighting. Provide special furniture.

- *Response Format Changes*   Allow the student to mark in the answer booklet, point to responses, answer orally, or answer on audiotape. Provide a word processor. Provide auditory amplification. Allow chubby or thin pencils, long pencils, different positions of paper or test-taking positions, colored stickers for visual cues, acetate color to reduce glare and increase contrast.

- *Assistive Devices*   Allow any assistive technology currently being used, including augmenting communication (e.g., letter boards, voice systems), assistive listening devices, magnifier, large-print or braille materials, mounting systems (e.g., slant boards), and calculators.

---

ing problem or visual impairment might have a reading passage read to him or her before answering reading comprehension items.

Exemption

Exemptions are instances when a student does not take the standardized achievement test. Exemptions are granted through a waiver process in which it is established that a validly interpreted test result is not possible due to a disabling condition that is judged to be severe. The disabling conditions may be mental, physical, or emotional. Another class of disabling conditions includes lack of facility in the English language and the second language is not accommodated. For example, as a temporary means until the child makes a transition to English, some states provide side-by-side (English and Spanish) versions of a test or translated versions to accommodate the measurement of achievement in a child's native language. The objective over time is to remove the reason for the exemption so that all students can be assessed fairly. The IDEA requires that these students be assessed by some alternative means that is linked to the content standards.

Appeal

An appeal is an instance where a score received can be challenged on the grounds that a proper accommodation or modification was not granted. Appeals also may involve a situation in which an exemption via a waiver should have been granted. As you can see from this partial list of accommodations, any change in testing can be very significant or very minor. All accommodations are designed to meet a serious student deficiency, and the modification is supposed to remove the factor that prevents the student from performing adequately.

More important, all students with disabilities need special education. It is important to note that these accommodations and modifications should also be present in daily schooling and classroom assessments. The student's IEP should be specific about the special needs in teaching and testing. Test scores simply show how successful we educators are with this special population. The test scores of students with disabilities highlight the need to improve instructional programs and services to the extent that these children improve. The ultimate goal of special education is to have these students function in society to the extent possible.

Guidelines for Testing Students with Disabilities

Throughout this book, reference has been made to the professional standards (American Educational Research Association, American Psychological Association, & National Council on Measurement in Education, 1999) for testing. These standards dedicate an entire chapter to testing students with disabilities. Although the standards are intended for testing specialists, they have practical value to teachers and other educators. Some of these standards include:

- The achievement domain being measured is not altered by any test accommodation. The intent is to remove the influence of the disability on the student's measure of knowledge and skills or ability being measured.
- The IEP team recommending the accommodation should be qualified by training and experience and familiarity with the student.
- If at all possible, the basis for making an accommodation should be prior research or experience with similar disabilities.
- Scores should be reported in context of the disability and any accommodation or modification.

In the case of a test modification, that which is being measured is being altered. This is a more significant change in the testing, but, again, the IEP committee is best suited to select the modification and interpret its meaning in light the student's prior learning history.

Getting a Student's Test Accommodated or Modified

Testing sponsors expect a procedure to be followed to accommodate a test. This procedure normally involves the student's IEP team, including the classroom teacher, who is central in activating this request for an accommodation. Documentation is a key factor. These steps include:

- State the disability.
- Make the accommodation request current, based on the child's condition over the past three years.
- Provide relevant educational, developmental, and medical history.
- Describe the testing done to arrive at a diagnosis for the disability.
- Describe the functional limitation of the disability.
- Describe the accommodation requested, using the list of approved accommodations provided by the test sponsor.
- Establish the credentials of the evaluator.

As you can see, accommodations and modifications are serious business. The best interests of the student are the main concern. The IEP team is best suited to develop this petition for accommodation, modification, or exemption, and the petition may have to be reinstated periodically to stay current.

Reporting and Interpreting Test Scores of Students with Disabilities

A common theme in this chapter and in Chapter 3 is that the public, policymakers, legislators, educators, and others are best served when a set of achievement scores from a large group is disaggregated into meaningful subgroups. Therefore, it is critical to provide the most accurate description of each student's achievement. When testing conditions include accommodation or when tests are modified, the test result is usually flagged and is best interpreted by the IEP team, since the team members have the context and understanding of the student's level of learning. Flagging of scores might stigmatize the student, so if the accommodation or modification is well documented and considered valid, then flagging should not be done.

Exemptions present another problem. According to a study by Rivera and Stansfield (2000), states vary considerably in their inclusion and exemption policies. Thus, state-to-state comparisons, which in Chapter 3 were argued to be invalid, are further justified as invalid, simply because not all states exclude students with severe disabilities to the same extent. Because states differ in their exemption policies, the validity of interpretations of students with disabilities must also differ. One solution is for all states to have the same policy about excluding students with disabilities.

Students Living in Poverty

Poverty has a pervasive effect on all elements of life, and achievement testing is no exception. According to a report from the National Center for Educational Statistics (1996), 21.2 percent of U.S. children live in poverty. Most of these children (55 percent) have single parents. A report by the Educational Research Council (National Center for

Fair and Open Testing, Fall 1994) showed that 89 percent of the variation in state average NAEP scores were explained by poverty. This figure, 89 percent, is equivalent to a correlation of .94 (see Chapter 2). Virtually every cognitive test shows results like those given in Table 9.2. For the ACT Assessment, the pattern is unmistakably strong in its association with family income.

The official government designation for students living in poverty involves eligibility for the free-lunch program. Families with school-age children below the poverty line so qualify. These children form a statistical category that is useful for studying the achievement of children living in poverty. The government also has another system of rating the poverty of people in the United States: a complex statistical model that includes education, income, and occupation. This model, which identifies low income as the lowest 25 percent of the population, is also useful for studying children living in poverty.

Quite a bit is known about students living in poverty (Rothstein, 2001). Because of poverty, they often lack basic life necessities, such as shelter and proper nutrition. This group includes homeless children and those with itinerant lifestyles. Poor children learn less outside of school than more affluent students, because the latter group has many opportunities for culturally enriching activities, such as movies, vacations, camps, plays, tutoring, child care, preschool, fairs, museums, and much more. The quality of instruction is generally poor in schools in poverty-ridden areas. Teachers are often eager to leave such areas, and the very best teachers can easily and will gladly make this kind of move. The high-stakes, higher-standards movement tends to push these students out of school or create the expectation that they are not good enough for society.

A research report by Terenzini, Cabrera, and Bernal (2001) shows that college students and graduates are unlikely to come from poverty. Those college students who

TABLE 9.2   *Family Income and ACT Scores*

Family Income	Average ACT
Less than $18,000	18.3
$18,000 to $24,000	19.1
$24,000 to $30,000	19.8
$30,000 to $36,000	20.4
$36,000 to $42,000	20.7
$42,000 to $50,000	21.1
$50,000 to $60,000	21.6
$60,000 to $80,000	22.1
$80,000 to $100,000	22.6
More than $100,000	23.4

do come from poverty are less likely to enroll in college, bring fewer academic credentials and qualifications into the college experience, are more susceptible to problems of financing college, are more likely to enroll in a community college, have a high risk of failure in college, and are less likely to attend college immediately after high school graduation. Once students from poverty are in college, they are less involved in extra-curricular activities, are more likely to work off campus (jeopardizing their achievement), are more likely to be debt ridden from college expenses, and are less likely to complete college (Singh & Ozturk, 2000). Students not completing college are less like to be employed 12 years later, earn less than college graduates, and are less likely to earn a professional degree. Thus, the few students from poverty who are actually qualified to go to college have many barriers to overcome to achieve what middle- and upper-class students commonly take for granted.

Poverty and Disabilities

A disturbing growing trend is that the percent of students with disabilities has been increasing. Between 1970 and 1994, the number rose from 11.7 percent to 14.4 percent (Fujiura & Kiyoshi, 2000). During the same time, poverty rates among adults remained stable, but the number of children living in poverty tripled between 1974 and 1994 from 5.2 percent to 16 percent. Those students living in poverty are more likely to have disabilities. In 1995, 42 percent of students living in poverty were identified as having one or more disabilities, as compared with 13 percent in the general population. Factors that may contribute to this sorry state of affairs are low birth weight, asthma, chronic illness, environmental trauma, and drug or alcohol problems.

Testing Students Living in Poverty

If you have constructed a model like the one in Chapter 1, you are likely to see poor children in a context of causes and effects that explain their low scores. Rather than focus on the teacher as the main problem that causes these students' low scores, the problem in educating children living in poverty calls for a concerted effort from the school, social agencies, and the often fragmented family of these students. The contrast in social conditions in nonpoverty areas is obvious. Students living in poverty should be considered as students living with a disability.

Students in poverty-stricken areas often attend schools that provide not only education but also social services. These might include breakfast programs, lunch programs, after-school recreation, clothing, and medical and health services. Domestic abuse and violence, drug and alcohol addiction, crime, and other social problems are more prevalent. The school serves more as a community center and home.

Evaluation of the educational success with this special population should not be limited to test scores alone, which are typically very low. In most circumstances, simply getting students to school is an achievement. Mobility rates also tend to be high among those living in poverty.

An important subpopulation of those living in poverty are the homeless. This increasing population includes children who do not necessarily have a regular school experience and suffer from serious emotional complications due to their poverty and homelessness. The added burdens with this subpopulation makes their education even more challenging than those living in poverty who have a home.

When standardized achievement tests are given, it is very important to keep in mind that these tests should help students learn. It is important to know how students living in poverty are doing educationally and what disabilities they suffer and what resources are needed to help them learn. Simply lumping these students with other students obscures the needs of this special population. Policymakers and the public should not use state-to-state or district-to-district comparisons when poverty is involved, because this factor undermines any effort to evaluate how a specific state or school district is doing. Since poverty is pervasive (ranging between 20 and 30 percent) in states, and with a disproportionate number of children living in poverty due to fragmented families, poverty, it can be argued, is a significant cause of underachievement in school.

Disaggregated Reporting

As discussed earlier regarding testing special education students, reporting of test results must be done separately for children living in poverty. Because poverty is a pernicious social condition, reporting the status of these students as a group calls attention to their urgent need and provides accurate and fair reporting of how schools are doing with respect to helping this troubled group of students. Legislators and school boards have a responsibility to provide equal opportunities for students. Clearly, this group needs higher-quality education to realize their potential. Standardized achievement testing provides a dependable indicator of the seriousness of the problem of students living in poverty.

Students with Limited English Proficiency (LEP)

Limited English proficiency (LEP) is an official government term that represents a concept used to identify students whose language background is not English. Usually, these students are immigrants to the United States, but some students born in the United States also qualify due to the setting in which they live, such as a barrio, ghetto, reservation, or other social/ethnic/racial enclave. Other terms used to described students whose native language is not English are *English as a second language (ESL)* and *English language learner (ELL)*. In this section, the term *LEP* will be used consistently. Another term you might see in literature relating to LEP students is *language minority*. One of the best sources of information about LEP education is the website of the Office of Bilingual Education and Minority Language Affairs (http://www.ed.gov/offices/ OBEMLA/).

The Bilingual Education Act, reauthorized in 1988 as Public Law 100-297 defines LEP students as (1) those born outside the United States whose native language is not English, (2) those coming from an environment or home where English is not the spoken language, or (3) those who are Native American or Alaska Native and who have a significant English language disability.

A distinction that affects testing of LEP students is the native language. Some languages are related to English (e.g., French, Italian, and Spanish) and others have less connection to English. Another distinction is that some LEP students live in a bilingual environment where one of the languages is English, or students may be immigrants, forced to learn English to survive in their new country. The teaching and learning of English and performance on achievement tests may be compounded by the types of LEP students you have.

Limited English proficient students are a fairly large and growing population, representing 14 percent of the K–12 school population (Abedi & Hofstetter, undated conference paper). California represents one of the largest states in terms of LEP student population, where about 50 percent speak a language in the home other than English. Most of these children are Spanish speakers (73 percent) but the balance speak a variety of Asian, African, and European languages. In fact, the diversity of languages spoken in some U.S. homes is flabbergasting (see Figure 9.2 for a sample from a single state). As a result, any tests administered in English involve translation for these students.

Many of concepts and principles about testing and assessment that apply to students with disabilities also apply to LEP students. Therefore, it is important to discuss accommodations and modifications to tests for LEP students.

Accommodations for LEP Students: Methods and Research

You learned in Chapter 7 that standardized achievement tests can underestimate a student's achievement if the student is not English proficient. Thus, accommodations should be provided to this population to ensure that the estimate of achievement is as accurate as possible. The accommodations that are offered to LEP students derive from

FIGURE 9.2 *Oregon's Linguistic Communities (1997–98)*

Spanish	Serbo-Croatian	Pashtu
Russian	Mandarin	Haitian
Vietnamese	Hindi	Fijan
Cantonese	French	Dari
Korean	Tingrinya	Burmese
Hmong	Portugese	Armenian
Cambodian	Creole	Farsi
Lao	Navajo	Thai
Japanese	Somalian	Nepalese
Mien	Punjabi	Mixteca
Tagalog	Finnish	Gugarati
Romanian	Maldavian	Liberian
Ukaranian	Norwegian	Dutch
Arabic	Czech	Chau Chu
Marshallese	Siouan	Albanian

Source: Haladyna (2001).

the accommodations offered to students with disabilities. Rivera and Stansfield (2000) characterized these accommodations as falling into four categories: (1) presentation, (2) response, (3) setting, and (4) timing and scheduling. However, these authors contended that the most offered accommodations from these categories fail to deal with linguistic deficiencies of these students.

To make valid interpretations for an achievement test, for instance, reading comprehension requires a test where the student reads a passage and selects the answers for reading comprehension test items. One action is to translate a test. But a translation is not necessarily successful. Also, offering a translation for one language might unfairly limit other LEP students who do not get a translated test. Most reading comprehension tests have a context or scenario drawn from American life. Many LEP students may not have this context; the test stimuli are therefore very foreign to them. Oregon has experimented with tests where test items are presented in two languages (called *side-by-side* testing). Thus, a native Spanish speaker can answer the item using the English or the Spanish version of the test. This is one promising direction for helping LEP students take tests.

Another accommodation is language simplification, where the vocabulary in the test is simplified so LEP students can translate better in their new language. Abedi, Lord, Hofstetter, and Baker (2000) have launched a very important programmatic study of language simplification for standardized testing that has great promise. They experimented with various accommodations with LEP students, such as (1) simplified English language on the test, (2) a glossary explaining the most difficult terms on the test, (3) extra time, and (4) glossary plus extra time. On a 35-item NAEP test, LEP students were helped by most of these accommodations, glossary only being the exception. In another study, glossary and extra time proved to be the most effective accommodation. Research by Abedi and colleagues shows that the issue of language simplification and these other accommodations is complexly related to other variables. Their research also confirms that these accommodations are much needed. Ironically, their research indicates that *all* students can benefit from these accommodations.

Research has shown that there are many reasons why test scores from LEP students may be invalidly interpreted due to underestimation:

1. If the test is timed, the student may not have enough time to finish the test, because the thought processes for translation require extra time.
2. The English reading comprehension level of the test may be too difficult, so the test becomes a measure of English reading comprehension instead of a measure of achievement.
3. The educational program of a transplanted student is not likely to be very strong, resulting in lower achievement and lower test scores.
4. The teaching quality may be inferior, especially if a bilingual teacher is needed.
5. If teaching is done in English and the student's English language proficiency is not good, not only is the child failing to learn English but he or she also is not keeping up in other areas of study.
6. If these students attend schools in school districts with limited services (e.g., poverty-stricken areas), they are less likely to receive the special attention that more affluent school districts provide. Underfunded schools tend to have underfunded programs for the neediest children.

7. If these students live in social or cultural isolation, they are likely to under-achieve.

Using a variety of conditions, Garcia (1991) analyzed the reading comprehension of 51 Hispanic and 53 Anglo students in fifth- and sixth-grade classrooms. She concluded that the Hispanic students were affected by limited knowledge of topics tested, implicit questions that required background knowledge, unfamiliarity with vocabulary, and literal interpretation. Giving the Hispanic students more time did not close the gap between the two groups of students. Garcia evaluated students' reading comprehension during interviews and concluded that they provided more information about the test passage than when tested formally. Since virtually all achievement tests require some degree of reading comprehension, Garcia argues that students with LEP underperform on formal reading comprehension tests and that new approaches are needed that better grapple with the LEP students' reading comprehension.

Fitzgerald (1995) produced one of the largest and most comprehensive reviews of research on LEP students. She drew some important conclusions, one of which was that LEP students learn to read English very much like native English speakers learn to read, but Fitzgerald did warn that teachers need to be patient with LEP students, because these students are slow readers who are less likely to react or respond in class settings. Also, teachers and test makers need to word questions carefully and provide sufficient background knowledge for students to respond, particularly when the background knowledge may include a cultural setting unfamiliar to the immigrant LEP student.

A new field of study is cross-language testing such as that seen with the international testing discussed in Chapter 5 and that is beginning to evolve with LEP student testing. The methods used to link tests given in different languages provide many challenges, and very little is known about how to do this (Sireci, 1997). Thus, it is not safe to assume that cross-language testing is the answer to properly assessing LEP student achievement.

The problem of testing LEP students is part of a larger problem. English language teaching is a hotly contested topic that not only involves pedagogy but also social and political issues. To understand the educational achievement of LEP students, one must put them in a context of federal, state, and school district policies, resources, and programs. Any test score is only a crude estimate of achievement and must be evaluated in terms of threats to valid interpretation.

State Policies and the Testing of LEP Students

According to a study by Rivera and Stansfield (2000), almost all states have testing policies governing the testing of LEP students, but the policies vary greatly and provide little specific guidance to school districts. Since the United States has consistently had a large immigrant population, the testing of students whose English is limited creates problems that are seldom solved. For instance, inconsistent testing policies within a state or school district can distort scores significantly, as a recent CRESST (2000) report indicated. Who is tested governs the class or school or school district mean. In this age of accountability via test scores, the more LEP students excluded, the better the school (the district, the state, the class) looks.

The lack of uniformity across the United States causes students most in need of special education not to be well served when it comes to standardized achievement testing. Abedi and colleagues (2000) reported that about 55 percent of the states provide accommodation for LEP students, even though federal laws state that all children should be given educational experiences to meet standards and fair assessments of their achievement. Given the new accommodation methods and recent research on language accommodations, states have a long way to go to provide fair assessments to LEP students.

Interpreting and Reporting Scores of Students from At-Risk Populations

This section discusses several interrelated issues and principles that address the problem of interpreting test scores of students from any of these three intermingled populations. If assessments of student learning should guide teachers in teaching better, what can guide teachers in better assessments with these students?

The most important step to take in understanding why a student is not learning adequately is to know the context surrounding each student's performance. Chapter 1 provided ideas about the ideal outcomes of schooling and the external and internal causes of student learning. The general causal model presented in Chapter 1 expresses the belief that there are many desired outcomes of schooling. These causes are either internal or external to schools. The reporting of test scores in a "naked" version in the newspaper or in other reports does a disservice to noneducators because the explanatory nature of reporting test scores is missing. As a result, noneducators are prone to develop their own working causal models, the most simplistic being:

Cause	*Effect*
Teacher	Test score

This model is flawed for many reasons (discussed in Chapter 1).

Another model is the one generally specified in Chapter 1. In this model, the contributions of internal and external causes of student learning are acknowledged. One might adopt a test based on a state's content standards, which still falls short of specifying a complete model of outcomes, but is often better than a publisher's standardized achievement test, which is unlikely to be correlated to the content standards.

Internal Causes	*External Causes*	*Outcomes*
Quality and quantity of instruction School leadership	Intelligence Social capital	Knowledge and skills Fluid abilities

This causal model is excellent for understanding that the reasons for poor performance may be due to disabilities, low social capital, and language proficiency. Educators need valid information to diagnose a learning difficulty. For students with disabilities, there are special education and federal laws supporting educators in providing the student with an individual education plan. For students in poverty, there might be special programs that in some way enrich or compensate these students for the deficits provided outside of school. For students with LEP, more effective instruction and fairer assessments are needed.

Disaggregated Reporting

All three populations discussed in this chapter should have their test scores reported according to membership in their group. Sometimes, these reports might include ethnicity, LEP, migrant status, and disabled versus nondisabled. All of these reporting categories in some way share this concern for telling the truth about the groups of students who are most at risk of not receiving an adequate education or of meeting a state's or school district's standards for success: promotion and eventually high school graduation. Disaggregated reporting tells the truth about how schools are doing and informs the public about the progress being made with one of the three major at-risk groups of students in the United States at the class, school, school district, and state levels.

Report Cards

The report card is a reporting device that shows the number of students in basic reporting categories for a specific subject matter widely used in schools, school districts, and states. These report cards can show a reporting unit's status for a specific year. Growth over several years can be monitored to see if the students in the reporting unit are making satisfactory gains in the subject matters tested, usually reading, writing, and mathematics (see Figure 9.3).

These contextualized reports recognize the role that socioeconomic status plays in score reports and permits school districts to measure student progress against themselves instead of against each other. But at the same time, normative information is available so that schools and school districts can compare themselves to similar schools or to the state's average. Over several years of monitoring student achievement, it is possible to note the degree of change. Thus, schools and their personnel truly have a yardstick to measure student progress.

Summary

This chapter has discussed the testing problems associated with students with disabilities, students living in poverty, and students with LEP. The argument was made that these students are at risk because they typically have low achievement. Unless there is significant intervention, their chances for finishing their education and obtaining gainful employment and a sense of empowerment in society are extremely small. Standard-

FIGURE 9.3   Example of a State Report Card Providing Contextual Information: Mathematics Problem Solving

School District	County	Percent Meeting Performance Standards				Students Tested		
		D	C	M	E	SES	Rank	N%
05 **State Total**		**36**	**7**	**55**	**2**	**1–734**	**40185**	**93%**
05 Brooklyn	Baker SD 5J	44	11	40	5	336	57	86%
05 Haines	Baker SD 5J	64	0	36	0	302	11	100%
05 North Baker	Baker SD 5J	23	8	67	2	460	60	95%
05 South Baker	Baker SD 5J	29	3	63	6	271	35	76%
05 Fairplay	Corvallis SD 509J	21	3	69	7	476	29	97%
05 Franklin	Corvallis SD 509J	15	15	70	0	710	27	96%
05 Garfield	Corvallis SD 509J	22	9	67	2	355	58	87%
05 Harding	Corvallis SD 509J	35	7	56	2	626	57	100%
05 Hoover	Corvallis SD 509J	14	4	76	6	697	49	91%

D = does not meet the standard; C = close to the standard; M = meets or exceeds the standard; E = greatly exceeds the standard. SES = socioeconomic status; N% = percentage of students tested. A low percentage would alert concern as to why so many students were excluded.

Source: Reprinted in part from webpage (http://www.ode.state.or.us/asmt/results/2000/download.htm).

ized achievement testing is not necessarily an evil with these students. However, this testing should be used in ways that help educators and noneducators understand the students' problems and deal more effectively with their lack of progress.

Accommodations, modifications, and exemptions help students through difficult times, but none of these is a safeguard that will ensure better performance through significant student learning. Disaggregated reporting pinpoints specific learning problems and helps schools and their personnel better plan instructional programs that will help these students. Also, the unwarranted attack on teachers and education under the ruse of accountability is somewhat dampened by responsible reporting that shows which students are learning adequately and which are not. Standardized achievement testing should help teachers better pinpoint the learning difficulties of these at-risk populations and plan better instruction.

10

How Can Standardized Achievement Test Results Help Students Learn?

A guiding tenet in this book has been that standardized achievement test scores should help students learn. This last chapter reviews basic concepts and principles governing the valid interpreting and using of standardized achievement test scores. Each section of this chapter address a question regarding how standardized achievement test results can and should help students learn. These questions are:

- Why do we have standardized achievement tests?
- What context do we have for interpreting and using standardized achievement test scores?
- How can we make student assessment work?
- How do we assess the validity of interpretations and uses of test scores?
- How should we sensibly and ethically prepare students for these tests?
- How do we lower test anxiety?
- What about test-based accountability and high stakes testing?

Why Do We Have Standardized Achievement Test Scores?

Accountability seems to be the most important reason for testing students. The public wants to know how the schools are doing, and the public has a right to know this. Elected officials representing the public respond by legally mandating a standardized achievement test policy and allocating resources to support this kind of testing. This action typically occurs at a state level but may also occur in a school district. Parents are often in support of such testing, but reports as to their motivation are not always clear cut, perhaps in part because parents do not fully understand the consequences of standardized testing.

The public also supports higher standards, thus there are initiatives in all 50 states for content standards and related testing programs. The second major use of test scores seems to be *high-stakes pass/fail decisions* affecting grade-level promotion as well as high school certification and graduation.

Another important use of test scores is to provide information to teachers, parents, and students about how well each student is learning so that this team can evaluate and plan each student's future studies. Thus, this third important use is to *help students learn.* Although educators may not fully agree with the first two uses, the majority of educators likely agree with this third use.

Chapter 3 identified many other uses of test scores, some seemingly reputable and others questionable or downright objectionable. Each and every use of a test score is subject to the same rules: logical argument and validity evidence supporting that use.

What Context Do We Have for Interpreting and Using Standardized Achievement Tests?

Chapter 1 introduced a list of student outcomes and a set of causes that exist internal and external to schooling. The proposed model is drawn from many essays and discussions by various educators interested in the "big picture" surrounding American education. The issue for all U.S. citizens is an open discussion of what outcomes are most important, what actions are best suited for achieving these outcomes, what resources the nation will provide for achieving these outcomes, and what are the positive and negative consequences of these actions. School reform is at the heart of change, but the reform should be well thought out and discussed by the broadest audience possible, not solely by a single special-interest group, such as politicians (Hall & Hord, 2001).

This model of school learning will surely pinpoint four language abilities: reading, writing, speaking, and listening. The model will also likely identify mathematical and scientific problem solving. Some model designers will appreciate critical thinking and incorporate it into their personal models. Society recognizes the value of creative abilities in the visual and performing arts, as well as creative abilities applied to all aspects of life. Nevertheless, the model grows richer as other abilities and the knowledge and skills supporting each ability are valued. The model will also identify the causes both inside and outside school that influence the development of abilities. Any discussion of student achievement should take into consideration both internal and external causes of student achievement. Context makes a difference. It is important to know the influence of intelligence and social capital on student learning, and then to know what can be done in schools to make a difference in student learning, given the conditions existing outside of school.

In short, your model for learning should answer the following questions:

What should students learn?	What factors in school are most important in determining what and how well students learn?	What factors outside of school are most important in determining what and how well students learn?

How Can We Make Student Assessment Work?

This section reviews some principles that leading educators have promoted as healthy, positive measures regarding standardized achievement testing. James Popham (1999), a highly respected testing expert and leading proponent of modern, progressive assessment reforms for more than 40 years, offered this guiding principle, which has been adopted and applied thematically throughout this book: *Standardized achievement testing can be useful only to the extent that it helps teachers plan instruction and thereby improves each child's learning.*

This statement should become a mantra for educators, parents, students, and others interested in American education. Toward the objective of making this guiding principle true, what should be done about standardized achievement testing in the United States? Testing should involve collaborative planning, be meaningful, linked to learning theory, have a developmental nature, and be multidimensional.

Collaborative Planning

Those responsible for determining if standardized achievement testing is needed and which test will be used include elected representatives of the people—namely, state legislators and school board members. By way of surveys, the public has assured these elected officials that standardized achievement testing is needed. Standardized testing is likely to have the greatest positive effect if all stakeholders are involved in the planning of the test, including parents, teachers, other educators, and other members of the public. Too often, however, the legislative assembly does the planning without consultation of those involved stakeholders. The exclusion of any group renders the assessment program less viable. Thus, collaborative planning is inclusive and shares in the process of building a consensus about what is to be tested, how the test is to be given, and how results are interpreted and used.

Meaningful Testing

Not all learning is drudgery, as the phrase *drill and practice* conveys. Yet, there is a persistent feeling among some of the public that much of learning is a form of mental exercise, as if the mind is a muscle and one has to exercise that muscle by performing meaningless learning tasks. It is important to be clear about the real outcomes of education. As Chapter 1 identified, student abilities seem to be at the heart of these outcomes. More focused attention is needed for student abilities such as reading, writing, speaking, listening, mathematical and scientific problem solving, critical thinking, and creative abilities. An obsession with knowledge and skills is misguided unless one identifies the connections of knowledge and skills to the development of these abilities. Thus, the way one applies personal knowledge and skills to meaningful encounters in one's life is what is important.

A newer approach to testing is embodied in the phrase *authentic assessment*. Although this term is often criticized, the phrase conveys that what students are learning is meaningful and valued in its own right. Consider these two performance tasks:

In two pages, prepare a plan for a field trip to the Desert Rock Museum for 33 students in this class. Make a budget. You have $600 to spend on this trip. Include in your plan the destination; transportation and food costs for everyone, including the teacher and one parent; and a schedule of activities. No spelling, grammar, or punctuation errors will be tolerated.

Contrast this with the following problem:

The student will add, subtract, multiply, and divide whole numbers.

The first exercise has the appeal of relevance to students: No plan, no trip. It is real, lifelike, and meaningful. For the second task, imagine pages and pages of addition, subtraction, multiplication, and division problems. The second exercise requires the same mathematics skills, but the first exercise requires the complex application of knowledge and skill before the student correctly adds, subtracts, multiplies, or divides.

Meaningful assessments are very difficult to create. In a writing assessment, writing experts believe that students should choose among a variety of writing prompts to best maximize their opportunities. Testing specialists warn that offering choices may accomplish what they hope but evidence suggests that offering choices introduces test score pollution because the choices offered differ in difficulty. What should you do? The choice is between eliminating test score pollution versus validly and meaningfully measuring something important. These issues are never easy to resolve.

Cognitive learning theory and the social/constructivist learning theory seem to favor teaching and testing that happen in a natural context where students see the merits of what they are learning. If your orientation is in that direction, then you will favor the kind of testing that appears to provide this meaningfulness. Generally, the kind of testing you choose will require performance, which is scarce in the standardized achievement tests reviewed in this book.

Testing Linked to Learning Theory

As mentioned several times throughout this book, a dominant learning theory of the last century was behaviorism. This theory views learning as the accumulation of knowledge and skills. Criterion-referenced testing was the trademark of behavioral learning theory. Each test item was keyed to a student learning objective. Teachers covered objectives and hoped that students would perform successfully on items reflecting each objective. These objectives were not necessarily linked in any logical way to the development of abilities.

A more recent emphasis is cognitive learning theory, in which student abilities are the focus of learning. Students may still have objectives and acquire knowledge and skills, just like before, but there is more emphasis on the application of knowledge in problem solving and in critical and creative thinking. The focus is on abilities instead of knowledge and skills. A student's ability is assessed in a meaningful context.

The state-adopted or school district-adopted standardized achievement test carries with it an implicit understanding that a certain type of learning theory is being used as the basis for teaching. States that emphasize writing assessments involving writing prompts and analytic or holistic scoring rubrics infer acceptance of a cognitive learning theory. When Vermont initiated a controversial portfolio assessment, policymakers seemed to support the social/constructivist viewpoint. Any state employing a traditional achievement test is probably well grounded in this traditional behavioral learning theory. Although traditionalists and reformers may argue about the merits and deficiencies of various learning theories, the fact remains that we educators are greatly divided on this issue. Standardized achievement testing seems to fit all learning theories but seldom equally well.

Your problem is to identify the theory that aligns well with your beliefs and to ensure that your chosen learning theory, teaching, and testing are consistent with your idea about student learning. As you can see, whatever theory you choose, you are likely to collide with government-imposed policies and tests that are disagreeable with your personal beliefs.

Developmental Nature

Many types of complex learning, as expressed in abilities such as writing and reading, have a developmental nature or theme that can be appropriately expressed in developmental terms. Writing portfolios are one way to measure this developmental nature or writing ability, but most standardized tests have little chance of capturing development without a change from multiple-choice questions to a more direct assessment found in performance testing.

Through this developmental perspective, we teachers can see our role as helping students move along a continuum through stages of growth as indicated in many current assessment programs:

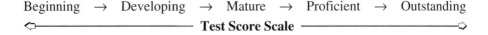

Beginning → Developing → Mature → Proficient → Outstanding
⟸——————————— **Test Score Scale** ———————————⟹

The focus for this criterion is on progress in a developmental stream from one level to the next. The emphasis here is not on competition, for everyone is competing against the same standard and everyone needs to achieve as much as possible. The threatening nature of testing is reduced because tests are used to verify effort to learn and growth is traced along this lifelong continuum that exists for each ability. This shift in thinking moves educators into a model for students that follows personal growth throughout the student's lifetime into adulthood.

Multidimensional Nature of Achievement

In the past, achievement testing was reduced to one score per subject matter, as if one score could capture the complexity of learning. Newer approaches see learning as richer and more complex than ever. Prior knowledge, motivation, developmental status, and learning opportunities are part of the consideration of the student in a learning process. To use only a single standardized achievement test score treats learning simplistically. Instead, the "big picture" in student learning must be regarded by considering a child's development status, learning history, and motivation, among other factors. A more comprehensive understanding of this comes from the model you constructed for yourself after reading Chapter 1. This model governs how you think about student learning and the strategies you use to help students learn.

One realization after pondering Chapter 1 should be that all people need basic verbal, quantitative, and analytical abilities to allow us to function effectively in various life roles, such as workers, citizens, partners, parents, and friends, among other roles.

Summary

What makes assessments work for you? Teachers, administrators, policymakers, legislators, and others need to work together to build assessment systems that include state, school district, and classroom assessment working in concert for the same student abilities we want to develop. These assessments should be intrinsically important and meaningful to students. As teachers, we want our teaching and testing to be well grounded in a learning theory that makes sense to us. We recognize that learning is developmental, seldom smooth, and very uneven. We want to help all students move along the developmental continuum at any speed at which they are capable. Finally, we recognize that learning is much more complex than any test can capture. We have some faith in test scores, but we need to consider other indicators of student learning, such as the emotional side of learning and how students deal with problems they encounter in life.

How Do We Assess the Validity of Interpretations and Uses of Test Scores?

This section of the chapter assesses the validity of interpretations and uses of tests, drawing heavily from Chapter 3. Remember that every interpretation and use of a test score requires separate validation. Test publishers and test sponsors have the responsibility of ensuring that evidence supports each interpretation and use of a test score.

Interpretations

The kind of interpretation being made of test scores must always be identified and the interpretation must always be valid. The interpreter must present a cogent case for an interpretation and the interpretation should be backed by evidence of the truth of interpretation. Simply put, a standardized achievement test score is supposed to measure student learning in a specific subject matter, such as reading. Is it valid to assert that the score reflects a child's level of performance in reading ability? Or did another factor come into play that affected that score and the accuracy of the interpretation? How confident can one be that an interpretation is correct? You learned in Chapter 7 that test scores can be flawed or polluted. You should approach all standardized achievement test scores with a caution due to a fear of pollution.

If the desired interpretation is to assess what the student has learned during his or her education to date, most standardized achievement tests do a good job of measuring the basic knowledge and skills needed to function in society. These tests are *not* good measures of the amount of learning that has occurred in a single year, however, unless the test is closely matched to content standards and instruction and an equivalent form is given the following year. Norm-referenced interpretations of these test scores address the amount of knowledge and skills each student has relative to all others at the same grade level.

If the desired interpretation is to assess a student's abilities, most of these tests fail to measure abilities. The writing assessment is the obvious exception.

If the desired interpretation is to assess what a student learned during a single year of school, most of these standardized achievement tests do *not* do a good job. Why? Simply because for such an interpretation, one must match what teachers teach and what a test measures. If there is a match, then one might obtain a good description of learning for a time frame. If there is a mismatch, then what has been learned about the student? Some students score high because they have a rich, positive learning history; some students score low because they have a poor, negative learning history. History must be considered in interpreting the achievement test score. Thus, you should always know the context for test score interpretation.

Uses

As Chapter 3 suggested, there are many uses of test scores. As an educator, you have a responsibility to use test scores responsibly and to guard against misuse. It has been suggested that certain uses of test scores may be invalid because there is an illogical argument behind the use or there is a lack of sufficient validity evidence supporting that use. Table 10.1 lists some questionable uses of test scores, a brief precis of the logical argument, and a description of the kind of evidence that might be needed. Table 10.2 lists the same criteria but for more defensible uses of test scores.

TABLE 10.1   *Some Questionable Uses of Test Scores*

Use	Logical Argument	Primary Validity Evidence Needed
Making comparisons to evaluate the quality of education in a state, school district, school, or class	Several testing experts have argued that this kind of comparison is illogical. Most states and school districts are too diverse and lack a common quality to make valid comparisons.	We need a test that is commonly adopted and linked to curriculum and instruction in each unit being compared. We need controls for external factors that influence student learning. The differences we see among students, classes, schools, and school districts are often explained by demographic variables such as parental education.
Teacher evaluation	Testing experts argue that test-based teacher evaluation is invalid because no test is adequate for measuring the outcomes of education. Also, external factors are very influential in student learning and need to be considered. Teaching is so complex that it can't be adequately assessed with a single test.	Research needs to show that effective teaching has a marked difference on some criterion achievement tests. We would have to define and measure teaching as part of this research. The test would have to be a very sound, comprehensive measure of student learning for a school year. External factors affecting student learning must be considered.
Evaluating real estate	As absurd as this seems, real estate agents in some cities have color-coded maps showing neighborhood test scores so that newcomers to the city can select the place with the "best schools." This is nothing more than finding places where family income and parental education are highest. This practice has nothing to do with the quality of schools.	Evidence would have to show the qualities of good schools and a link between that school and validly measured achievement. We would have to consider the external factors affecting student learning.
Test-based accountability and intervention in a school or school district	Schools that consistently fail to meet standards should face interventions (such as reconstitution) and penalties (including the possibility of being closed down). Teachers whose students consistently fail to meet standards should also face retraining or termination. Students, teachers, and schools should enjoy rewards for high performance (http://www.edexcellence.net/topics/standards.html).	We would need evidence that students' performance is less than expected given their external situations (social capital and intelligence) and that educational programs were inferior. The intervention would have to have proven success to be implemented.
Promotion, graduation	Standards and tests must be coupled with consequences. Students should be promoted only when they have met the academic standards required.	Narrow test-based accountability fails to account for the total achievement of the student. Evidence needs to be presented that each student in jeopardy of failing has received equal and adequate opportunities to learn with appropriate remedial programs.

TABLE 10.2   *More Defensible Uses of Test Scores*

Use	Logical Argument	Primary Validity Evidence Needed
Accountability	The public has a right to know how schools are doing. The legislature has to make decisions about policies and resources, so student achievement information is crucial.	We need a broad array of indicators of achievement. A test must be developed to match the curriculum (content standards) and instruction occurring; otherwise, we cannot make valid interpretations. We need to know context (social capital and intelligence) in interpreting test scores.
Evaluation of instructional program	The best criterion for evaluating an instructional program is student achievement.	If a test is a good survey measure of student achievement, as defined in a state or school district, then periodic assessments are an effective way to study the benefits of an instructional program. Other information should supplement your evaluation information.
Evaluation of curriculum	The best criterion for evaluating a curriculum is student achievement.	If a test is going to be used, that test must provide useful diagnostic subscores that relate to parts of the curriculum. Additionally, the test should be matched to the curriculum or content standards adopted and to instruction.
Placement, grouping, or selecting	We need to place students in groups where they receive the most beneficial instruction. An achievement test can help us do this job. Also, if we are going to select someone for a program, the right test can help us choose who is best qualified for this program.	As with most uses here, the test must be matched to our curriculum and content standards as well as to instruction. Students placed, grouped, or selected should be followed and retested to ensure that the placement, grouping, and selection has actually benefited the student.
Prediction	The best prediction of future achievement is past achievement.	Correlations of the test must be made from one year (or time period) to the next year (or time period).

How Should We Sensibly and Ethically Prepare Students for These Tests?

Given that you have identified a standardized achievement test that measures what you want it to measure, and you have decided that your students are going to take this test, how should you prepare your students for this test? Two relevant standards were proposed by a leading test specialist, James Popham (1991), that are worth citing:

- No test preparation activity should violate the ethical standards of the education profession. We might think of this as any practice that if exposed to the public would shame us as educators.
- No test preparation practice should increase students' test scores without simultaneously increasing student mastery of the content domain to be tested. In other words, the standardized test is intended to sample from a large domain of knowledge. If an increase in a student's score does NOT correspond with a similar increase in overall learning, then this standard is violated.

These points have been made repeatedly in the testing literature and in this book, but, because the violation of these principles seems to be at epidemic levels in U.S. education, it is worth making these points again and again.

This final section is devoted to advice on how to get students ready for taking the annual standardized achievement test that is mandated in a school district by the school district or the state. Consistent with a theme throughout this book, the test *must* be linked to state content standards, and the reporting of test results should be consistent with principles identified throughout this book. The main purpose of giving any achievement test is to improve student learning.

Advice to Parents about Mental and Health Issues Affecting Testing

Parents play a vital role in preparing students for any standardized achievement test. If the test is truly intended to help students learn, then students need to do their best. The best general advice to parents is to focus their child on the importance of learning and to learn throughout life. This is simply good parenting. Parents should be encouraged to get their children physically and mentally ready for the test.

Physical Preparation. Good test preparation includes assuring that students get a good night's sleep the night before a test, are reasonably motivated, and eat properly the night before and in the morning. Getting properly hydrated before a testing session is good, and staying away from caffeine is recommended. Students should dress comfortably for the testing session. For those children who wear glasses, be sure the lenses are clean.

Mental Preparation. Students should be coached about their state of mind and be well prepared in the psychological and physical health issues affecting test taking. If there is tension or anxiety during the testing period, employ relaxation techniques by taking a few slow, deep breaths and closing the eyes and resting momentarily. All distracting thoughts should be released from the mind. Also, practice body relaxation techniques by taking stretches, yawning, or deep breathing.

Curriculum

If a standardized achievement test is mandated in your school district or school, then asking the most basic question seems fair: How does this test measure up to our school district curriculum or the state content standards? As was pointed out in a study by Noggle (1987), only a 27 percent correlation existed between the Arizona's Iowa Test of Basic Skills and Arizona's content standards. One experiment I conducted in a small school district in an Oregon coastal community was to have the teachers parse the Iowa Test of Basic Skills into two parts: items that reflected content taught by them and items that reflected content not taught by them. When item norms were examined (showing how the larger national sample performed on each item), the teachers and I found that the students did quite well with instructionally relevant items but quite poorly with instructionally irrelevant items. The obvious message here is that most published standardized achievement tests lack the match to the curriculum and therefore have limited interpretive usefulness.

Test Practice

All students need to know and be given practice in how to take standardized tests. Practice sessions might be scheduled using test item formats used on the actual test. That way, students know what to expect and will not be surprised or confused. Teachers might offer students extensive practice in all types of item formats, to increase their sophistication in test taking. This kind of test preparation does not seem to violate either standard and seems like good advice for all school leaders and teachers. Such an approach is nonpolluting and reflects what assessment experts think is appropriate for any classroom teacher. This practice extends to the students' use of scoring guides (rubrics) that are used to score writing performance or mathematical problem solving.

Haladyna (1997) identified 7 multiple-choice formats and more than 20 performance item formats. Students should be adept at handling any and all of these formats. Classroom teachers should be well schooled in how these formats link to their state content standards and be willing to use each format at the appropriate time to give students the full experience of handling all test item formats in classroom tests rather than in separate formats.

Test-Taking Strategies

Teachers and parents can prepare children for taking a standardized achievement test by giving them instruction on test taking. Testing specialists call this *testwiseness*. As has been stated repeatedly, all students should learn the same test-taking strategies, because if only some do, then test score pollution is potentially introduced. One of the best sources of advice on test taking comes from Sarnacki (1979). His advice for taking multiple-choice tests comes in useful categories:

Time-Using Strategies
- Work as rapidly as you can, answering the easy items quickly.
- Set up a schedule using the time assigned, so you have enough time to finish.
- Work at a pace that gets you through the test with a little time left over to review harder items.
- Guess at items that you cannot answer definitely (see Guessing Strategies as one of these categories)
- Mark items that require more time.
- Use extra time later to answer these harder items.

Error-Avoidance Strategies
- Read or listen to directions/instructions carefully. Make sure you understand how to take the test and mark your answers.
- Read each item carefully to ensure you understand.
- As you read the stem, think of the right answer before you read the options.
- Mark or identify key words or phrases that help you understand what the item requires.
- Ask the person giving the test for help in understanding the item.
- Eliminate implausible choices as right answers.
- Erase stray marks on the answer sheet.
- Make sure that all test items have only one choice marked.
- Check all answers for correctness; change answers if you feel justified.

Guessing Strategies
- Always guess if you don't know the right choice (unless there is a penalty for guessing).
- Don't look for patterns in the answers you choose (good testmakers don't have answer patterns).

Deductive Reasoning Strategies
- Eliminate choices that are obviously wrong and choose from the remaining choices.
- If two choices are similar or identical, don't choose either one.
- If two choices are overlapping, don't choose either one.
- Use information from other items, if possible, to help you answer an item.

Advice on Taking a Performance Test

Not all standardized achievement tests are multiple choice in format. An increasing number of these tests require student performance. Writing assessments are the most numerous, but mathematics performance tests are also increasing in use. Mehrens, Popham, and Ryan (1998) offer some advice to test-takers who are preparing for a performance test. They think that teachers should not teach to a specific performance but instead concentrate on a "domain" of possible tasks the student might encounter. There is also the danger of practicing a performance at the expense of other important learning. Students should never be surprised at a performance test format. Teachers regularly need to give students practice in the format they are going to use and teachers should also introduce the scoring guide (rubric) to students. Students should know the basis for grading and be prepared to perform with the full knowledge of these scoring guides.

In addition to this wise advice, here is some specific advice that may be helpful:

Performance Test-Taking Advice
1. Always read the instructions or listen carefully as the instructions are read to you.
2. Use your time profitably. Don't waste time on one test item.
3. Study the item carefully and underline key words or phrases to help you understand what the test item is asking you to do. For example:
   * *Discuss*—Provide reasoning behind. Give different points of views.
   * *Describe*—Give a description of a concept, principle, or procedure.
   * *Compare*—Show how two or more things are similar. Provide examples.
   * *Contrast*—Show how two or more things are different. Provide examples.
   * *Explain*—Clarify or simplify a concept, principle, or procedure. Give a rationale.
   * *Justify*—Argue in favor of or defend.
   * *Critique*—Argue against or attack.
   * *List*—Simply give a list. Make sure the list is long enough.
   * *Outline*—Give a list but show its organization. Use an outline.
4. Before writing your answer, use an outline or other organizational strategy.
5. Organize your paragraphs from your outline.
6. Form a clear thesis statement and use supporting documentation.
7. Paraphrase key points in the original question as part of your introductory sentence to help you organize your thoughts.
8. Use logic or reasoning in writing your answer.
9. Provide examples to show your understanding.
10. Although writing may not be the object of the performance, use principles of good writing.
11. Do not use a big vocabulary, as judges are not impressed by vocabulary. But if your topic is technical or scienific, use the vocabulary that is appropriate.
12. Write clearly and legibly. Help the reader/judge understand what you are communicating.

Summary

Test taking is a skill that all students should learn and learn well. Teachers and parents should ensure that all children are well prepared. Daily classroom lessons may be embedded with opportunities to improve test-taking skills by using a variety of assessment formats and giving students ideas and encouragement about how fairly and honestly they can improve their test performance.

How Do We Lower Test Anxiety?

Test anxiety can pollute test scores. About one of four students have some degree of test anxiety that results in lower-than-deserved scores, thus this student malady should be addressed. As a teacher, you should be alert for this problem and help students through this stressful time.

The physical signs or symptoms of test anxiety are headaches, nausea, faintness, excessive perspiration, and bladder or bowel accidents. The emotional signs of test anxiety are unusual emotions, crying or laughing inappropriately, anger, helplessness, and agitation. No matter what the symptoms are, the result is performance that is lower than you would predict from seeing the student perform in the classroom. Sometimes, a student will miss an inordinate number of items in a row.

What can a teacher do to lower test anxiety?

- Urge the students to apply appropriate test preparation practices as advocated in this chapter.
- Teach the students to remain calm and composed during the test.
- Teach the students to remain focused on the task and not to wander.
- Urge the students to avoid discussing the test with other students.
- Tell the students not to be concerned with how other students are doing (e.g., finishing earlier). Speed is not a predictor of test performance.

If simple remedies fail, invalidate the test score because it does not represent the student's true level of learning. Test anxiety can be treated by a therapist. The treatment will serve the child well throughout life, as he or she continues to take tests into adulthood.

What about Test-Based Accountability and High-Stakes Testing?

Throughout this book, it has been argued that test-based accountability in a high-stakes testing environment is not good. True accountability involves a shared responsibility among everyone in society for providing clear learning outcomes, equal opportunities for learning, and measures of student learning that accurately show student achievement. One approach to accountability is the use of context variables to frame student achievement and to better evaluate teachers, schools, school districts, and states. The idea behind this kind of contextualizing is to consider the social conditions of the class or school being studied and make adjustment in scores, much like handicapping is done in horse racing or golf. Such contextualizing, although a good idea basically, is fraught with threats to validity. First, the tests used may be too specific and lead to a narrowing of the curriculum. Second, like Tennessee, the basis for contextualizing may overlook important variables, such as socioeconomic status or parents' education. Third, the approach limits the evaluation to test scores alone instead of broadening the view about an educated child. According to a report by Bracey (2000), Tennessee has used such a model since 1992 but the model ignores family education and family income factors and simply looks at gain on a test of questionable validity. Given that poverty and other conditions, such as LEP and disabilities, contribute to low achievement, this model ignores these three potent factors.

Standardized achievement tests will continue to be administered because the public and elected officials (legislators and school board members) want them as indicators for accountability. Nevertheless, the critical issue that remains is that test scores need to be interpreted and used in ways that help students learn instead of harming students. Chapter 6 discussed high-stakes testing for elementary and secondary school students and for those preparing for a career in any profession, such as teaching. Several organizations have studied and discussed principles that they support in the interpretation and use of high-stakes test scores (AERA, 2000). The National Center for Fair and Open Testing (1999–2000c) advocates many of the following principles:

1. *Base all state and district tests of student achievement on clear content standards.* Many states have adopted content standards that have much in common with each other. The idea of having the achievement test content matched to the state's content standards or the school district's curriculum is one of the most vital conditions of effective achievement testing.

2. *Employ multiple methods of testing, knowing that no single test or item format will capture the full range of possible student behavior being learned.* While we teachers are being encouraged to use this full range of tests and item formats in teaching, standardized achievement testing continues to rely primarily on multiple-choice tests that reflect mainly knowledge. The tendency is for us to teach to the content most likely to be found on the test instead of teaching to the broader content, much of which is untested. When we teach to the test, we nullify the validity of the test score interpretation or use.

3. *Make achievement tests require complex thinking that involves the application of knowledge and skills.* Such testing is not easy to accomplish with multiple-choice items; thus, better multiple-choice tests must be created or ways to use performance formats must be found that accomplish this end.

4. *Resist using the publishers' test results unless these tests are aligned with each state or school district's content standards.* Some states, such as Arizona and California, give tests that are not aligned with their content standards, yet legislators and other elected officials will attempt to fool the public into thinking that teachers have failed because they did not align their teaching to the nonaligned test.

5. *Avoid making pass/fail decisions on the basis of a single test.* Use weighted composites of results from a variety of sources. Such composites tend to measure more aspects of learning and tend to produce more reliable scores.

6. *Provide alternate assessments when justified, accommodating students with identifiable disabilities.* Federal legislation (ADA and IDEA) provide the legal basis for providing alternative assessments to students with disabilities. States and school districts need similar or identical policies that specify what disabilities will be accommodated and how tests might be modified in extreme circumstances.

7. *Provide opportunities for retesting if the result is undesirable.* Virtually all graduation, certification, and licensing testing programs allow for retesting if a failing decision is reached based on test performance. These test forms should cover the same content and have the same difficulty, since the passing score is the same from time to time.

8. *When making high-stakes, pass/fail decisions, test scores should be very reliable.* Although *reliable* is a technical, theoretical term, the estimation of reliability is routine. This coefficient should be high enough to generate confidence that making a pass/fail decision is defensible from ethical and legal standpoints.

9. *Include all students in testing,* even those from special populations, such as students with disabilities, students learning to speak English, and students with inadequate preparation for schooling. Yet, at the same time, provide responsible reports that indicate not only the status of students from these special populations but also the conditions surrounding their performance and the plans and resources provided or needed to remedy their plight. A corollary of this guideline is that the policies for exclusion of students should be the same for all school districts in a state or all schools in a school district.

10. *High-stakes testing programs should be annually reviewed to assure that tests are being validly interpreted and used* (Downing & Haladyna, 1997). Get professional advice about the quality of the testing program and the validity of interpreting and using test scores. Find out what needs to be done to improve the testing program.

11. *Observe the ethical standards and principles of professional societies concerned about test score validity* (American Educational Research Association, American Psychological Association, & National Council on Measurement in Education, 1999). Major educational organizations have position statements, policies, or standards about testing. Check with organizations to which you belong and see what they are advocating. Generally, their statements agree with statements from other organizations.

12. *For each use of a test score, separate validation is needed.* Do not allow users of test scores to assume a particular use if it is not validated. Publishers usually provide validity evidence for test score uses they believe are appropriate. Sometimes, users of test results, such as legislators or school boards, want to use test scores for purposes not supported by validity evidence or the test publishers. Insist on validity evidence in support of each and every test score use.

13. *Provide all students and professionals preparing to take a high-stakes test with adequate opportunity to learn.* Lack of this opportunity is inexcusable. In many settings, lack of opportunity is grounds for a successful lawsuit against the test sponsor.

14. *When students or professionals fail a high-stakes test, provide a humane remedial program* that will significantly increase their chances for a successful retest and the benefits of more education.

15. *Testing programs with high-stakes decisions will have positive and negative consequences.* These consequences should be known and evaluated. In the end, educators will want to weigh the good against the bad when they decide to continue or abandon the testing program.

16. *Passing scores should be set in valid ways.* These methods should be well documented and available to the public. Setting unrealistically high scores will result in many students failing; setting unrealistically low scores permits virtually anyone to pass, despite their level of learning. Some standard-setting methods are unethical or actually illegal, such as setting quotas or simply arbitrarily pulling a number out of the air, such as 75 percent. Instead, use a well-documented standard-setting method that is consistent with the intended use.

17. *One of the biggest threats to validity is the inability to read, write, speak, and listen in the English language.* English language learners typically score very low on high-stakes tests. Thus, incorrect interpretations about their learning are likely to be made until teachers are certain that English is mastered. Then their level of learning can be properly assessed.

18. *Students with mental, emotional, and physical disabilities typically score low on standardized achievement tests,* as Chapter 9 discussed. Not only are these students legally entitled to special education but testing must provide accommodations and modifications in their tests as befits their disabilities. Many of these students have multiple disabilities as well as language learning problems, and many of these students with multiple disabilities live in poverty, which only further compounds their problems. Their test scores should always be separated from other groups and their situations should be contextualized. What is being done to help them learn?

19. *Firm, explicit rules should be used to decide who is tested.* It is very easy to pollute group test score interpretations by selecting or eliminating students to be tested. By having a common set of rules about who is tested, one is more likely to make valid interpretations of test scores. The best example of what happens when this rule is not followed was discussed in Chapter 8. Remember that excluding many low-scoring students is effective in raising your class, school, or school district average; however, this is very deceptive to the public.

A Final Note on Educational Reform and Achievement Testing

A persistent theme in this book has been that achievement testing should be used to help students learn, but, as you have seen, in the hands of legislators, policymakers, and school boards, achievement testing has been often misinterpreted and misused or used invalidly. A national obsession with test scores has reduced learning to the score on a short test. According to French (1998), this narrow view of student learning leads to a natural tendency for large organizations (e.g., states or school boards) to mandate educational reform that is very autocratic and undemocratic. Educators are typically not involved in reform policies as part of the solution. In many instances, educators are identified as the problem, referred to as "educrats" by their harshest critics or the "educational establishment" by reform-minded legislators. French described the reform effort in Massachusetts as one that had a firm democratic basis and that was proceeding smoothly to systemic change that included sensible achievement testing. Then, the politics in the state changed. The state had developed, through consensus, state curriculum frameworks (content standards), inquiry-based and project-based learning, interdisciplinary curricula, and assessments of complex thinking, but all of this was retired, and a new system was created. Conservative board members drafted new content standards and a single high-stakes test was created for making pass/fail high school graduation decisions. The curriculum was narrowed to fit the test. French argued that such "reform" is like throwing gasoline on a fire.

What has been learned from experience, learning theory, and research is that reform must have important pieces in place, such as the following:

- Full participation of educators, working on curriculum framework and assessments and their interpretations and valid uses
- Broad, comprehensive academic standards that focus on important abilities instead of knowledge and skills, acknowledging that knowledge and skills are crucial to the formation of these abilities
- An emphasis on the application of knowledge and skills to solve problems and to think critically and creatively
- A developmental perspective that tracks each student's growth from the time he or she enters school to the time he or she performs adequately to leave school for work or for further education
- A commitment to professionalism of teachers
- An emphasis on democratic principles to flourish, instead of heavy-handed, autocratic, mandated testing programs
- Allowing autonomy and self-determination in school districts but also having in place fair assessments that provide true accountability
- Equal funding for schools and school districts, and adequate funding for schools dealing with neglected student populations

The narrow authoritarian approach depicted in many states and other locales results in small, meaningless achievement in a narrow domain of learning at the expense of developing the abilities of gifted students and at the abandonment of neglected students. Thus, standardized achievement might realize the dreams of many Americans for a good education or high-stakes standardized achievement testing might increase the lack of opportunity to learn and increase the problems seen with these neglected populations.

Summary

This chapter has reviewed the justification for standardized testing and the context in which test scores should be interpreted. Despite the many problems encountered in standardized achievement testing, it can work. But classroom assessments are an important part of this puzzle. Classroom assessment and standardized achievement testing must work together to coordinate and monitor student learning. Many interpretations and uses of these test scores may be valid, based on logic and existing evidence, but several interpretations and uses are not logically based or lack validity evidence. Finally, the chapter discussed ethical preparation for the testing session. Accountability and high-stakes testing can be managed in an environment that helps students. The guidelines on high-stakes testing of the American Educational Research Association regarding how high-stakes test should be developed were reviewed.

Epilogue

This book has attempted to portray standardized achievement testing honestly and critically. As you have seen, standardized achievement testing is very extensive and, in fact, growing in the United States and in the world. Accountability, regulation, and higher standards contribute to its growth. As a teacher-in-training, teacher, educator, parent, legislator, school board member, or simply citizen, you can play an active role in shaping educational policies, allocating resources to education, and ensuring that students and others are well served by these standardized achievement testing programs. At stake is the welfare and future of the country's children and those who serve them—our educators.

Certain common understandings are needed to guide us in interpreting and using test scores:

- Know the context for student learning. That context includes factors internal and external to schooling.
- Know what a test measures. We need a clear definition of what a test is supposed to measure; content standards and curriculum are good referents.
- Know the basis for validity. That basis includes a logical argument concerning why a test score intepretation or use is valid and evidence that supports that argument. Without the argument and evidence, we should be very leery about the validity of any interpretation or use.
- Know about test score pollution. We should be very cautious about any test score. There is considerable evidence that any test score might be polluted by any of a multitude of factors.
- Know the consequences. Growing evidence shows that narrow test-based accountability and high-stakes testing are harmful to students and to the educative process.
- Know the standards. We have standards to follow that might improve the interpretation and use of test scores and make the consequences more positive and beneficial.

Standardized achievement testing has the potential to be a positive force in American education, but only when test scores are validly interpreted and used.

References

Abedi, J., & Hofstetter, C. (undated). *Language background variables as powerful predictors of students' NAEP math performance.* Paper presented at the annual meeting of the American Educational Research Association.

Abedi, J., Lord, C., Hofstetter, C., & Baker, E. (2000). Impact of accommodation strategies on English language learners' test performance. *Educational Measurement: Issues and Practice, 19*(3), 16–26.

Allington, R. L., & McGill-Franzen, A. (1992). Does high-stakes testing improve school effectiveness? *ERS Spectrum, 10,* 3–12.

Alspaugh, J. W. (1999). Achievement loss associated with the transition to middle school and high school. *Journal of Educational Research, 92*(1), 20–26.

American Educational Research Association. (2000). Position statement of the American Educational Research Association concerning high-stakes testing in pre K–12 education. *Educational Researcher, 29,* 24–25.

American Educational Research Association, American Psychological Association, & National Council on Measurement in Education. (1999). *Standards for educational and psychological testing.* Washington, DC: American Psychological Association.

American Psychological Association Task Force. (1996). *American Psychologist, 51*(2), 77–99.

Arizona Republic, The. (December 9, 1990). Disrupted families tied to child woes, p. A3.

Arizona Republic, The. (December 8, 1991). 1.5 million start school unprepared, report says, p. A4.

Arizona Republic, The. (November 24, 1998). U.S. outpaced by 22 nations in graduation rates, p. A3.

Bailey, L. (May/June 1998). Should high-stakes tests drive mathematics curriculum and instruction? *Mathematics Education Dialogues,* p. 8.

Bangert-Drowns, R. L., Kulik, J. A., & Kulik, C-L. C. (1983). Effects of coaching programs on achievement test performance. *Review of Educational Research, 53,* 571–585.

Barrett, J. (November 25, 1998). Reprieve for teachers too. *The Arizona Republic,* pp. A1, A18.

Bemiller, A. (1993). Lake Woebegone revisited: On diversity and education. *Educational Researcher, 22,* 7–12.

Berk, R. (1988). Fifty reasons why student achievement gain does not mean teacher effectiveness. *Journal of Personnel Evaluation in Education, 1,* 345–363.

Berliner, D. C., & Biddle, B. J. (1995). *The manufactured crisis: Myths, fraud, and the attack on America's public schools.* Reading, MA: Addison-Wesley.

Bland, K. (April 22, 2001). Too young for kindergarten? *The Arizona Republic,* pp. A1, A10.

Bloom, B. S. (Ed). (1956). *Taxonomy of educational objectives. Handbook I, Cognitive domain.* New York: David McKay.

Bloom, B. S. (1976). *Human characteristics and school learning.* New York: McGraw-Hill.

Bloom, B. S., Engelhart, M. D., Furst, E. J., Hill, W. H., & Krathwohl, D. R. (1956). *Taxonomy of educational objectives.* New York: Longmans Green.

Bodenhausen, J. (May/June 1998). High-stakes tests. *Mathematics Education Dialogues,* p. 9.

Bracey, G. (1998). Back to Coleman. *Phi Delta Kappan, 80*(1), 88–89.

Bracey, G. (2000). Value added, value lost. *Fairtest Examiner, 14*(3), 9–12.

Bridgeman, B., McCamley-Jenkins, L., & Ervin, N. (2000). *Predictions of freshman grade-point average from the revised and recentered SAT1: Reasoning test: Research report 2000–1.* New York: The College Board.

Brookover, W. B., Schweitzer, J. H., Schneider, J. M., Beady, C. H., Flood, F. K., & Wisinbaker, J. M. (1978). Elementary school social climate and school achievement. *American Educational Research Journal, 15,* 301–318.

Caldas, S. J., & Bankston, C. L. (1999). Multilevel examination of student, school and district level effects on academic achievement. *Journal of Educational Research, 93*(2), 91–100, 395–415.

Cannell, J. J. (1989). *How public educators cheat on standardized achievement tests.* Albuquerque, NM: Friends for Education.

Carroll, J. B. (1963). A model for school learning. *Teachers College Record, 64,* 723–733.

Carroll, J. B. (1985). A model of school learning. In C. W. Fisher & D. C. Berliner (Eds.), *Perspectives on instructional time* (pp. 59–72). White Plains, NY: Longman.

Carroll, J. B. (1993). *Human cognitive abilities: A survey of factor analytic studies.* New York: Cambridge University Press.

Cashen, V. M., & Ramseyer, G. C. (1969). *Journal of Educational Measurement, 6*(3), 155–158.

Cizek, G. J. (1998). *Filling in the blanks: Putting standardized testing to the test.* Washington, DC: Thomas B. Fordham Foundation.

Cizek, G. J. (1999). *Cheating on tests: How to do it, detect it, and prevent it.* Mahwah, NJ: Lawrence Erlbaum.

Cizek, G. J. (Ed.). (2001). *Setting performance standards: Concepts, methods, and perspectives.* Mahwah, NJ: Lawrence Erlbaum.

Cohn, A. (2000). *The case against standardized testing: Raising the scores, ruining the schools.* Portsmouth, NH: Heinemann.

Cole, N. S. (1990). Conceptions of educational achievement. *Educational Researcher, 19,* 2–7.

Cole, N. S., & Moss, P. A. (1989). Bias in test use. In R. L. Linn (Ed.), *Educational measurement* (3rd ed., pp. 201–220). New York: American Council on Education and Macmillan.

Coleman, J. S. (1987). Families and schools. *Educational Researcher, 16,* 32–38.

College Board. (June 1999). *Research note 07: Concordance between the SAT1 and ACT scores for individual students.* New York: Author.

College Board. (1999). *College-board seniors national report.* New York: Author.

Cooley, W. W. (1991). State-wide student assessment. *Educational Measurement: Issues and Practices, 10,* 3–6, 15.

Cooper, H. (1989). *Homework.* New York: Longman.

CRESST. (2000). *The CRESST Line: Newsletter of the National Center for Research on Evaluation, Standards, and Student Testing.* Los Angeles: UCLA.

Crouse, J., & Trusheim, D. (1988). *The case against the SAT.* Chicago: University of Chicago Press.

Darling-Hammond, L. (November 1991). The implications of testing policy for quality and equality. *Phi Delta Kappan,* pp. 220–225.

Deaton, W. L., Halpin, G., & Alford, T. (1987). Coaching effects of the California achievement tests. *Journal of Educational Research, 80,* 149–155.

Dorn, S. (January 1998). The political legacy of school accountability systems. *Educational Policy Analysis Archives, 6*(1).

Downing, S. M., & Haladyna, T. M. (1997). Test item development: Validity evidence from quality assurance procedures. *Applied Measurement in Education, 15,* 5–12.

Dwyer, C. A. (1994). *Development of the knowledge base for the PRAXIS III: Classroom performance assessment criteria.* Princeton, NJ: Educational Testing Service.

Edelman, J. (1981). The impact of the mandated testing program on classroom practices: Teacher perspectives. *Education, 102,* 56–59.

Educational Testing Service. (1980). *Test scores and family income: A response to charges in the Nader/Nairn Report on ETS.* Princeton, NJ: Author.

Educational Testing Service. (1999). *Catalog of research reports.* Princeton, NJ: Author.

Estrin, E. T., & Nelson-Barber, S. (1995). Issues in cross-cultural assessment: American Indian and Alaska Native students. *Knowledge Brief, 12.* San Francisco: Far West Laboratory.

Fisher, C. W., & Berliner, D. C. (Eds.). (1985). *Perspectives on instructional time.* White Plains, NY: Longman.

Fitzgerald, J. (1995). English-as-a-second-language learners' cognitive reading processes: A review of research in the United States. *Review of Educational Research, 65,* 145–190.

Flynn, J. R. (1998). IQ gains over time: Toward finding the causes. In U. Neisser (Ed.), *The rising curve: Long-term gains in IQ and related measures* (pp. 25–66). Washington, DC: American Psychological Association.

Frederiksen, N. (1984). The real test bias: Influences of testing on teaching and learning. *American Psychologist, 39,* 193–202.

Freeman, D. J., Belli, G. M., Porter, A. C., Floden, R. E., Schmidt, W. H., & Schwille, J. R. (1983). The influence of different styles of textbook use on the instructional validity of standardized tests. *Journal of Educational Measurement, 20*(3), 259–270.

Freeman, D. J., Kuhs, T. M., Porter, A. C., Floden, R. E., Schmidt, W. H., & Schwille J. R. (1983). Do textbooks and tests define a national curriculum in elementary school mathematics? *The Elementary School Journal, 83,* 501–513.

Freeman, D. J., & Porter, A. C. (1989). Do textbooks dictate the content of mathematics instruction in elementary schools? *American Educational Research Journal, 26*(1), 403–421.

French, D. (1998). The state's role in shaping a progressive vision of public education. *Phi Delta Kappan, 80*(3), 184–194.

Fujiura, G. T., & Kiyoshi, Y. (2000). Trends in demography of childhood poverty and disability. *Exceptional Children, 66*(2), 187–199.

Garcia, G. E. (1991). Factors influencing the English reading test performance of Spanish-speaking Hispanic children. *Reading Research Quarterly, 26,* 371–391.

Gardner, H. (1983). *Frames of mind: The theory of multiple intelligences.* New York: Basic Books.

Gardner, H. (1986). *The mind's new science: A history of the cognitive revolution.* New York: Basic Books.

Gardner, H., & Hatch, T. (1989). Multiple intelligences go to school. *Educational Researcher, 18,* 4–10.

Glasser, J. E. (1999). Tenement of failures: A teacher's lament. *English Journal, 88*(5), 16–17.

Goleman, D. (1995). *Emotional intelligence.* New York: Bantam.

Good, T. L., & Brophy, J. E. (1987). *Looking in classrooms.* New York: Harper & Row.

Goodlad, J. I. (1984). *A place called school.* New York: McGraw-Hill.

Gould, S. J. (1996). *The mismeasure of man.* New York: Norton.

Goyins, T. (1998). High-stakes testing and student empowerment. *Mathematics Education Dialogues,* p. 7.

Guilford, J. P. (1967). *The nature of human intelligence.* New York: McGraw-Hill.

Haas, N. S., Haladyna, T. M., & Nolen, S. B. (April 1990). *War stories from the trenches: What teachers and administrators say about the test.* Paper presented at a symposium at the annual meeting of the National Council on Measurement in Education, Boston.

Haertel, E. (1986). The valid use of student performance measures for teacher evaluation. *Educational Evaluation and Policy Analysis, 8,* 45–60.

Haertel, E., & Calfee, R. (1983). School achievement: Thinking about what to test. *Journal of Educational Measurement, 20*(2), 119–131.

Haladyna, T. M. (1997). *Writing test items to evaluate higher order thinking.* Boston: Allyn and Bacon.

Haladyna, T. M. (1998). Review of the *Stanford Achievement Test, Ninth Edition.* In J. C. Impara & B. S. Plake (Eds.), *The thirteenth mental measurements yearbook.* Lincoln, NE: The Buros Institute of Mental Measurement, University of Nebraska–Lincoln.

Haladyna, T. M. (1999). *A comprehensive guide to student grading.* Boston: Allyn and Bacon.

Haladyna, T. M. (2001). *Evaluation of the Oregon statewide assessment program.* Salem, OR: Oregon Department of Education.

Haladyna, T. M. (2002). Supporting documentation: Assuring more valid test score interpretations and uses. In G. Tindal & T. M. Haladyna (Eds.), *Large scale assessment programs for all students: Validity, technical adequacy, and implementation issues* (pp. 89–108). Mahwah, NJ: Lawrence Erlbaum.

Haladyna, T. M., Downing, S. M., & Rodriguez, M. C. (in press). A review of multiple-choice item-writing guidelines for classroom assessment. *Applied Measurement in Education.*

Haladyna, T. M., Haas, N. S., & Allison, J. (1998). Tensions in standardized testing. *Childhood Education, 74,* 262–273.

Haladyna, T. M., & Hess, R. K. (1999). Conjunctive and compensatory standard setting models in high-stakes testing. *Educational Assessment, 6*(2), 129–153.

Haladyna, T. M., Nolen, S. B., & Haas, N. S. (1991). Raising standardized achievement test scores and the origins of test score pollution. *Educational Researcher, 20,* 2–7.

Haladyna, T. M., & Ryan, J. (April 2001). The influence of rater severity of whether a student passes or fails a performance test. In T. Haladyna (Chair), *The rater effect in performance testing.* Symposium conducted at the annual meeting of the American Educational Research Association, Seattle.

Haladyna, T. M., & Thomas, G. P. (1979). The affective reporting system. *Journal of Educational Measurement, 16,* 49–54.

Hall, G. E., & Hord, S. M. (2001). *Implementing change: Patterns, principles, and potholes.* Boston: Allyn and Bacon.

Herman, J., & Golan, S. (1993). The effects of testing on teaching and schools. *Educational Measurement: Issues and Practice, 12,* 20–25, 41.

Herman, J., Klein, D. C. D., & Abedi, J. (2001). Assessing students' opportunity to learn: Teacher and student perspectives. *Educational Measurement: Issues and Practice, 19*(4), 16–24.

Herrnstein, R. J., & Murray, C. (1994). *The bell curve: Intelligence and class structure in American life.* New York: The Free Press.

Heubert, J. P., & Hauser, R. M. (Eds.). (1999). *High stakes: Testing for tracking, promotion, and graduation.* Washington, DC: National Academy Press.

Hicken, S. (1992). The pre-professional skills test: How it affects teacher aspirants and predicts performance in teacher preparation programs. *The Urban Review, 24*(4), 253–261.

Hill, K. (1984). Debilitating motivation and testing: A major educational problem, possible solutions, and policy applications. In R. E. Ames & C. Ames (Eds.), *Research on motivation in education* (Vol. 1, pp. 245–274). New York: Academic Press.

Hill, K., & Horton, M. W. (April 1986). *Teaching and testing solutions to the problem of debilitating effects of test anxiety on test performance.* Paper presented at the annual meeting of the American Educational Research Association, Atlanta.

Hill, K., & Wigfield, A. (1984). Test anxiety: A major educational problem and what can be done about it. *The Elementary School Journal, 85,* 105–126.

Hixson, B. K. (January 25, 2000). How tests change a teacher. *New York Times,* p. A27.

Hollenbeck, K. (in press). Determining when test changes are valid accommodations or modifications for large-scale assessment. In G. Tindal & T. Haladyna (Eds.), *Large-scale assessment programs for all students: Development, implementation, and analysis.* Mahwah, NJ: Lawrence Erlbaum.

Horn, J. L. (1985). *Remodelling old models of intelligence.* In B. Wolman (Ed.), *Handbook of intelligence: Theories, measurements, and applications* (pp. 267–300). New York: Wiley.

House, E. R. (1991). Big policy, little policy. *Educational Researcher, 20,* 21–26.

Husen, T., & Tuijnman, A. (1991). The contributions of formal schooling to the increase in intellectual capital. *Educational Researcher, 20*(7), 17–25.

Impara, J. C., & Plake, B. S. (Eds.). (1998). *The thirteenth mental measurements yearbook.* Lincoln, NE: Buros Institute of Mental Measurement, University of Nebraska–Lincoln.

Jensen, A. R. (1969). Environment, heredity, and intelligence. *Reprint Series No. 2. Compiled from the Harvard Educational Review.* Cambridge, MA: Harvard Educational Review.

Jensen, A. R. (1980). *Bias in mental testing.* New York: The Free Press.

Jensen, A. R. (1986). g: Artifact or reality. *Journal of Vocational Behavior, 29,* 301–331.

Joint Committee on Fair Testing Practices. (1988). *The code of fair testing practices.* Washington, DC: American Psychological Association.

Kantrowitz, B. (March 5, 2001). The SAT showdown. *Newsweek,* pp. 48–50.

Katzman, J., & Hodas, S. (April 9, 2000). The trouble with tests. *Education Life,* p. 36.

Kean, M. H. (June 7, 1992). National testing won't work until we improve teaching. *The Philadelphia Inquirer,* p. C-1.

Kelley, M., & Haladyna, T. M. (April 2001). Trials and tribulations of correcting for the rater effect in evaluating a career ladder, teacher portfolio. In T. Haladyna (Chair), *The rater effect in performance testing.* Symposium conducted at the annual meeting of the American Educational Research Association, Seattle.

Kelley, T. L., Ruch, G. M., & Terman, L. M. (1923). *Stanford Achievement Test (first edition).* Yonkers, NY: World Book Company.

Klein, S. P., Hamilton, L. S., McCaffrey, D. F., & Stecher, B. M. (1996). *What do test scores in Texas tell us*? Rand Corporation. (http://www.rand.org/publications/IP/IP202/)

Kohn, A. (2000). *The case against standardized testing. Raising the scores, ruining the schools.* Portsmouth, NH: Heinemann.

Koretz, D. M., Linn, R. L., Dunbar, S. B., & Shepard, L. A. (April 1991). *The effects of high-stakes testing on achievement: Preliminary findings about generalization across tests.* Paper presented at the annual meeting of the American Educational Research Association, Chicago.

Kulik, J. A., Bangert-Drowns, R. L., & Kulik, C. C. (1984). Effectiveness of coaching for aptitude tests. *Psychological Bulletin, 95*(2), 179–188.

Kurtz, M. (April 14, 1999). AISD tried to improve dropout rate data. (Austin, TX) *American-Statesman,* pp. A1, A11.

LaTendre, G. K. (1999). The problem of Japan: Qualitative studies and international educational comparisons. *Educational Researcher, 28,* 38–45.

Lee, W. E., & Loeb, S. (2000). School size in Chicago elementary schools: Effects on teachers' attitudes and students' achievement. *American Educational Research Journal, 37*(1), 3–31.

Leinhardt, G., & Seewald, A. M. (1981). Overlap: What's tested, what's taught? *Journal of Educational Measurement, 18,* 85–96.

Linn, R. L. (1990). Admission testing: Recommended uses, validity, differential predicting, and coaching. *Applied Measurement in Education, 3,* 297–318.

Linn, R. L. (2000). Assessments and accountability. *Educational Researcher, 29*(2), 4–16.

Linn, R. L., & Gronlund, N. (2001). *Measurement and assessment in teaching* (7th ed.). Columbus, OH: Merrill.

Lohman, D. F. (1993). Teaching and testing to develop fluid abilities. *Educational Researcher, 22,* 12–23.

Lomax, R. G., West, M. M., Harmon, M. C., Viator, K. A., & Madaus, G. F. (1995). The impact of mandated standardized testing on minority students. *Journal of Negro Education, 64,* 171–185.

Lord, M. (April 3, 2000). High-stakes testing: It's backlash time. *U.S. News and World Report,* p. 54.

Mayer, J. D., & Salovey, P. (1997). What is emotional intelligence? In J. D. Mayer & P. Salovey (Eds.), *Emotional development and emotional intelligence: Implications for educators* (pp. 3–31). New York: Basic Books.

McGill-Franzen, A., & Allington, R. L. (1993). Flunk 'em or get them classified: The contamination of primary grade accountability data. *Educational Researcher, 22,* 19–22.

McGuinn, D. (May 17, 1999). Cramming for "the test." *Newsweek,* pp. 74–75.

McNeil, L. M., & Valenzuela, A. (2000). *The harmful impact of the TAAS system of testing in Texas: Beneath the accountability rhetoric.* Cambridge, MA: Harvard University Civil Rights Project. (www.law.harvard.edu/groups/civilrights/testing.html)

Mehrens, W. A. (1991). Facts about samples, fantasies about domains. *Educational Measurement: Issues and Practices, 10,* 23–26.

Mehrens, W. A. (1995). Legal and professional bases for licensure testing. In J. C. Impara (Ed.), *Licensure testing: Purposes, procedures, and practices* (pp. 33–58). Lincoln, NE: Buros Institute of Mental Measurements, University of Nebraska–Lincoln.

Mehrens, W. A. (1998). How to prepare for performance assessments. *Educational Measurement: Issues and Practices, 17,* 18–22.

Mehrens, W. A. (in press). Consequences of assessment: What is the evidence? In G. Tindal & T. Haladyna (Eds.), *Large-scale assessment programs for all students: Development, implementation, and analysis.* Mahwah, NJ: Lawrence Erlbaum.

Mehrens, W. A., & Kaminski, J. (1989). Methods for improving standardized test scores: Fruitful, fruitless, or fraudulent? *Educational Measurement: Issues and Practices, 8,* 14–22.

Mehrens, W. A., & Lehman, I. J. (1987). *Using standardized tests in education* (4th ed.). New York: Longman.

Mehrens, W. A., & Phillips, S. E. (1986). Detecting impacts of curricular differences in achievement test data. *Journal of Educational Measurement, 23,* 185–196.

Mehrens, W. A., Popham, W. J., & Ryan, J. M. (1998). How to prepare students for performance assessment. *Educational Measurement: Issues and Practice, 17*(1), 18–22.

Messick, S. (1984). The psychology of educational measurement. *Journal of Educational Measurement, 21,* 215–237.

Messick, S. (1989). Validity. In R. L. Linn (Ed.), *Educational measurement* (3rd ed., pp. 13–104). New York: American Council on Education and Macmillan.

Messick, S. (1994). The interplay of evidence and consequences in the validation of performance assessments. *Educational Measurement: Issues and Practices, 23*(2), 13–23.

Messick, S. (1995a). Validity of psychological assessment: Validation of inferences from persons' responses and performances as scientific inquiry into score meaning. *American Psychologist, 50,* 741–749.

Messick, S. (1995b). Standards of validity and the validity of standards in performance assessment. *Educational Measurement: Issues and Practice, 14*(4), 5–8.

Miyasaka, J. R. (April 2000). *A framework for evaluating the validity of test preparation practices.* Paper presented in the symposium titled, Instructionally corrupt test preparation: Can it be detected or deterred? at the annual meeting of the American Educational Research Association, New Orleans.

Monroe, W. S. (1918). Existing tests and standards. In G. M. Whipple (Ed.), *The seventeenth yearbook of the National Society for the Study of Education. Part II: The measurement of educational products.* Bloomington, IL: Public School Publishing Company.

Moos, R. H. (1979). *Evaluating educational environments.* San Francisco: Jossey-Bass.

Murphy, L. L., Impara, J. C., & Plake, B. S. (Eds.). (1999). *Tests in print V.* Lincoln, NE: Buros Institute.

Nairn, A., & Associates. (1980). *The reign of ETS: The corporation that makes up minds.* Washington, DC: Author.

National Center for Educational Statistics. (1996). *Youth indicators 1996: Trends in the well-being of American youth.* Washington, DC: U.S. Department of Education.

National Center for Educational Statistics. (2000). *The conditions of education.* NCES 2000-62. Washington, DC: U.S. Department of Education.

National Center for Fair and Open Testing. (Summer 1988). Civil rights, feminist leaders challenge National Merit formula. *Fair Test Examiner, 2*(3), 3, 4.

National Center for Fair and Open Testing. (Fall 1994). NAEP measures poverty, not educational quality. *FairTest Examiner, 8.*

National Center for Fair and Open Testing. (Summer 1998). N.C. lawmakers alter testing plan. *FairTest Examiner, 12*(3), 6.

National Center for Fair and Open Testing. (Fall 1998a). Most appalling news contest. *FairTest Examiner, 12*(4), 3, 16.

National Center for Fair and Open Testing. (Fall 1998b). NRC criticizes high-stakes testing. *FairTest Examiner,* 12(4), 1, 4.

National Center for Fair and Open Testing. (Fall 1998c). N.C. teachers criticize test. *FairTest Examiner, 12*(4), 3, 14.

National Center for Fair and Open Testing. (Fall 1998d). Tests and grade retention. *FairTest Examiner, 12*(4), 3, 7, 14.

National Center for Fair and Open Testing. (Winter 1999–2000a). Test-based grade retention program fails in Chicago. *FairTest Examiner, 14,* 6.

National Center for Fair and Open Testing. (Winter 1999–2000b). Classroom impact of TAAS. *FairTest Examiner, 14,* 9.

National Center for Fair and Open Testing. (Winter 1999–2000c). NCTE & IRA oppose high-stakes testing. *FairTest Examiner, 14,* 12.

National Center for Fair and Open Testing. (Spring 2000a). More colleges embrace test-score optional admissions. *FairTest Examiner, 14*(2), 1, 11.

National Center for Fair and Open Testing. (Spring 2000b). Mt. Holyoke goes "SAT" optional. *FairTest Examiner, 14*(2), 1, 11.

National Center for Fair and Open Testing. (Spring 2000c). Wellstone. *FairTest Examiner, 14,* 9.

National Center for Fair and Open Testing. (Summer 2000a). Score delays paralyze planning. *FairTest Examiner, 14,* 4.

National Center for Fair and Open Testing. (Summer 2000b). Separate, unequal, and substandard: Exposing the Texas myth. *FairTest Examiner, 14,* 16, 10.

National Center for Fair and Open Testing. (Summer 2000c). Cheating and test coaching. *Fair-Test Examiner, 14,* 5.

National Center for Fair and Open Testing. (Fall 2000a). Annual ACT/SAT score fixation. *FairTest Examiner, 14,* 10.

National Center for Fair and Open Testing. (Fall 2000b). NJ school supers call for test halt. *FairTest Examiner, 14,* 10.

National Center for Fair and Open Testing. (Fall 2000c). Cheating and test coaching. *FairTest Examiner, 14,* 5.

National Center for Fair and Open Testing. (Fall 2000d). Parents win victory in Chicago. *Fair-Test Examiner, 14,* 1, 10.

National Center for Fair and Open Testing. (Fall 2000e). Polls shows skepticism about testing. *FairTest Examiner, 14,* 4.

National Center for Fair and Open Testing. (Fall 2000f). Teacher test cheating. *FairTest Examiner, 14,* 14.

National Center for Fair and Open Testing. (Winter 2000–2001a). Massachusetts exam under attack. *FairTest Examiner, 15*(1), 4, 8.

National Center for Fair and Open Testing. (Winter 2000–2001b). More states retreat from testing. *FairTest Examiner, 15*(1), 3, 13.

National Institutes of Health. (November 16–18, 1988). Diagnosis and treatment of attention deficit hyperactivity disorder. *NIH Consensus Statement, 16*(2). Bethesda, MD: Author.

Neisser, U. (Ed.). (1998). *The rising curve: Long-term gains in IQ and related measures.* Washington, DC: American Psychological Association.

Noggle, N. L. (October 1987). *Report on the match of the standardized tests to the Arizona Essential Skills.* Tempe: Arizona State University, College of Education.

Nolen, S. B., Haladyna, T. M., & Haas, N. S. (1992). Uses and abuses of achievement test scores. *Educational Measurement: Issues and Practices, 11,* 9–15.

Oakes, J. (1992). Can tracking research inform practice? Technical, normative, and political considerations. *Educational Researcher, 21*(4), 12–21.

Owen, D. (1985). *None of the above: Behind the myth of the scholastic aptitude test.* Boston: Houghton Mifflin.

Paris, S., Lawton, T. A., Turner, J. C., & Roth, J. L. (1991). A developmental perspective on standardized achievement testing. *Educational Researcher, 20,* 12–20, 40.

Payne, K. J., & Biddle, B. J. (1999). Poor school funding, child poverty, and mathematics achievement. *Educational Researcher, 28*(6), 4–13.

Peterson, B. (Summer 2000). Is there value in value-added testing? *Rethinking Schools, 14.* (http://www.rethinkingschools.org/Archives/14_04/val144.htm)

Phelps, R. P. (1998). The demand for standardized testing. *Educational Measurement: Issues and Practice, 17*(3), 5–19.

Phelps, R. P. (2000). Trends in large-scale testing outside the United States. *Educational Measurement: Issues and Practice, 19*(1), 11–21.

Phillips, S. E. (in press). Legal issues affecting special populations in large-scale testing programs. In G. Tindal & T. M. Haladyna (Eds.), *Large-scale assessment programs for all students: Validity, technical adequacy, and implementation issues.* Mahwah, NJ: Lawrence Erlbaum.

Plake, B. S., & Impara, J. C. (Eds.). (2001). *The fourteenth mental measurements yearbook.* Lincoln, NE: Buros Institute.

Plass, J. A., & Hill, K. T. (1986). Children's achievement strategies and test performance: The role of time pressure, evaluation anxiety, and sex. *Developmental Psychology, 22*(1), 31–36.

Popham, W. J. (1991). Appropriateness of teachers' test-preparation practices. *Educational Measurement: Issues and Practice, 10*(4), 12–16.

Popham, W. J. (2000a). *Testing, testing! What every parent should know about school tests.* Boston: Allyn and Bacon.

Popham, W. J. (April 2000b). *Why the score-boosting game is, for teachers, a no-win contest.* Paper presented at the annual meeting of the American Education Research Association, New Orleans.

Popham, W. J., & Husek, T. R. (1969). Implications of criterion-referenced measurement. *Journal of Educational Measurement, 6,* 1–9.

Porter, A. (1995). The uses and misuses of opportunity-to-learn standards. *Educational Researcher, 24,* 21–27.

Qualls, A. L. (2001). Can knowledge of erasure behavior be used as an indicator of cheating? *Educational Measurement: Issues and Practice, 20*(1), 9–16.

Ree, M. J., & Carretta, T. R. (1994). Factor analysis of ASVAB: Confirming a Vernon-like structure. *Educational and Psychological Measurement, 54,* 457–461.

Richmond, M. (May/June 1998). *Mathematics Education Dialogues,* p. 13.

Rivera, C., & Stansfield, C. W. (September 2000). States' progress toward testing LEP students evaluated. *NCME Newsletter, 8,* 2–3.

Rodriguez, M. (2002). Choosing an item format. In G. Tindal & T. M. Haladyna (Eds.), *Large-scale assessment programs for all students: Validity, technical adequacy, and implementation issues* (pp. 211–229). Mahwah, NJ: Lawrence Erlbaum.

Rothstein, R. (January 3, 2001). Poverty and achievement, and great misconceptions. *The New York Times on the Web.* (http://www.nytimes.com/2001/01/03/national/03LESS.html)

Rumberger, R. W., & Larson, K. A. (1988). Student mobility and the increased risk of high school dropout. *American Journal of Education, 107*(1), 1–35.

Ryan, J. M., & Demark, S. (2002). Variation in achievement scores related to gender, item format and content area tested. In G. A. Tindal & T. M. Haladyna (Eds.), *Large-scale assessment programs for all students: Development, implementation, and analysis* (pp. 67–88). Mahwah, NJ: Lawrence Erlbaum.

Salvia, J., & Ysseldyke, J. E. (2001). *Assessment in special and remedial education* (8th ed.). Boston: Houghton Mifflin.

Samson, G. E. (1985). Effects of training in test-taking skills on achievement. *Journal of Educational Research, 78,* 261–266.

Sarnacki, R. (1979). An examination of test-wiseness in the cognitive test domain. *Review of Educational Research, 49*(2), 252–279.

Schmitt, K. (1995). What is licensure? In J. C. Impara (Ed.), *Licensure testing: Purposes, procedures, and practices* (pp. 3–32). Lincoln, NE: Buros Institute of Mental Measurements, University of Nebraska–Lincoln, Dept. of Educational Psychology.

Scholes, R. J., & McCoy, T. (April 1998). *The effects of type, length, and content of test preparation activities on ACT assessment scores.* Paper presented at the annual meeting of the American Educational Research Association, San Diego.

Scholes, R. J., & McCoy, T. (April 1999). *Differential effects of test preparation activities and subject content on ACT assessment scores.* Paper presented at the annual meeting of the American Educational Research Association, Montreal.

Seddon, G. M. (1978). The properties of Bloom's taxonomy of educational objectives for the cognitive domain. *Review of Educational Research, 48,* 303–323.

Shavelson, R. J., Bolus, R., & Keesling, J. W. (1980). Self-concept: Recent developments in theory and research. In D. A. Payne (Ed.), *Recent developments in affective measurement.* San Francisco: Jossey-Bass.

Shepard, L. A. (1990). Inflated test score gains: Is the problem old norms or teaching the test? *Educational Measurement: Issues and Practice, 9*(3), 15–22.

Shepard, L. A. (1991). Psychometrician's beliefs about learning. *Educational Researcher, 20,* 2–9.

Singh, K., & Ozturk, M. (2000). Effect of part-time work on high school mathematics and science course taking. *The Journal of Educational Research, 94*(2), 67–74.

Sireci, S. G. (1997). Problems and issues in linking assessments across languages. *Educational Measurement: Issues and Practices, 16,* 12–19.

Smith, M. L. (1991a). Meanings of test preparation. *American Educational Research Association, 28*(3), 521–542.

Smith, M. L. (1991b). Put to the test: The effects of external testing on teachers. *Educational Researcher, 20,* 8–11.

Snow, R. E. (1989). Toward assessment of cognitive and conative structures in learning. *Educational Researcher, 18,* 8–14.

Snow, R. E., & Lohman, D. F. (1989). Implications of cognitive psychology for educational measurement. In R. L. Linn (Ed.), *Educational measurement* (3rd ed., pp. 263–332). New York: American Council on Education and Macmillan.

Sowell, T. (1994). *Race and culture: A world view.* New York: Basic Books.

Spearman, C. E. (1904). "General intelligence" objectively determined and measured. *American Journal of Psychology, 15,* 201–293.

Spearman, C. E. (1927). *The abilities of man.* London: Macmillan.

Stallings, J. (1980). Allocated academic learning time revisited, or beyond time on task. *Educational Researcher, 9,* 11–15.

Sterman, M. B. (2000). EEG markers for attention deficit disorder: Pharmacological and neurofeedback application. *Child Study Journal, 30*(1), 1–23.

Sternberg, R. J. (1985). *Beyond IQ: A triarchic theory of human intelligence.* New York: Cambridge University Press.

Sternberg, R. J. (1988). *The triarchic mind: A new theory of human intelligence.* New York: Penguin.

Sternberg, R. J. (1998). Abilities are forms of developing expertise. *Educational Researcher, 27*(3), 11–20.

Sternberg, R. J. (Ed.). (2000). *Handbook of intelligence.* Cambridge: Cambridge University Press.

Sternberg, R. J., & Grigorenko, E. (1997). *Intelligence, heredity, and the environment.* Melbourne, Australia: Cambridge University Press.

Stevenson, H. W. (Summer 1987). The Asian advantage: The case of mathematics. *American Educator,* pp. 26–32.

Stiggins, R. J., Griswold, M. M., & Wikelund, K. R. (1989). Measuring thinking skills through classroom assessment. *Journal of Educational Measurement, 26,* 233–246.

Taylor, H. G., Klein, N., Minich, N. M., & Hack, M. (2000). Middle school-age outcomes in children with <750 gm birth weight. *Child Development, 71*(6), 1495–1511.

Terenzini, P. T., Cabrera, A. F., & Bernal, E. M. (2001). *Swimming against the tide: The poor in American higher education. Research Report No. 2001-1.* New York: The College Board.

Terman, L. M. (1916). *The measure of intelligence.* Boston: Houghton Mifflin.

Terman, L. M., & Oden, M. (1959). *The gifted group at mid-life.* Stanford, CA: Stanford University Press.

Thurstone, L. L. (1938). *Primary mental abilities.* Chicago: University of Chicago Press. (Reprinted in 1968 by the Psychometric Society).

Tyler, R. (1950). *Basic principles of curriculum and instruction.* Chicago: University of Chicago Press.

United States Department of Education. (1987). *What works: Research about teaching and learning.* Washington, DC: Author.

vos Savant, M. (1988). Interview with the smartest woman in the world. *National Forum, LXVIII* (2), 17.

Watson, N. (June 1998). What are the high stakes for you and your students? How do they affect your teaching? *Mathematics Education Dialogues,* pp. 5–6.

Whitehead, B. D. (April 1993). Dan Quayle was right. *The Atlantic Monthly,* pp. 47–50ff.

Wigfield, A., & Eccles, J. S. (1989). Test anxiety in elementary and secondary school students. *Educational Psychologist, 24*(2), 159–183.

Wiggins, G. (1989). Teaching to the (authentic) test. *Educational Leadership, 76,* 41–47.

Wiggins, G. (1993). *Assessing student performance.* San Francisco: Jossey-Bass.

Wittrock, M. C. (1986). *Handbook of research on teaching* (3rd ed.). New York: Macmillan.

Zwick, R. (1999). Eliminating standardized tests in college admissions: The new affirmative action? *Phi Delta Kappan, 81,* 320–324.

Zwick, R. (December 17, 2000). The standard bearers. *San Francisco Chronicle*, Section cc, pp. 1–4.

Author Index

Subject Index